Jane C. Croly

Jennie June's American Cookery Book

Containing upwards of twelve hundred choice and carefully tested receipts,

embracing all the popular dishes, and the best results of modern science

Jane C. Croly

Jennie June's American Cookery Book
Containing upwards of twelve hundred choice and carefully tested receipts, embracing all the popular dishes, and the best results of modern science

ISBN/EAN: 9783744785136

Printed in Europe, USA, Canada, Australia, Japan

Cover: Foto ©Lupo / pixelio.de

More available books at **www.hansebooks.com**

JENNIE JUNE'S

AMERICAN COOKERY BOOK,

CONTAINING UPWARDS OF TWELVE HUNDRED CHOICE AND CAREFULLY
TESTED RECEIPTS; EMBRACING ALL THE POPULAR DISHES,
AND THE BEST RESULTS OF MODERN SCIENCE, RE-
DUCED TO A SIMPLE AND PRACTICAL FORM.

ALSO,

A CHAPTER FOR INVALIDS, FOR INFANTS, ONE ON JEWISH COOKERY;
AND A VARIETY OF MISCELLANEOUS RECEIPTS OF SPECIAL
VALUE TO HOUSEKEEPERS GENERALLY.

BY MRS. J. C. CROLY, (JENNIE JUNE.)
AUTHOR OF "TALKS ON WOMEN'S TOPICS," ETC.

"What does cookery mean?"
"It means the knowledge of Medea, and of Circe, and of Calypso, and of Helen, and of Rebekah, and of the Queen of Sheba. It means the knowledge of all fruits, and herbs, and balms, and spices—and of all that is healing, and sweet in fields, and groves, and savory in meats—it means carefulness, and inventiveness, and watchfulness, and willingness, and readiness of appliance It means the economy of your great-grandmothers, and the science of modern chemists—it means much tasting, and no wasting—it means English thoroughness, and French art, and Arabian hospitality, and it means in fine, that you are to be perfectly, and always 'ladies,'—'loaf givers,' and as you are to see imperatively that everybody has something pretty to put on,—so you are to see, even yet more imperatively, that everybody has something nice to eat."—RUSKIN.

NEW YORK:
THE AMERICAN NEWS COMPANY,
119 & 121 NASSAU STREET.
1866.

Dedicated

TO THE YOUNG HOUSEKEEPERS OF AMERICA.

INTRODUCTION.

"Why another cook-book, when there are already so many?"

Well, for several reasons, one of which is, that when an inquiry was made for a good, practical cook-book, we knew not which to recommend. We examined a great many, and found some good for one thing, and some for another; but few containing just what young, middle class housekeepers want to know—arranged in a clear, available form, unencumbered with unnecessary and wordy details.

A very small number of the printed cookery and house-keeping books have been written by women, and still less by persons possessing any practical knowledge of the subject of which they were treating. The majority are clumsy compilations of all kinds of receipts—good, bad, and indifferent, collected from various sources, and put together with an ignorance as profound, of their results, as if they had been written in an unknown language.

There are certain "high art" cookery books that are very good and complete, in their way; but they are too elaborate and pretentious for the class for whom this was written. They go into the mysteries of French dishes, and tell how to get up grand dinners, but they leave the poor young wife, who wants to cook a chop or a chicken, stuff a piece of veal, and make a pudding, or a loaf of bread for the first time in her life, quite in the dark.

It is not claimed for the present volume, by the author, that it fully meets the necessities of the case, or has satisfactorily accomplished its task, even within the modest limits assigned to it. It is one thing to think how something may be done, and another thing to do it; but it is claimed that the object of the work has been constantly kept in view, that it has been executed lovingly, with a strong appreciation of the benefit and pleasure to be derived from good cooking, from the intermingling of the finer with the grosser elements, with a pleasant remembrance of good times spent in the kitchen, and with an earnest wish to make these duties seem attractive to the conscientious young wives who would willingly perform their part, if they but knew how.

Nearly all the receipts and recommendations in the following pages have been carefully tested and found sensible and practical. We have omitted some things, which nearly all cook-books contain, such as directions for carving, setting table, etc.; because it seemed a waste of valuable space. Carving is partly a gift of nature, and partly of grace; it is never learned from a book. Directions of this kind, moreover, are useless without illustrations; and these did not come within the scope of the present work. Information as to how to put the knives and forks on a dinner table is another work of supererogation. Few persons who use a cookery book are so benighted as not to have seen a table neatly set sometime or other, and if they have, it is worth more to them than a dozen printed rules. Young housekeepers will, however, find a great many hints,—the result of experience and observation,—which we hope will prove useful to them, and help to keep them from the errors and perplexities of many who have preceded them.

Dear friends,—for it is you, for whom this book is written, and to whom it is dedicated,—I believe in you, I sympathize with you, because I am one of you. I see you in your lovely young wife-hood, so happy in your treasures of pantry and closet, so proud of your first culinary success, and of your lord and master's high appreciation of it; and I would, if it were possible, extend the loving halo which glorifies every act of affection during these first happy months, to all your future; so that no weariness, no pain, no distrust, no loss of anything that now makes life beautiful, might ever come near you. But this is out of my power. I can only wish for every one no more clouds than is necessary, to vary and make beautiful the matrimonial sky, and so dear friends,

FAREWELL.

GENERAL PRINCIPLES OF COOKING.

1. The object of cooking is to make food healthful, and palatable; the secret is therefore, how to combine elements and flavors, so as to produce the best results.

2. The best meat requires the simplest preparation.

3. A cardinal principle in cooking is cleanliness; a dirty cook cannot be a good cook, because all her dishes, no matter how distinct in quality, or costly in material, will taste as if, to use a common expression, they were "cooked in one pot."

4. As a general rule, to which there are very few exceptions, cook long and slowly, to cook well, and let the heat reach every part as evenly as possible.

5. Fresh meats, and fish are better than corned, pickled, or smoked provisions; and the flesh of grown animals, (beef or mutton) is to be preferred to young beasts, such as veal or lamb.

6. The natural order in cooking meats or fish, excepting oysters, is first to broil, second to boil, third to roast, fourth to stew, fifth to bake, and sixth to fry; and never to fry, as long as there is another method left.

7. To retain the jucies in boiled meat, keep it in mass and plunge it in boiling water; this coagulates the outer coating and prevents the escape of the jucies, or soluable matter. To extract the jucies for soup, cut it up in small pieces, and put it in cold water; this draws out all the strength, making good soup, but poor meat.

8. Air should have access to roasting meat, hence spit roasting before a fire, is found much better than roasting in a closed oven.

9. Always retain as much as possible of the distinct flavor of every article of food used; mixtures which make all dishes taste alike, are dyspepsia breeding, as well as appetite killing.

10. Carefully avoid placing articles in contact, which have no

affinity, such as fish and meat, etc. It is sufficient for people to do that in their stomachs.

11. A light hand in making, a quick step in baking, maketh a good conscience for eating bread, puddings, and pies.

12. Food for the well, is better than physic for the sick. Bad cooking is a crime; it is the cause of dyspepsia, and a host of other evils. A woman convicted of it ought to be arraigned for manslaughter.

HOUSEKEEPING.

The great question when a young couple are going to be married is, whether they shall keep house or board. The gentleman, as a general rule, wishes to keep house, he is tired of boarding; moreover, he had anticipated so much enjoyment in a snug little house of their own, and so much pride and pleasure in seeing his pretty Nellie at the head of his table, doing the honors to the choicest of his friends.

But Nellie has quite different ideas; in the first place, she knows nothing about cooking. She has, with the help of her mother, or the cook, made cake once or twice, or possibly blanc-mange, which was very much praised; but of the practical details required in the getting up of the most ordinary breakfast, dinner, or supper, she knows nothing, and has not the remotest intention or inclination to become acquainted with them.

The final result is, that they go to "board" in some highly genteel establishment, where the prices are high in proportion to the gentility and lack of real comfort, and some fine morning the young gentleman wakes up to the knowledge that he is tied to a wife who doubles his expenses, but has added nothing to his happiness, or at any rate, nothing to the real value and usefulness of his life.

This is a matrimonial swindle. Girls ought not to marry until they are ready and willing to accept the position of head of a household, and capable of making a home what it should be to husband and children.

If a man can find a woman to act as his mistress for her board and clothes, well and good — there is no law to prevent it; but for a woman bearing the honored name of wife to hold so dependent and humilating a position, is fearful degradation.

The marriage relation is one of reciprocal interests, duties, and responsibilities; and no young lady ought to marry until she is willing to assume her share of them. True affection on the part of the husband will lighten, and make duties pleasures, but whatever aspect they bear, she must not shrink from them. If she has not received the training necessary to fit her for the position, it is her misfortune; but it will be her fault, if she does not try as far as possible to remedy the evil.

Want of means constitutes no sort of reason why young married people should not go to housekeeping. What we spend on foolish and useless gewgaws and presents would, in nine cases out of ten, if usefully applied, set them up in a style quite in accordance with their means, if not their inclination.

But it is not for themselves they fear. They are willing, or at least they think so, to live together in an attic; but society! Well, what has society got to do with it? Society will not pay your butcher's and grocer's bills, nor care a copper whether they are paid or not. Society will eat ice-cream, oysters, and cake of your providing, but that is not what you are marrying for.

You have chosen a comparatively poor man, your business is to adapt yourself to his circumstances, to make the most of his means in providing a pleasant home, and bringing up carefully and conscientiously the children which may be given you. If society find you out, or if you find it worth while to fill up any of the chinks or interstices with occasional glimpses of the false, glittering, outside world — good! you will come back to your sweet home with so much the more relish; but do not *marry* it, do not sacrifice your own sense of duty, and the happiness and welfare of husband and family to it.

Talk of happiness,—there is none like that of an intelligent, affectionate family circle. There is no pleasure, no enjoyment equal to that of a mother ministering to the wants, or gratifying the natural and innocent tastes of her children. The pleasure is all the greater, because it is a *surprise*.

Young women very often dread the exacting care of a family, and expect to find wifely and maternal duties irksome and wearisome; that is the reason why they would so willingly escape them, as they fancy, by boarding, and not having children.

But unfortunately, or fortunately, God has managed it so that we cannot take the pleasures of life without bearing its pains; we cannot shirk a plain line of duty, without incurring the penalty. But we can, and do, by taking upon ourselves bravely, its burdens, find an exaltation of womanhood, and a hight and depth of happiness, such as we never before dreamed of.

Exceptions are said to exist to every general rule; but there are very few to this, that when people marry, they ought to set right about making a home of their own. If you can only afford two rooms, live in two rooms. If your means will compass a small house, but not a large one, then take the small one, and be happy and thankful.

I would not give a wisp of straw for a young woman who does not want, on her marriage, to occupy her own little domain; who does not revel in anticipation over the contents of kitchen and closet, if there is only a small cook stove in one, and a set of delf in the other. But this suggests a matter of some importance.

KITCHEN FURNISHING.

In selecting a house to live in, particularly if it is a small one, give the preference to a pleasant, sunny kitchen, which will at least look clean when it is clean, and into which it will not be disagreeable to enter.

As a general rule, buy as little as possible on first going to housekeeping; it is easy to add more when experience has discovered to you precisely what you want; but if you should indulge in any extravagance, let it be in the kitchen furnishing.

It is a real pleasure to get a glimpse of an orderly kitchen and neat closets, newly fitted up with all the useful modern contrivances for saving labor, and making it agreeable, and as the whole cost would not amount to more than one expensive carpet, it is not worth while to do without them.

It is economical, moreover, to have all kitchen utensils of the best quality; cheap pans, brushes, pails, earthenware and the like, are not only an "eyesore" in a house, and bad or disagreeable to use, but they are good for nothing; they eternally want replacing, while a really good article is not only taken better care of, but will stand infinitely more of hard usage.

Oil cloth is the best material for covering a kitchen floor; it is easily kept clean, and does not absorb the dirt and grease.

Short, white muslin curtains to kitchen windows are considered "nonsense" by some people, but they are tidy, and the cost and washing are not much.

Of course the kitchen will be supplied with dresser, table with drawer, and ironing table. As to chairs, three and a common rocker are sufficient; but I would enliven the walls with a picture or two, if possible, and encourage the cook, or maid of all work, to have her monthly rose or pot of geranium in the window.

Under the shelves of the kitchen closets, it is a good plan to have narrow strips of board, in which nails or tacks can be inserted, for the purpose of hanging up all sorts of small articles, such as iron and wooden spoons, sugar and flour sifters, tin strainers, lemon squeezer, lemon grater, egg beater, skewers, small sauce pans, cake turner, rolling pin, and such things as one is most likely to want, and which it is convenient to have in sight.

The floors of all closets should be covered with oil-cloth, so that they can be easily washed up, and kept neat and clean.

HOUSEHOLD MANAGEMENT.

Women are sometimes accused of managing too much, and sometimes of not managing at all; but the most perfect system of management is, undoubtedly, that which outwardly betrays itself least, and in the results of which, there is not suspected to have been any management at all.

Regularity is the pivot upon which all household management turns; where there is a lack of system there is a lack of comfort, that no amount of individual effort can supply. Forethought also is necessary, so that the work may be all arranged beforehand; done in its proper order, and at the right time. Never, except in cases of extreme emergency, allow Monday's washing to be put off till Tuesday; Tuesday's ironing till Wednesday, or Wednesday's finishing up and "setting to rights," till Thursday. Leave Thursday for extra work; or when that is not required, for resting day, or half holiday, and as a preparation for the up stairs' sweeping and dusting of Friday, and the downstairs' baking and scrubbing of Saturday.

Arrange work so as to save fuel as much as possible. Mix bread at night, so that it will be ready to bake with that "first fire" which always makes the oven hot in the morning. Prepare fruit over night, so that pies or other things can be quickly made and baked immediately after. Prepare hashes for breakfast, over night. Have the kitchen and dining room put in order before retiring to rest. Have kindlings and whatever is needed for building fires laid ready, and the fire in the kitchen raked down, so that it can be built up in the shortest possible space of time. This is not only a saving in the morning, but will be found useful in case of illness in the night, when a fire is often required at a moment's notice.

Try to buy in as large quantities as possible, so as to save the perpetual running out to the grocery. Supplies on hand also enable the housekeeper to provide a more varied table, with far greater economy than is possible where every thing is bought by the half a pound, more or less.

Every family that can possibly find means to do it, or a place to properly keep the articles, should commence winter with fuel, potatoes, apples, flour, and butter, enough to last till Spring. A good supply of hominy, rice, farina, Indian meal, preserved fish, and other staples, including sugar, should also be laid in, not forgetting a box of raisins, one of currants, a third of soap, and a fourth of starch.

There is such an immense saving in soap well dried, that it is surprising so many housekeepers content themselves with buying it in damp bars. Starch also is frightfully wasted by quarter, and half pound purchases, which are frequently all absorbed at one time, by careless girls, in doing the washing for a small family.

But in most American families, the largest amount of waste, probably, takes place in the use of fuel. Heretofore, fuel of all kinds has been comparatively cheap, and very little supervision has been exercised over its use. At present rates however, it is an item of considerable importance; and it is quite time that servants were taught how to employ it to the best advantage.

In nine out of ten kitchens, when there is any cooking to be done the range is made red hot; when the cooking is done, the fire is left to go down to ashes, and is then raised by means of a wasteful pile of kindling wood. When no cooking is going on, and a large fire is not needed, the dampers will frequently be left open, and the fuel allowed to blaze itself out up the chimney instead of being kept in reserve for actual service.

The general principle of construction upon which American kitchen stoves and ranges is based, renders them either very economical, or very much otherwise, according to the way they are managed. After the fire is first built in an ordinary stove, or range, the dampers ought all to be closed up and not opened again during the day, except while broiling, or something of that sort. If the grate is kept clear, and the fire replenished with a small quantity of coal, before it begins to get low, both the oven, and the top of the range will be kept sufficiently hot for any kind of cooking, and it will be done all the better for being done somewhat more slowly, than is customary with the well meaning, but terribly blundering, and irresponsible race of wild Irish girls, who officiate as the high priestesses of our domestic altars.

The strictest attention on the part of a house-keeper, is necessary, to see that certain articles are kept for their proper use; for instance, that the dish cloth is not used for a floor cloth, that the napkins are not used to wipe up the dishes, the dish towels as dusters, a new broom to sweep out the back yard, and the best new enamelled sauce pan, for melting down grease.

Where the lady of the house attends partly to her own work, she will naturally see to all these things; but where it is left wholly to servants, there are always complaints of missing articles, and an inspection of the kitchen, or ironing table drawer, would generally bring them all to light, although in a state almost unrecognizable, from dirt, and their contiguity to whitening, hair oil, candle grease, combs and brushes, and other articles, all of which it is found "handy" to keep in a drawer in the kitchen, with mats, table cloths, towels, and other things destined for family use.

It is hardly necessary after this to say that a kitchen being once provided with necessary and convenient articles for cleaning and cooking, the presiding genius should be held to a strict accountability for them. Pudding cloths should be forthcoming whenever wanted, — dry, clean, and free from stains; towels, napkins, pans, bowls, and cooking utensils, should be kept strictly to their uses, and not put away till perfectly clean and dry.

Ironing sheets, blankets, skirt board, bosom board, iron holder, rubber, and the like, should be kept smoothly folded in the drawer of the ironing table, when not in use.

The shelves of kitchen, dining-room, and other closets, should be covered with fresh paper, neatly cut out on the edges, once in two weeks, and dusted down twice a week.

Pot closets, safes, and refrigerators, should be thoroughly scrubbed out every week, and the latter aired every day.

Good brooms and brushes will last a long time if care is taken of them. When first bought they should be allowed to stand in cold water for twelve hours, and then thoroughly dried before using When not in use, they should be hung up by a loop of twine, or cord, so that the weight may not rest on the edge of the splinters, and break them. Four large brooms should be provided, one for the kitchen, one for the parlor, one for the sleeping rooms, and one for the family, or "living" room. A "whisk" will be required for every room in the house, besides one for the hall.

As soon as the kitchen broom is worn down so as to render it unfit to sweep the floor with ease and comfort, take it for the cellar, door steps, and back yard; take the one from the sitting room for the kitchen, the one from the parlor to the sitting room, and get a new one for the parlor.

Exact punctuality in serving the meals, and punctual attendance at them; it is oftener the fault of the family, than the servants, that meals are served at irregular hours. Where the members make a practice of sitting down any time, and food is kept waiting until it suits their pleasure or convenience to partake of it, irrespective of household necessities, servants, or any one else, will naturally become careless and neglectful.

HOUSEHOLD MEMORANDA.

Dried herbs should be tied each separately in a paper bag, and hung against the wall in the store-room. Mint, pennyroyal, catnip, sage, thyme, summer-savory and parsley, are all good to have in the house.

Parsley should be bunched before it goes to seed, and hung up to dry. In a week, or two, it may be put in paper bags, and is ready for use, for soup, stuffing, or fricassee.

PIECE BAGS.

Out of an old calico dress make three piece bags, and label each one of them with its written name upon a small square piece of white muslin, which must be sewn upon the side of the bag. One should be the "rag-bag," another the "white piece-bag," a third, the "colored piece-bag," — they will be found very useful.

DUSTERS

Provide a duster, as well as a feather brush, and a whisk broom, for every room in the house, and see that they are kept in their place, when not in use.

KITCHEN HOLDERS.

Make three kitchen holders, one to put away with the ironing apparatus, two others, to be hung up, one each side, under the kitchen mantle piece, so as to be ready for lifting pots and kettles off the fire, or taking hold of the hot handle of a sauce pan, or skillet. Small squares of old, or new carpet, are best, with an inner lining of old cloth, and an outer one of dark twilled cotton, which may either be sewed to the edge of the carpet, or the whole may be bound with worsted binding. Add a loop to hang it up by.

PAPER AND STRING.

When parcels are brought to the house, take the nice white, or brown tissue paper, in which the goods have been wrapped, fold it and put it away in a drawer, with the string tied round it, to be ready for use in case of emergency.

MENDING

When you put the clean clothes away for the family, examine every piece, and see if a string, or a button needs replacing, or a fracture requires mending. Pile all together, and repair them at once, remembering that a stitch in time saves nine.

MENDING STOCKINGS.

Mending stockings for a large family, is a somewhat onerous, and not altogether agreeable duty. As soon as the daughters are old enough they should be set to mending their own; but even then, there is sometimes a large pile for "mother's" work basket. Do not hurry them; however, mend them conscientiously, if it is only one pair at a time. Have needle and darning cotton of the proper size, take a large area in every direction beyond the hole, leave loops at each end of the thread, as it is drawn out, for shrinkage—and darn carefully and extensively over all the thin places. Hose mended in this way will not require the process more than twice, during their existence, provided the quality in the first place was the best. Cheap hose are not worth buying at all.

RAINY DAYS.

Make the house look as bright as possible inside, have something good for tea, put on a pretty dress, light up early, romp with the children, tell them stories, and determine at least to have sunshine in the house, if you cannot have it outside.

PACKING AWAY SUMMER OR WINTER CLOTHES.

Before packing away summer or winter clothes, devote a day to an examination of them; mend, and clean any spots off that may require it, brush, and shake them well, fold up smoothly, and sprinkle between every fold a little gum camphor, unless you are so fortunate as to have cedar chests, and then you will not need it. Sprinkle a little gum camphor also on the bottom of common trunks or chests, pack closely, filling up all the crevices, with small articles such as stockings, gloves, scarfs, hoods and the like, reserving the body part of the box for the larger garments.

Nice dresses, velvet cloaks, opera cloaks, furs, and the like, should be folded in sheets, or towels, pinned tightly down, and be placed in the trays, or hollow part of trunks, by themselves, if possible.

CAKE BOX.

Have a japanned box, or large jar, for cake, which will shut down tight. Cover it with a linen cloth, which should be put in the wash once in two weeks. Empty the box, scald it out, and let it dry in the sun, or before the fire, every week.

CHAMBER, MANTEL, AND TOILET COVERS.

White Marseilles, thin *pique* or Allendale quilting, edged with white ball, or twisted fringe, makes nice covers for toilet stands, or chamber mantels, especially where cottage furniture is used. If the furniture is very handsome black walnut, or rosewood, elegant mantel covers may be made, by tacking patent maroon velvet on a thin board, and edging it with bullion fringe.

TO CLEAN LOOKING GLASSES.

Divide a newspaper in two halves, fold up one in a small square and dip it in cold water. Rub the glass first with the wet half of the paper, and dry with the other. Fly specks, and all other dirty marks will disappear as if by magic.

TO TAKE OUT SCORCH.

If a shirt bosom, or any other article has unfortunately been scorched in ironing, lay it where bright sunshine will fall straight upon it. It will take it entirely out, leaving it clean and white as snow.

LABEL CHILDREN.

Into the crowns of the hats or bonnets of little children, sew a square of writing paper, stating age, and residence. This will save them from any danger of being lost.

WASH RAGS.

Small squares of crash hemmed, make very nice wash rags, or small, coarse tea napkins, fringed on the sides; very good ones may also be made out of the best part of old dinner napkins, or tablecloths. Be careful always to supply them to every sleeping-room with the towels, and see that they are changed once a week.

NIGHT CLOTHES.

Never wear anything at night that you have worn during the day, nor during the day, that you have worn at night.

TO PUT OUT FIRE.

In all such cases, great promptitude and quickness is necessary. The thing to be done is, to *crush* it out; either with rugs, mats, blankets, or whatever else is handy.

If the fire is in a chimney, fire a pistol into it, or put salt on it, and close up the draft of the fire-place, by pinning a quilt up over it. This last precaution alone will generally prevent danger, unless there should happen to be a high wind.

SHEETS.

When sheets are beginning to wear in the middle, sew the selvage sides together, tear them in two, and hem down the sides; they will last enough longer to pay for the trouble, especially at present price of muslin.

PAY AS YOU GO.

Keep no books, and never run accounts with stores; *pay for what you buy when you buy it*, and so save much money and trouble and prevent many very disagreeable mistakes.

HOW TO CLEAR A TABLE.

Collect all the food together first, and dispose of it, neatly, and carefully. Put all the spoons together, all the forks together, and all the knives together. If you have a small pitcher partly full of warm water on the table, put the knives into that, blades down. Scrape the plates clean, and empty all the slops from the tea and coffee cups, into the slop bowl. Have ready your clean light wooden tub, two thirds full of hot water, little mop, piece of soap, and tin pan of warm water for rinsing. Wash the glasses first, with a little soap, and rinse them, then the spoons, then the cups and saucers, then the silver forks, then the plates, lastly, the larger dishes. Dry quickly with nice large fine linen crash towels. Be careful not to put the handle of knives into hot water, or silver knives where they can touch the forks, as that will scratch them. The quicker the whole operation is performed, the brighter and nicer the ware will be.

MATTRESSES.

Mattresses are used universally now in preference to feather beds; and to save trouble, some people straighten the clothes over them, just as they rise. This is very bad, they ought to be turned every day, and exposed to the air some time before the bed is made up.

HINTS ON ECONOMY.

PROVIDE ON SATURDAY for Monday, so as not to take up the fire with cooking, or time in running errands, any more than is possible on washing day.

WAIT TILL ARTICLES, fruit, fish, poultry and vegetables, are in full season, before purchasing. They are then not only much lower in price than when first brought to market, but finer in quality and flavor.

OUTSIDE GARMENTS, bonnets, cloaks, hats, shawls, scarfs and the like, will last clean and fresh much longer, if the dust is carefully removed from them by brushing and shaking after returning from a ride or a walk.

WHEN YOUR APPLES begin to rot, pick the specked ones out carefully; stew them up with cider and sugar, and fill all your empty self-sealing cans. In this way you may keep in nice apple sauce till apples come again.

PICKLE OR PRESERVE JARS should be washed in lukewarm or cold water, and dried in the sun or near the fire. Hot water cracks the polished surface of the inside, and renders them unfit for their specific use.

NEVER ALLOW CHILDREN to eat butter with meat or gravy; it is both wasteful and injurious.

HOT BUCKWHEAT CAKES will go farther and last longer than any other single article of food. A celebrated judge declared that he could remain in court all day, without feeling a symptom of hunger, after a breakfast of buckwheat cakes.

A STEW is not a bad dish for a family dinner, once a week; make it of good meat, and savory with sweet herbs, and the most fastidious will not object to it.

RISE EARLY on fine summer mornings, and throw all the windows of the house open, so that it may exchange its close atmosphere, for the cool, fresh air. Have the work done before the heat of the day comes on, and save it as much as possible during the warmest weather.

TAKE CARE OF THE FOOD that is brought into the house, and see that none of it is wasted; but do not be always on the lookout for *cheap* things. Beans are cheap, and very good sometimes; corn meal is cheap too, and even more available, because it can be made into a great variety of dishes, but people would not care to live on beans and corn meal all the time, because they are cheap. Eating is intended as a means of enjoyment, as well as of sustaining life; and it is right to avail ourselves of the abundant resources provided, as far as we can consistently.

USE TEA LEAVES, or short, freshly cut grass, to sprinkle upon carpets before sweeping. It will freshen up the colors, and save the usual cloud of dust.

HAVE EVERYTHING CLEAN, on Saturday night, something nice for tea, and also for Sunday morning breakfast. Let the approach of the Sabbath be anticipated in all things, with pleasure. Stay at home with the children on Sabbath evening, and finish the day with a sacred concert.

ALLOW NO HOLES, or corners in the house, in drawers, on shelves, or in closets, for the stowing away of dirty rags, old bottles, grease-pots, and broken crockery. When bottles are emptied, let them be cleaned, and put down in the cellar, until they are wanted. Harbor no dirty grease pots, and when an article is broken past recovery, throw it away at once; there is no use in keeping it to collect dust, and cobwebs.

MAKE A POINT of examining safe, refrigerator, closets, drawers, and all receptacles for food, and kitchen articles, at least as often as once a week, either Saturday, or washing day. Look into pickle jars, bread jars, cake jars, butter tubs, apple, and potato barrels, everything in fact, examine their condition, see if they are kept covered and clean, and that food put away, is not left to spoil, or be wasted.

THE FEWER SERVANTS THE BETTER—two requires a third to wait upon them, and so on *ad infinitum*. Have good servants however, pay good wages, and make them responsible for their work.

IF IT IS POSSIBLE, and when there is a will there is a way, call your household together, after breakfast every morning, and have domestic worship, be it ever so short. A verse of a hymn, a passage from the Bible, and just a few words of heartfelt prayer, and praise, sets everything right for the day, smooths ruffled tempers, and puts the domestic machine in nicely running order. It is also no bad preparation for the temptations and annoyances of business.

BEFORE SWEEPING a room, have the furniture, and especially all the small articles, dusted and removed. This keeps them looking fresh, and new.

WEAR PRETTY MORNING DRESSES; they are inexpensive, and easily preserved from injury, by a large calico apron enveloping the skirt of the dress, and sleeves of the same kind, gathered into a band, top, and bottom, and extending over the elbows. These can be slipped on and off in a minute, and with a bib added to the apron in front, affords complete protection, while engaged in dusting, making pastry, and the like.

ALWAYS HAVE YOUR TABLE served neatly, and then if friends "happen in," you will not be ashamed to ask them to share your meal. Be hospitable, if it is only a crust, and a cup of cold water; if it is clean and good of its kind, there is no reason to blush for it; the hearty welcome will make amends for the absence of rich viands.

IF CHILDREN WANT ANYTHING between meals, which they should not, give them a cracker, or an apple; do not encourage an irregular and unhealthy appetite, by giving them pie, cake, or gingerbread.

RULES FOR EATING

1. Eat slowly as if it was a pleasure you desired to prolong, rather than a duty to be got rid of as quickly as possible.
2. Don't bring your prejudices, your dislikes, your annoyances, your past misfortunes, or future forebodings, to the table — they would spoil the best dinner.
3. Respect the hours of meals, you have no right to injure the temper of the cook, destroy the flavor of the viands, and the comfort of the family, by your want of punctuality.
4. Have as much variety in your food as possible, but not many dishes served at one time.
5. Find as little fault with the food prepared as possible, and praise whenever you can.
6. Finally, be thankful, if you have not meat, that you have at least an appetite, and hope for something more and better in the future.

THE USE OF FUEL.

There is no department of housekeeping in which our national spirit of waste and extravagance is more clearly exemplified, than in our use of fuel. Even the enormous advance in prices has led to no retrenchment or reform in this respect. Coal and wood are just as recklessly as ever, shovelled into the cellar. Bridget makes the same blazing fires, subject to no supervision, except a faint, general direction, to " sift the cinders every morning ; " and Bridget says " yes'm " as usual, but there being nobody to see, or know whether she does or not, in nineteen cases out of twenty, she does not do it.

Every little while through the day, the fires are raked down, and fresh coal put on, the dampers of stove or range left wide open, and for so much cooking as a cup of tea, or a dish of potatoes, a fresh fire built with range made red hot, and as much fuel wasted as would have cooked a thanksgiving dinner.

GRATE FIRES.

These are generally considered as requiring a great deal of coal, and so they do, under the usual system of management in this country. But let us see how they manage grate fires in England.

The grate is cleared, with the exception of a few scattering cinders, which forms a sort of body, for the paper, which is torn up in small pieces, and crushed down, and the wood, which is neatly and compactly laid "across and across." When the largest and best cinders remaining are picked out and thrown on, a match is applied, cinders are still put on wherever they are needed to catch the blaze, and when the wood is burnt down, and the cinders are all a-glow, fresh coal is used to fill up the grate. The ashes are then sifted, the cinders, which are fine and small, damped, and when the fire has burned red through, *without the use of the blower*, the wet cinders are thrown on the top. In this way a grate fire will last through a whole day with once replenishing, and keep a room warmer than we do, without blaze, our frequent use of the blower, and reckless waste of fuel.

KITCHEN RANGES.

Nearly all of these are built on the air tight principle, and should be kept closed up tight all the time. The fire will be found to burn equally well, though more moderately; the oven will be always hot, and cooking can be done slowly, as it ought, on the top of the range, with much less trouble, and infinitely better than if "rushed through," at a red heat.

PARLOR HEATERS.

These new heaters are very good for small houses; we used one for years, with great satisfaction, and found it quite as efficient, and much safer, more convenient and more economical than a furnace.

Parlor heaters are fitted into the wall, and take up no more room than a grate; they should be attended to with regularity, and then the fire will hardly ever need to go out; once in two months is quite as often as it requires to be made up fresh. At night, wetted cinders should be thrown on the fire so as to thickly cover it while it is good, and the dampers shut up close; these will keep the fire almost intact till the next morning, when a thorough raking down will be needed. A parlor heater properly managed, burns out about as much coal as one large grate or two small stoves; but excepting in the very coldest weather, it will comfortably heat the whole house.

SPRING FUEL.

Coke is excellent fuel for spring and fall, if it is carefully and rightly used; but if it is mixed with hard coal and thrown on a kitchen fire by a reckless servant, at discretion, it becomes equally extravagant and useless. Coke makes a bright, hot fire, kindles easily, and goes out easily; but it can also be made to last a long while, by packing it a little on top, and neglecting to rake it down. This is the method for early spring, when fires are required in the morning and evening, but not much through the sunshiny part of the day.

A great saving is effected in spring fuel, by putting the "slack" from coal, in a heap by itself, and with it, ashes from which the cinders have not been taken. Dampen the heap occasionally with a little water, and add to it, whenever there is material. Doing this through the coldest weather will form a sort of compost, hard and insoluble, which can be broken apart, and furnishes splendid fuel for spring grate fires, or for parlor heaters

SOUPS.

STOCKS.

Stock is the foundation of soups, and also of good gravies, sauces, and the like. A French cook can do nothing without the stock pot, and keeps it supplied in a way that is both useful, and economical.

Stock can be made to keep for a considerable time, and be used for many purposes, if occasional additions are made, and the whole of the liquor re-scalded. It may be made from meat, or from bones, or from both, or it may be made from bones with the addition of refuse meat, the trimmings of regular joints. Chicken and turkey bones may be thrown in, and will help to enrich, and give flavor to the preparation. Any kind of bones with a little meat upon them, will make good stock, if they are *simmered*, not boiled, long enough, and beef, mutton, veal, poultry, and other bones may be stewed together. In stewing them down, use the liquor if you have it, in which other meat has been boiled, so that nothing may be wasted. Shank bones, trimmings from chops, any thing of this sort may be thrown in, simmered all day, then poured into a jar, and the fat removed the next morning. It is then frequently a jelly, and ready to convert into soup, with the aid of herbs, and vegetables—or kept for other uses. Stock sours very soon after the vegetables have been boiled in it, so it is best not to put the vegetables in till needed for soup.

If your stock is made of meat, or partly of meat, cut it up fine, and always put it on in cold water, if the water is hard, put a pinch of soda in it. This will extract all the pieces of the bones and meat. If on the contrary, you want to boil meat, and retain its pieces, put it on in boiling water. [See the Principles of Cooking.]

STOCK FROM BONES.

Take the bones of a sirloin of beef, break them into half a dozen pieces or more, put them in the stock pot with a gallon of cold water; and let them simmer gently for five or six hours. Then take it off, strain it—it ought to make about two quarts—and set it aside for several hours, or over night. When cold, skim off the fat. Then return it to the pot with a turnip, and a large carrot cut up in two or three pieces, two onions, a bunch of sweet herbs, a sprig or two of parsley, and a head of celery if it can be obtained, or a teaspoonful of celery-seed tied in a piece of muslin. Let these simmer together gently for two hours, adding boiling water to keep the quantity two quarts, and putting in also while boiling a little salt and a large lump of sugar; when done, strain it off into a jar, and you have a good stock, which can be kept several days, in a cool place in winter, or by being boiled over each day, in summer.

STOCK WITHOUT MEAT.

Put into a stew pan ten carrots, as many turnips and onions cut in small pieces, two lettuces, two sticks of celery, a handful of chervil, half a cabbage and a parsnip cut in slices; add to these three ounces of butter and a quart of water; stew them till the liquid is nearly dried up, and then fill the stewpan with water; add a quart of peas, green or dried, according to the season, two chives, some pepper and salt; stew slowly three or four hours and strain through a colander for use.

BRAN STOCK.

Put a large handful of bran into a quart of water, boil and leave to simmer till the quantity is reduced to half. This will do excellently for the thickening of meat soup. It will make very good soup of itself, if onions, salt and pepper, with a few vegetables, are mixed in it. It will also be good sweetened with molasses or honey.

COW HEEL STOCK.

A cow heel in two quarts of water will make first rate stock, but do not get boiled cow heels. The others take more boiling, but make much richer stock, and may be used more than once.

FOUR QUARTS OF BROWN STOCK.

Heat an iron pot and rub the bottom with garlic. Put in ten pounds of shin of beef, fresh killed, and a pint of water; let it stand by the fire for an hour, then add three quarters of a pound of lean ham, three onions, three carrots, a small head of celery, four cloves, six allspice, ten peppercorns, a table-spoonful of brown sugar, a tea-spoonful of mustard, a tea-spoonful of salt, a large black onion, and six quarts of water. Simmer and skim frequently for six hours. Strain into an earthen dish, and when cold, remove the fat; a fine hair sieve dipped in cold water is good to strain it with.

FOUR QUARTS OF WHITE STOCK.

Put into an iron pot a knuckle of veal, about seven pounds, a cowheel, and an old fowl; add a turnip, two onions, a lettuce, a blade of mace, quarter of a nutmeg, half a pound of lean ham, a tea-spoonful of salt, a small bunch of sweet herbs, and six quarts of water. Simmer gently, and skim frequently, for six hours. Strain into an earthen dish, and when cold, take off the fat.

COMMON SOUP.

Take the neck, shanks, scraps of fresh meat, or old fowls. Let your meat, beef, mutton, fowls, or game, be cut into small pieces, and the bones cracked up well. Put the pieces into a pot and cover them with as much water as will stew them into rags; stew them very slowly, then pour in some boiling water, and keep the soup boiling to within a few minutes of serving. Skim it entirely free from grease. Take out whatever you wish to set away for the next day before you put in the vegetables. Now cut up vegetables (previously cooked by themselves), in it slice potatoes, okra, turnips, carrots, any vegetable you like, or rice or barley. If there is any vegetable,—for instance, onions, cabbage, or tomatoes,— which you wish to give distinctive character to your soup, use that vegetable entirely, in connection with potatoes and okra, which give consistency without any very discernible taste. If your soup lacks richness, a few spoonfuls of drawn butter will help; if consistency, some gelatine may be dissolved in it. A bouquet of sweet herbs is indispensable. A rich soup is sometimes flavored with wine or catsup. It is as well to offer these articles to each person, as also the castor at the table. Vermicelli or macaroni may be used as a substitute for okra.

SOUP OR STOCK FROM ONE POUND OF BEEF.

Take one pound of lean beef, free from fat, mince it finely and add to it its own weight of cold water; heat it very slowly to boiling, two or three hours is not too much, let it boil briskly a minute or two, strain it through a towel. Mix the liquid with salt and other seasoning, tinge it darker with roast onions or burnt sugar. Dr. Liebig says this forms the best soup that can be prepared from one pound of flesh.

FISH SOUPS.

A variety of good soups can be made of fish by stewing them down in the same manner as meat, with the same addition of vegetables and herbs. If the skin is coarse, strip it off before using the fish, and when stewing skim off the oily particles.

WINTER SOUP.

Take a shin of beef, boil it in two gallons of water down to one gallon; pour it out after removing the bones, and let it cool. This will be one mass of jelly, from which as much can be taken daily as may be needed in the quantity of soup desired. Stew the vegetables or cook the rice, split peas, beans, and add all together with as much water as may be necessary, and let it boil well.

SORREL SOUP WITHOUT MEAT.

Wash a handful of sorrel, add some chervil, lettuce, and leeks; chop all very fine, and stew with salt and butter; when the vegetables are done enough, add some stock without meat or water. Let it stew again, and before you serve, add the yolks of three or four eggs well beaten, with some cream or good milk, taking care it does not boil after the eggs are added. Season to taste. Sorrel is prepared for winter in jars, first chopped, then pounded and seasoned. It must be closely covered.

RABBIT SOUP.

Cut up your rabbit and put it into a soup-pot, with a ham bone, a bunch of sweet herbs, a bay leaf, an onion stuck with cloves, some whole pepper, and let it simmer till the meat is tender, then cut off the meat into neat squares, return the bones and trimmings into the soup, and let it simmer till the meat is in rags; then strain it, and thicken it with flour and butter, mixed on the fire, without being browned; add a pint of highly seasoned stock, or if desired a pint of red wine—port is best—season to taste and let all simmer together with the meat that was cut off. Serve hot.

SPRING SOUP.

Cut an equal quantity of carrots, turnips, onions and leeks; stew them in some good stock; then add some French beans, peas, bean cucumbers, asparagus tops, lettuces, sorrel and chervil; add a little bit of white sugar; let these reduce to nearly a glaze; then add them to some stock thickened with green peas rubbed through a tammy. The soup might be thickened, to vary it, with asparagus rubbed through a tammy; in this case all the vegetables should be strained off, and some asparagus tops served only in the soup.

SOUP FOR INVALIDS.

Boil two pounds of lean veal and a quarter of a pound of pearl barley in a quart of water very slowly, until it becomes of the consistency of cream. Pass it through a fine sieve and salt it to taste. Flavor it with celery seed, if the taste be liked, or use fresh celery, if in season,—a very small quantity would suffice. It should simmer very slowly. This soup is very nourishing.

GUMBO.

Take a large fowl, cut in pieces, beat up and fry very brown, and make with it a highly seasoned and rich gravy. Cut into it a half gallon of tender green okra, as many ripe tomatoes, and pour on three pints of boiling water; boil until the vegetables are of the softest consistency, and chicken in rags. Stir in a heaping tablespoon of young sassafras leaves, dried and reduced to a powder. Strain into your dish hot. When well made this will almost rope like candy. Pepper, onions, and sweet herbs are used profusely in this soup, with salt to savor it.

WHITE SOUP.

Put four or five turnips, four leeks, two heads of celery, washed and sliced, into the saucepan with a piece of butter and a knuckle of ham; add a quart of stock, and let all stew together till tender. When nearly done, put in a pint of milk and some small pieces of bread; boil up two or three times, strain it and serve it hot.

MOCK TURTLE SOUP.

Parboil a calf's head divided, and cut all the meat in small pieces; then break the bones and boil them in some beef broth; fry some shalots in butter, add flour to thicken, and stir it in; skim it carefully while it boils up, and add a pint of white wine; let it simmer till the meat is perfectly tender, then put in some chives, parsley, basil, salt, cayenne, soy, and mushroom catsup to your taste, and boil it in for ten minutes; squeeze a little lemon juice into your tureen, pour your soup on it, and serve with force meat balls.

SHEEP'S-HEAD SOUP.

Cut the liver and lights into pieces, and stew them in four quarts of water, with some onions, carrots, and turnips, half pound of pearl barley, pepper, salt, cloves, and a little marjoram, parsley and thyme. Stew all these until nearly done enough, then put in the head and boil it until quite tender, then it should be taken out and everything strained from the liquor. Let this stand till cool, then take off the fat, and thicken it with butter and flour in the same way as mock turtle. A glass of wine may be put into the tureen if desired, before pouring in the soup.

CONCORD SOUP.

Three pounds of neck of beef, one cowheel, one pennyworth of carrots and turnips, part of a head of celery, one bunch of tied up sweet herbs, four onions browned, one pint of peas, all put together into three quarts of water. After boiling for some hours, to be well strained before serving up

CALF'S HEAD SOUP BROWNED.

Strain the liquor the head was boiled in, and set it away until next day; take off all the fat; fry an onion in a little butter in the soup pot, dredge in a little flour, stir until brown; cut up two carrots, two onions, two turnips, and whatever is left of the head, in inch pieces, put them in with the stock, a dozen cloves, pepper and salt; boil it about two hours; braid up a little flour and butter, stir it into the soup, and boil about ten minutes; add, if desired, half a tumbler of red wine; serve hot.

BROWN GRAVY SOUP.

Cut a few onions in pieces, fry them in dripping brown; cut three pounds of beef in pieces, brown this also, stirring and turning both meat and onions as they fry, then put them in the saucepan with a carrot, a turnip cut small, and a little celery if you have it, or two seeds of celery, add three quarts of water to this, stir all together with a little pepper and salt; simmer very slowly and skim off what rises; in three or four hours the soup will be clear. When served, add a little vermicelli, which should have previously been boiled in water; the liquor should be carefully poured off through a sieve.

CHICKEN SOUP.

Take two large old fat chickens; chop up the pieces and mash the bones. Put in a few slices of boiled ham if not too strong. Stew slowly until in rags. Then pour on three quarts of boiling water, and boil it down to half a gallon. Chop up the chickens' hearts, the yolks of four hard boiled eggs, and stir, with a tea cup half full of grated bread crumbs, into a cup of rich sweet cream; strain the soup, return it to the kettle with a bouquet of herbs, boil five minutes, stir in the cream, etc., and take it off quickly. Any soup of fowl or game may be made in the same way. Instead of the thickening prepared as above, you may boil in it some rice, or use vermicelli, or macaroni, previously simmered until soft.

OYSTER SOUP.—1.

Take a shin of veal, put it in a pot with three quarts of water, and a head of celery, pepper, and salt; boil it three hours; then strain it all through a sieve; add a small piece of butter, braided in a table-spoonful of flour; stir it in and give it one boil; have ready, washed out of the liquor, one gallon of oysters; strain the liquor into the soup, let it boil up, then put in the oysters with a spoonful of mushroon sauce; give it one boil and send it to the table very hot.

OYSTER SOUP.—2.

Slice some onions, fry them a light brown in a quarter of a pound of butter, then put them on the fire to stew in some stock, as much as required for your soup,—about half an hour is sufficient; before you serve, add two or three dozen of oysters, with their liquor strained. Thicken with the yolks of three eggs, and season it with white pepper, mace, and salt; it must not boil after the eggs are put in, but thicken like custard. Any kind of good broth or stock makes the foundation. Some add to this before the eggs are put in, a glass of white wine.

OYSTER SOUP.—3.

Mix one pint of water with whatever liquor you can drain from two quarts of fresh oysters. When this liquor comes to a full boil, put the oysters in, and boil until nearly done; then pour in a quart of fresh milk. Season with salt, pepper, and a blade of mace. If you prefer the soup a little thick, powder a half dozen crackers fine, and sift them into it.

OYSTER MOUTH SOUP.

First make a rich mutton broth, pour it on the oysters. Add a small piece of butter rolled in flour, let it simmer gently for about quarter of an hour. then serve it in a dish with crackers in the bottom.

ASPARAGUS SOUP WITH GREEN PEAS.

After cutting the greenest part of the asparagus into pieces about an inch or two long, blanch them in boiling water until quite done; add some good stock to it and strain it. Boil the pieces separately, add them to the soup and serve toasted bread with it, if desired.

GREEN PEA SOUP

Take some young carrots, turnips, onions, celery, and cabbage lettuces; cut them in slices, and put them into a stewpan with a little butter, and some lean ham cut in pieces. Cover them closely and let them stew for a short time. Fill up with stock sufficient for the soup required, and let it boil until the vegetables are quite soft, adding a few leaves of mint and the crust of a roll; pound all, and having boiled a quart of peas, as green as you can, strain them off and pound them also; mix them with the rest of the ingredients and pass through a sieve. Heat it, and season with salt, pepper and sugar; add a few young boiled peas, and use the spinach to restore it.

PEA SOUP WITHOUT MEAT.

Boil a pint of split peas in two quarts of water for four or five hours, or until quite tender. Then add two turnips, two carrots, a stick of celery, and some potatoes all cut in pieces. When tender, pulp it through a sieve. Cut a large onion in slices and fry it in butter and flour, to thicken the soup. Season to taste. If desired, a ham bone or a piece of beef can be stewed with the peas, to be taken out when the soup is pulped through the sieve. Serve with the soup pieces of bread fried crisp in butter.

ENGLISH PEA SOUP.

Take a half of a shin of beef, some beef and ham bones, and, if possible, a knuckle of veal, and boil all together, in a gallon of water, with a little salt. Clear it of the scum, as it rises, and have ready a quart of split peas, which have been soaked in cold water over night. Boil the meat very slowly, for two hours, then put in the peas, which will have absorbed the water, with a root of celery, and two or three carrots scraped, and cut in pieces. Sift in, also, a little dried mint, and season to taste. Cook slowly, stirring often with a wooden spoon, for four hours.

SOUPS.

ARTICHOKE SOUP.

Have a knuckle of veal (weighing about five pounds) for dinner. When all have dined, return the bones into the stewpan, with the liquor in which it was boiled, a nice, white onion, and two turnips. Boil some Jerusalem artichokes in milk, (skim milk will do,) then beat up all with the liquor, which, of course, must be first strained, then thickened with a small quantity of flour rubbed smooth in a tea cup, with a little milk. Use white pepper for the seasoning, to keep the color pure.

PARSNIP SOUP.

Cut in pieces half a dozen parsnips, a head of celery, and two onions; stew them in two quarts of stock until they are tender, take them out and pulp them through a coarse sieve, and pour the pulp back into the soup, flavor with pepper and salt, and before serving pour in a little milk.

CARROT SOUP.

Take half a gallon of stock; add three turnips, six carrots, three or four onions, and let them stew till tender. Take out the vegetables, strain the soup; take off the red part of the carrots, and rub it through a colander, make the soup about as thick as cream, with the pulped carrot. Heat it well through and serve.

COLANDERED SOUP.

Boil in water some peas with salt, pepper, and any vegetables. When quite soft mash the whole and bray through a sieve or colander. Instead of split peas you may use carrots, turnips, asparagus, or green peas, etc., as the staple. Put your colandered vegetables back into the pot, and if you have any stock, thin the soup with it; if you have no stock, thin with water, or milk and water. Boil up, and your dish is fit for table.

BARLEY SOUP.

In four quarts of water put two pounds of trimmings or odd pieces of meat, a quarter of a pound of pearl barley, four sliced onions, salt and pepper, with a little parsley, if you have it. Simmer for three hours or more.

FRENCH SOUP.

Put first a gallon of water to a sheep's head nicely cleaned, then reduce it to half the quantity, and add a teacupful of pearl barley, half a dozen large onions, a turnip, a carrot, a bunch of sweet herbs, pepper, salt, cloves, and a little mushroom or walnut catsup. Strain all off, cut part of the head in pieces and serve it in the soup, with a small quantity of white wine.

PUMPKIN SOUP.

Take three pounds of ripe pumpkin, peel and remove the seeds, cut into pieces of moderate size, and place in a stewpan over the fire with a pint of water; let it boil slowly till soft, strain off all the water, and pass the pumpkin through a colander; return the pulp into the stew pan adding nearly three pints of milk, one ounce or more of butter, a pinch of salt and pepper, and a few lumps of loaf sugar; boil for ten minutes, stirring often. Pour it boiling into the dish, on very thin slices of bread. The sugar improves the flavor, but may be omitted. It can be seasoned with a blade of mace or a little nutmeg.

GOURD SOUP.

Cut two pounds of the gourd into large slices, put it into a pan with three ounces of butter, two tea-spoonfuls of salt, two of moist sugar, a little pepper, and half a pint of water; set on the fire and stew gently for twenty minutes. When reduced to a pulp, add two table-spoonfuls of flour, stir and moisten with three pints of new milk; boil with care ten minutes longer, and serve with toast in slices. Vegetable marrow is equally good, made into soup according to this receipt.

ONION SOUP WITH MILK.

Slice some onions into a stew pan, with a piece of dripping, or lard, and a little flour. When brown add a quart of boiling milk, pepper, salt, and any cold cooked vegetables at hand. Boil up once or twice, and you have a delicious food, without meat or stock.

ONION SOUP WITH WATER.

Slice some onions into a stewpan, with any grease at hand, and keep them moving about till half brown, then sift in a little flour or fine bread-crumbs, and brown well. Now add a quart of boiling hot water, with salt, pepper, and some cold cooked vegetables. This would be greatly improved if you could contrive to fry in grease a few bits of bread cut into small pieces, and add them to the soup when brown.

TOMATO SOUP.

Boil a shin of veal three hours, or take some soup stock. Cut up two onions, two carrots, and two turnips, and put with it; also pepper, salt and one dozen tomatoes. Boil this two hours, and strain it through a sieve. Toast some pieces of bread a light brown; cut them in dice form, and put them into the dish. The soup should be turned on to the toast just before it is taken to the table, as soaking long spoils it.

BREAD SOUP.

Set the stock on the fire to boil; let it simmer three or four hours. Place in a bowl bits of bread, no matter how hard and stale. Pour over them enough hot broth to soak them well; mash fine, and put the whole into the stock. Let it continue to simmer a few minutes more after the bread mash has been added.

VERMICELLI SOUP.

Put a shin of veal, one onion, two carrots, two turnips, and a little salt, into four quarts of water. Boil this three hours; add two cups of vermicelli, and boil it an hour and a half longer. Before serving take out the bone and vegetable.

JENNY LIND'S SOUP.

The following soup is stated by Miss Bremer, to be the soup constantly served to Mademoiselle Jenny Lind, as prepared by her own cook. The sago and eggs were found by her soothing to the chest, and beneficial to the voice. Wash a quarter of a pound of best pearl sago thoroughly, then stew it quite tender and very thick in water or thick broth; (it will require nearly or quite a quart of liquid, which should be poured to it cold and heated slowly;) then mix gradually with it a pint of good boiling cream or milk, and the yolks of four fresh eggs, and mingle the whole carefully with two quarts of strong veal or beef stock, which should always be kept ready boiling. Serve immediately.

GERMAN PANCAKE SOUP.

Make a batter with a pound of flour, a little salt, half a pint of milk; stir well, and add two eggs beaten; it should be of the consistency of cream. Make this into pancakes, fried very pale yellow. As each one is fried, lay it on a board and double over once. Roll each slightly, and cut into strips half an inch wide, and put them into the soup tureen and pour good stock, well seasoned and strained, over them. Serve hot.

SOUP JARDINIERE.

Put a bouquet of finely cut vegetables, consisting of celery, a carrot, an onion, tomatoes,—two if fresh, two table-spoonfuls if canned,—a leek, and a bunch of parsley, in a stew pan, with two ounces of butter, pepper, salt, and cover down for nearly an hour; when cooked soft in the butter add a quart or more of broth, and two table-spoonfuls of cold jelly gravy, and leave the whole to simmer together an hour longer, or until dinner time. During the process of coming to a boil, the butter or grease rising to the top should be skimmed off and preserved, to be clarified for further use.

AN INEXPENSIVE SOUP.

Take three pounds of the neck of beef, one cow heel, carrots and turnips, half a head of celery, one bunch of tied up sweet herbs, four onions browned, one pint of peas; put together into three quarts of water and, after boiling some hours, strain through a sieve. The best part of the cow heel may be cut in square pieces and served up in the soup.

BAKED SOUP.

When baking is more convenient, in four quarts of water put

one pound of trimmings or odd pieces of meat, two onions, and two sliced carrots, two ounces of rice or bits of bread, one pint of split peas, pepper and salt. Put the whole into a close jar, and bake slowly for four hours. This will make a good, wholesome food for a large family.

HOTCH POTCH.

Put a pint of peas into a quart of water; boil them until they are so tender as easily to be pulped through a sieve. Take of the leanest end of a loin of mutton three pounds, cut it into chops, put it into a saucepan with a gallon of water, four carrots, four turnips, cut in small pieces; season with pepper and salt. Boil until all the vegetables are quite tender; put in the pulped peas a head of celery and a sliced onion. Boil fifteen minutes, and serve.

SCOTCH MUTTON BROTH.

Take the scrag end of a large sized neck of mutton, reserving the best half for cutlets, put it into a stewpan and boil it with three quarts of water, half a pint of Scotch barley, three leeks, three onions, a little parsley and thyme. Skim it, and after it has boiled up, let it stand on the top of the stove and simmer for two hours, then skim again, and if it is too thick with barley add half a pint of boiling water, three or four turnips, a head of celery, and two carrots cut in pieces; after which, let it simmer slowly an hour and a half more; the barley should be almost wholly dissolved. The meat may be cut in pieces and served with the broth or served separately.

BROTH FOR AN INVALID.

Cut the chicken, veal, mutton or beef, up into pieces, and put into a jar with a cover; fill with water, adding a little salt; close down tight, and let it simmer all day on the stove or range; strain, and season to taste. This method extracts all the juices and strength of the meat, and is infinitely better than boiling.

MEATS.

TO BOIL BEEF.

If the beef is very salt put it in cold water; if it is only slightly corned put it in *boiling* water, and let it cook very slowly. This will render it quite as tender as if put into cold water, and at the same time all the juices of the meat will be retained. Boil until tender, but not until ragged, so that the meat will cut clean and clear, when cold.

Never buy poor, *cheap* pieces of corned beef, they are full of bone and gristle; there is no satisfaction in eating from them, and they prove the most costly in the end.

Fresh beef should never be boiled plain, unless it is boiled down for soup; it may be stewed, or cooked alamode, or stuffed and baked, provided the piece is not suitable for roasting.

STEWED BEEF.

Take six pounds of round of beef, place it in a deep kettle, with half a pint of water, half a pint of broth, a gill of good vinegar, a bunch of parsley, a few cloves, a sprig of sweet marjoram, and some salt, and pepper. Let it lay in this over night, turning it several times, if it is warm weather; it is best to give the mixture a boil up, putting the meat to it cold. The next day simmer four or five hours, adding two onions chopped small; take up the meat, add a tea spoonful of butter braided in flour to the strained liquor, with a dash of mushroom catsup. Pour it over the meat, and serve. If more liquid is required while stewing, put in broth or gravy, if you have it,—if not, water.

CURED BRISKET OF BEEF FOR CHRISTMAS.

At night rub fourteen pounds of brisket of beef, with one ounce of saltpetre pounded very fine; the next morning mix together half a pound of sugar, and four handfuls of common salt, and rub the beef well over with it. Let it remain in the pickle two weeks, turning and rubbing it every day; then take it out, and put it into an earthen pan, with some suet chopped fine to cover the bottom of the pan, and the same on the top of the beef, with a little water to keep the pan from burning. Bake it slowly for six hours. Eaten cold.

CURED BEEF, TO EAT COLD.

Put three fourths of a pound of coarse sugar, one pound of bay salt, nearly an ounce of allspice, a tea-spoonful or less of cloves, a small piece of saltpetre, and three cents worth of cochineal, into four quarts of water; let these all boil slowly together fully twenty minutes; then take from the fire, and let it stand till quite cool. Take a round of beef, from twenty to twenty-five pounds, and pour this pickle over it, turning it once or twice a day, continuing this for two or three weeks. At the end of this time it will be ready for use.

BOILED BEEF STEAKS.

It is not necessary to beat them; cut them half an inch thick and place them on the gridiron. The fire should be clear and brisk, the gridiron should be hot, the bars rubbed with suet. Sprinkle a little salt over the fire. Turn the steaks often, keeping a dish close to the fire, in which to drain the gravy from the top of the steak as you lift it. The gridiron is best set in a slanting direction, so that fat will not fall on the coals and make a smoke. If there is a smoke, take the steak off for a moment. Over a brisk fire of coals steaks will be done in ten minutes. Then lay them on a hot plate with a small slice of butter on each piece, pouring over them the gravy, and sprinkling on a very little salt.

BEEF ALAMODE.

Lard a round of beef with slices of fat bacon dipped in vinegar; roll it up with chopped seasoning, cloves, sage, parsley, thyme, pepper and green onions; bind it close and put it in a sauce pan. Turn it when half done, and let it stand for twelve hours on a stove. It can be eaten hot or cold.

BRAISED BEEF.

Take five or six pounds of rump, and cover down close in a pan, with enough butter or clarified dripping to prevent burning or sticking to the pan; let it cook slowly for an hour, then pour off the grease and put in a little broth, half a cup of rich gravy, a few drops of vinegar, and a little calf's-foot jelly, if convenient; cover down closely again and let it cook, with the heat all about it, for two hours longer, basting frequently; when it is quite tender, take it up, and mix half a table-spoonful of flour with a little cream, and put into the gravy, which season to taste, and then pour over the meat, that is to say, a part of it, for an economical cook will reserve part to assist in the preparation of next day's dinner.

BRISKET OF BEEF STUFFED.

A piece weighing eight pounds requires about five or six hours to boil. Make a dressing of bread crumbs, pepper, salt, sweet herbs, a little mace, and one onion chopped fine and mixed with an egg. Put the dressing in between the fat and the lean of the beef and sew it up tight; flour the cloth; pin the beef up very tight in it; boil it five or six hours. When it is done take the cloth off, and press it until it is cold. This is to be cut in thin slices and eaten cold.

MOCK DUCK.

Procure a steak cut from the rump of beef, and fill it with a dressing made of chopped bread, pork, sage, onions and sweet marjoram, and well seasoned; sew it up, put a slice or two of pork, or some of the dressing, on the top, and set it in a pan, into which pour a pint of water; cover down tight, and let it cook slowly in the oven three hours; then take off the lid, brown quickly, and serve hot.

OX CHEEK STUFFED AND BAKED.

Mash and soak thoroughly an ox cheek; put it into plenty of warm water and boil gently an hour, throwing in a large tea spoonful of salt and skimming occasionally. Lift it out, and when cool take out the bones. Put in a good roll of forcemeat; bind up the cheek securely, and bake it in a moderate oven an hour or an hour and a half, until it is quite tender clear through. Drain it from fat, unbind it, and serve it with a good brown gravy, or any sauce preferred, or with melted butter in a tureen, a cut lemon and cayenne.

SPICED BEEF.

This can be made from either the round, brisket or rump of beef, but ribs are the most tender eating. Procure from eight to ten pounds of the ribs of beef; those which have a good amount of fat upon them are the best; remove the bone, rub the meat well with one ounce of saltpetre pounded very finely, and three hours after this has been applied, rub on half a pound of moist sugar; let the meat lay in this for two days, then take one ounce of ground pepper, half an ounce of pounded mace, a few cloves well pounded, and a tea-spoonful of cayenne pepper. Mix all these ingredients well, and rub them well into the beef, particularly into the holes, adding occasionally a little salt. Roll up the meat as a round, and bind it with a strong fillet. Chop some suet very finely, cover the beef with it, and bake it in a moderately heated oven, from five to six hours. While baking, it may be placed either upon a meat tin, or in an earthen jar as nearly of its size as possible. In both cases there should be a cup full of gravy or water under the meat, to prevent it from burning; if a jar is used there should be a cover to it.

FILLETS OF BEEF.

Take two pounds of steak from a round of beef, cut thin, divide it into strips about three inches broad; beat them with a chopper till flat and tender, then chop finely some fresh gathered mushrooms, and add a little pepper, salt, and fresh butter in small pieces. Lay the mushrooms and seasoning half over the strips of steak; roll them up, fasten them with a coarse needle and thread, (or with very tiny skewers,) and lay the fillets in a pie dish to bake. The baking dish should be covered with another dish of the same size, to prevent the steam from evaporating, otherwise the outside of the meat will be dry. Thicken the gravy which is in the baking dish with flour and butter, and add mushroom catsup as a seasoning.

The fillets will require turning whilst baking. But a less troublesome plan of cooking a steak in this mode, is to have it dressed in one piece. The steak should be cut thin and rolled as described, but instead of mushrooms add a fine forcemeat or plain veal stuffing.

FILLETS OF BEEF WITH ANCHOVY.

Soak five or six anchovies in water for about two hours, split them and put the fillet with them, mixed with some bacon; boil it on a slow fire with a small quantity of broth, a glass of white wine, a clove of garlic, two cloves, and a bunch of herbs. When sufficiently done, strain the sauce, add to it a piece of butter rolled in flour, two spoonsful of cream, and a few capers; mix in a little yolk of egg, and pour it over the fillet.

FILLETS OF BEEF WITH FORCEMEAT.

Make forcemeat with fowls' livers, grated bacon, a little butter, parsley, shallots, three yolks of eggs, and spices. Cut a fillet of beef in two, flatten it with a cleaver, lard it through, then lay the forcemeat between it, and also about a pint of small mushrooms which have been previously stewed in a little butter; tie the meat up in a cloth, boil it in broth, with a glass of wine and a bunch of sweet herbs.

HUNTER'S BEEF.

Take a round of beef weighing fifteen pounds, and let it hang two or three days. Reduce to a very fine powder two ounces of saltpetre, two ounces of sugar, three quarters of an ounce of cloves, the same of nutmeg, one third of an ounce of allspice, two handsful of common salt. Bone the beef, and rub the spices well into it, and do so every day for two or three weeks. When you wish to dress the meat, wash the spices off the outside with cold water, bind it up tightly with tape, and place it in a pan with a tea-cupful of water at the bottom; cover the top of the meat with chopped suet; cover the pan with a coarse paste, and brown paper over that. Let it bake five hours, and when it is cold remove the paste and the tape. Some persons stuff the hole left by taking out the bone, with chopped parsley and sweet herbs.

HUNG BEEF.

Make a strong brine of bay salt, saltpetre and pump water. Place in it a piece of ribs of beef, and let it lie for nine days. Then hang it in a chimney in the smoke of wood or sawdust. When it is nearly dry, wash the outside with bullock's blood, and when this is dry, boil it and serve it with vegetables.

HAMBURGH PICKLE FOR BEEF, HAMS AND TONGUE.

Take two gallons of water, three pounds of bay salt, or if that cannot be got, five pounds of common salt, two pounds of coarse sugar, two ounces of saltpetre, and two ounces of black pepper bruised and tied in a fold of muslin; boil all together twenty minutes, removing the scum as it rises. Pour the pickle into a deep earthen jar, and when it is cold lay in the meat so that every part is covered. Turn the meat occasionally. A middling sized round of beef will be ready for the table in a fortnight.

MEAT PIE FOR LUNCH.

Place a thick rump steak well larded and rubbed with shallot in the bottom of a saucepan, cut up some game into small pieces without bones, and lay over the steak, mixed with pepper and salt and some pieces of bacon; stew them all well, and add chopped mushrooms and a rich gravy, before making them into the pie. The pie should have a thick ornamental crust round the sides and on the bottom. Let the top crust be loose, so that additional gravy can be poured in; and bake until it is a light brown.

BEEF BALLS.

Take a piece of beef boiled tender, chop it very finely with an onion, season with salt and pepper, add parsley, bread crumbs, lemon peel, and grated nutmeg; moisten it with an egg, mix well together, and roll it into balls. Then dip them in flour and fry them in boiling lard or fresh dripping. Serve them with thickened brown gravy, or fried bread crumbs.

BEEF CROQUETTES.

Mince some dressed beef very fine, melt a piece of butter in a stew pan, add three or four onions, chopped fine, and fried a pale brown; add a spoonful of flour, and moisten with a little good stock, or gravy, seasoned with pepper, salt, nutmeg, and a little parsley chopped fine. When the sauce is done enough, put in the minced beef; let it stew a short time till the sauce is dry, then form the meat into either balls or rolls; dip each into the beaten white of eggs; have some butter, or lard, hot; put each ball very gently into the frying pan, shaking a little flour over them, roll them about gently in the pan to brown them alike, and when a good color, drain them on a cloth, and serve on dressed parsley.

HASHED BEEF.

Take cold roast beef, cut in slices, and remove skin and gristle. Place in a stewpan a small piece of butter, an onion chopped fine, a table-spoonful of flour; put it on the fire and stir it till it browns, but be careful it does not burn. Then stir in gradually half a pint of stock, flavored with herbs, with a little salt, and let it boil up thick. Put in two table-spoonsful of hot green pickles chopped small, and the slices of beef. Heat them through and serve with sippets of toast.

COLD MINCED BEEF.

Having removed the fat and skin, mince the beef nearly to a paste: stew gently—if possible over night, so that the fat may be skimmed off. Season with pepper and salt, and sprinkle with oat-meal; chop a half handful of parsley and thyme and throw in; boil a large onion nearly tender, chop it and mix it in; add sufficent broth or skim-milk and water to cover the beef; let it simmer two hours; then thicken with a little oatmeal, and add a dessert spoonful of mushroom or walnut catsup; stir well, boil a minute and serve with pieces of bread toasted. The bones from which the meat is cut will do for the broth in which the meat is stewed, if broth is used. Even then, however, a tea-cupful of milk may be added with the thickening.

DRIED BEEF COOKED.

After being thinly sliced, as usual, freshen it in water; stew it in a little water until tender; then beat an egg with a little flour, put a lump of butter to the beef, stir in the egg and flour, and serve on toast bread with the gravy over it.

KEEPING BEEF.

Cut up the meat in pieces as large as you wish, and pack it in a barrel or cask. Then make a brine as follows: one pound and a half of salt to one gallon of water, one ounce of saltpetre to one hundred pounds of beef, one table-spoonful of ground pepper to one hundred pounds of beef. Put in the salt and saltpetre, heat it boiling hot, skim it, then add the pepper. Pour it on the beef boiling hot and cover closely.

TOUGH BEEF.

Carbonate of soda will remedy tough beef. Cut the steaks the day before using into slices about two inches thick; rub over them a small quantity of soda; wash off next morning, cut it into suitable thickness, and cook. The same process will answer for fowls, legs of mutton, etc.

A LEG OF MUTTON IN FOUR MEALS.

For the first meal, cut off a handsome knuckle and boil it; for the second meal, take as many cutlets as required for the family from the joint; for the third meal, roast the remainder of the joint. The remains of both the boiled and roasted meat, may then be hashed for a fourth meal.

BOILED LEG OF MUTTON.

Cut off the shank bone and trim the knuckle. Boil with salt in the water, skimming. If it weighs nine or ten pounds it will need to cook three hours. It may be served with parsley or celery and butter, or caper sauce, or pickled kidney beans and onion sauce; mashed turnips, spinach and potatoes are good with it.

ROAST LEG OF MUTTON.

A leg of mutton weighing ten pounds should be roasted two hours. When half done, turn the fat out of the roaster; then baste the meat with the dripping. Make the gravy the same as for roast beef, or add a few spoonsful of current jelly and a cup of red wine. Ten minutes more should be allowed for every extra pound of mutton.

LEG OF MUTTON WITH OYSTERS.

Parboil fat oysters and mix with them some parsley, minced onions, and sweet herbs, boiled and chopped fine, and the yolks of two hard boiled eggs. Cut five or six holes in the fleshy part of a leg of mutton, and put in the mixture; dress it as follows: Tie it up in a cloth and let it boil gently two and a half or three hours, according to the size.

ROAST SHOULDER OF LAMB.

A nice way to cook a shoulder of lamb is to bone it, and fill the space with a stuffing made of chopped mushrooms, parsley, salt pork, cracker crumbs, some sweet herbs, pepper and salt, and a raw egg. Braise it with some good stock gravy, and send it to table surrounded by spinach, garnished with slices of egg.

ROAST QUARTER OF LAMB.

To roast a quarter of lamb, lard it slightly with salt pork, and sprinkle it with bread crumbs and finely-chopped parsley. Make a sauce of some stock gravy, a table-spoonful of vinegar, chopped mint, a little yolk of egg, and mushroom catsup; pour over the joint, and let it stand in the oven a few moments. Serve with green peas, with which a little bunch of mint has been boiled.

ROAST JOINT OF MUTTON.

Roast the joint of a leg of mutton in the usual way; rub on a little salt, and also sprinkle on flour as the fat comes out. Have it nicely and evenly browned on every side, baste it well, and when ready, to take out, pour off the dripping and have ready a little boiling water, but do not drown the real juices of the meat. Serve with currant jelly if convenient.

BROILED MUTTON CHOPS.

Trim them; remove what fat is not required to cook with them; season and broil over a clear fire, turning often until done. Serve with small pieces of butter on them.

FRIED MUTTON CHOPS.

Trim them, season with pepper and salt, fry them in their own fat or pork fat, turn them often. Serve them hot. Brown a little butter and flour, add a little water, and pour the gravy over them.

MUTTON CHOPS WITH CUCUMBERS.

Slice cucumbers and lay them in a deep dish, sprinkled with salt and wet with vinegar. Fry the chops a nice brown, lay them in a stewpan, and put the cucumbers, drained, over them; add some chopped onions, pepper and salt, cover them with weak broth and stew them, skimming occasionally.

SAVORY MUTTON CHOPS.

Cut up the chops and beat them with the edge of a knife. Beat the yolks of a few eggs and dip the cutlets in them; season them with pepper, salt, nutmeg, and bread crumbs. Roll them in buttered papers and boil them. Use for sauce some good gravy, a piece of butter, crumbs of bread, capers, anchovies, with some nutmeg and a little vinegar. As soon as they are dressed, tear off the papers, and set them on the dish with the sauce.

COLD MUTTON BROILED.

Cut in thick slices cold boiled leg of mutton; it should not be cooked too much or it will fall into pieces; put on it salt and pepper, and then broil it. Let it be very hot, and add a thick sauce flavored with fresh tomatoes, or tomato sauce, and serve.

MUTTON PUDDING.

Take cold boiled mutton, or roast mutton if that is on hand, cut it into small slices, and slice a few potatoes. Dip the slices of meat into a mixture of salt, pepper, flour, and finely chopped onion; butter the basin, line it with suet crust, fill it with alternate layers of mutton and potatoes, pour in a tea-cupful of gravy, or stock, cover with crust and cook it.

FIRST RATE WESTERN STEW.

Part of a breast of mutton or lamb, cut in bits, as many potatoes, pepper and salt to taste; two onions, a bunch of parsley, a bunch of sweet herbs. Stew all together in barely sufficient water to cover them, for two hours, gently. Then put in a tea-cup of tomato catsup, and boil up again. Serve hot.

MUTTON CROQUETTES.

Cut the meat from a neck of mutton into pieces about as large as your finger, lard them through with ham bacon; let them simmer in some stock with sweet herbs; when done, take the pieces of meat out, reduce the gravy and strain it over them; cover each piece with good fowl seasoning, wrap it in a slice of bacon, wash them over with egg, strew them with bread crumbs, and bake them.

HASHED MUTTON.

At night cut cold boiled or roast mutton into slices, remove the solid fat, break the bones, and put it in a saucepan with a large onion sliced thin; pour in broth or stock to just cover over it, and let it simmer until at boiling heat, but do not let it boil. Pour it into an earthen dish and cover it for the night. In the morning, or sometime before dinner, skim off the fat, return it to the pot with seasoning and a little flour, and let it simmer, but not boil, a long time. As the meat gets dry, pour in milk. A quarter of an hour before serving, take away the bones and skin, add a dessert spoonful or more of walnut or mushroom catsup, thicken smoothly with flour, oat meal or Indian meal, wet with milk and liquor from the hash; boil a minute longer, add more seasoning if required, and serve with sippets of toasted bread.

UNCOOKED MUTTON MINCED.

Cut off two pounds from a leg of mutton, remove the fat, and chop it up finely, with a slice or two of bacon; season with pepper and salt, and put it into a saucepan with a tea-cupful of gravy, six ounces of butter. Chop three young lettuces; add a quart of young peas, an onion chopped small. Stir all together over a gentle fire until quite hot, then place the saucepan closely covered at the side of the fire, and let it stew gently for three hours. Serve in a hot dish, and place round it a wall of well-cooked rice.

HASHED MUTTON WITH MUSHROOMS.

Take nice slices of mutton, without skin or fat, and sprinkle each piece with flour on both sides. Put six large mushrooms, after having been trimmed and cut in four pieces, into a stewpan with a small piece of butter, to stew; add a little gravy, some pepper and salt, and when sufficiently done, put in the meat; let it heat through, slowly, stirring it the while that it may not burn, but not let it boil, or the meat will be hard. As soon as the hash thickens and the flour is all heat through and changed color, the hash is done. Serve immediately with sippets of neatly cut, thin toast, or fried bread, round the dish.

MINCED MUTTON.

Prepare a sauce by taking finely chopped onions, parsley, and sweet herbs; fry in butter, and add a table-spoonful of flour mixed in water or stock, and as much stock as required. Mince cold boiled or roast mutton, taking only the good parts, place it in the sauce and warm it through without boiling. This should be served with poached eggs on the top.

MINCED MUTTON WITH CUCUMBERS.

To prepare minced mutton and cucumber, the mutton should be minced as before, then a large cucumber should be pared, the seeds taken out, and cut up in small, square pieces about the size of a nutmeg. Stew till tender in savory brown sauce, and put in the minced mutton and some thickening, if necessary. Mix the mutton and cucumber well together, let it heat through, and serve it piled high on a dish, with sippets of fried bread round it.

THE EPICURE'S HASH.

Cut in slices about one pound of cold mutton; then put two sliced onions into a stew pan with a small piece of butter, and fry brown; then add half a pint of good flavored broth, a dessert-spoonful of Harvey sauce, the same spoon three times full of taragon vinegar, two tea-spoonsful of curry paste, a small lump of sugar, and a little pepper and salt to taste; let this sauce just boil up once and then simmer slowly by the fire for half an hour; stir it often, and thicken it with a table spoonful of flour, mixed smooth in a little cold water; or you can use corn starch, half the quantity will do. When the thickening has boiled thoroughly, and the sauce ready, put in the meat, let it heat through but not boil. Serve hot, with pieces of toast round the dish.

QUARTER OF LAMB AS A SAVORY DISH.

Procure a hind quarter of lamb, and cut off the shank from it. Raise the thick part of the flesh from the bone with a knife. Prepare some forcemeat, the same as for veal or any other white meat, and place it between the bone and flesh, and all underneath the kidney. Roast the lamb partially, then place it on a saucepan with a quart of mutton gravy; cover it up and let it stew gently. When it is sufficiently cooked, take it up and lay it upon a hot dish. Skim the fat from the gravy, and strain it; add a wine glass full of sherry or Maderia wine, a dessert spoonful of walnut catsup, two of browning, the juice of half a lemon, a little cayenne pepper, and half a pint of bearded oysters. Thicken with a little butter rolled in flour; pour the gravy hot over the lamb, and serve it up.

SHOULDER OF VEAL.

Put into an earthen pan a glass of water, two or three spoonsful of vinegar, three onions, sliced parsley, chives, two shallots, a bay leaf, a bit of thyme, two cloves, and about two ounces of butter; cover the pan close, and put a paste of coarse flour and water round the edges, to keep in the steam; let it bake three hours, strain the sauce and pour over the meat, after seasoning it with pepper and salt. Another way is to stuff it with bread crumbs, suet, or butter, parsley, a little thyme and lemon peel, pepper, salt and nutmeg; then lard it, and roast until brown, serving it with rich brown gravy.

STEWED LOIN OF VEAL.

Take part of a loin of veal, the chump end will do; put it into a large, thick, well tinned iron saucepan, or into a stewpan, two ounces of butter, and shake it over a moderate fire, until it begins to brown; flour the veal well all over, lay it into the saucepan, and when it is of a light brown, pour in gradually veal broth, gravy, or boiling water, to nearly half its depth; add a little salt, one or two sliced carrots, a small onion or more, and a bunch of parsley; stew the veal very gently for an hour or more; then turn and let it stew another hour until it is perfectly done. Dish the joint; skim all the fat from the gravy, and strain it over the meat, or keep the joint hot while it is rapidly reduced to a richer consistency.

BREAST OF VEAL STUFFED.

Cut off the gristle, raise the meat off the bones, then lay a good forcemeat, made of pounded veal, some sausage meat, parsley, and a few shallots chopped very fine, and seasoned with pepper, salt, and nutmeg; then roll the veal tightly, and sew it with the twine; lay some slices of fat bacon in a stewpan, and put the veal roll on it; add some stock, pepper, salt, and a bunch of sweet herbs; let it stew three hours; then cut out the twine, strain the sauce after skimming it, thicken it with brown flour; let it boil up once, and pour it over the veal; garnish with slices of lemon, each cut in four. A fillet of veal, first stuffed with forcemeat, can be dressed in the same manner, but it must first be roasted, so as to brown it a good color; and forcemeat balls, highly seasoned, should be served round the veal.

BREAST OF VEAL STEWED.

Brown the veal first, by half roasting it; remove as many of the bones as possible, and then put it in a stewpan with some stock, a glass of wine, a piece of lemon peel, a bunch of sweet herbs, a ham bone, and a carrot; let it simmer slowly in the oven about half an hour before it is served; strain off the sauce and remove the herbs, etc., put it then back with the veal, first thickening it with some flour browned with butter; let it boil up to take off the raw taste of the flour; then add some pickled mushrooms with their juice, and serve.

ROAST FILLET OF VEAL.

Take out or ask the butcher to do so, the bone from the center, and fill the cavity with a stuffing of bread crumbs, nice salt pork, an onion, sweet herbs, and pepper and salt to taste, all chopped up together until thoroughly blended; with the remainder fill up all the interstices and fasten with skewers; cover down in a bake-pan with a teacupful of water, for an hour and a half, basting occasionally; then remove the cover and roast until it becomes a rich brown. This dish is a universal favorite.

LOIN OF VEAL

This is best larded. Have every joint thoroughly cut, and between each one lay a slice of salt pork; roast a fine brown, and so that the upper sides of the pork will be crisp; baste often; season with pepper; the pork will make it sufficiently salt.

KNUCKLE OF VEAL.

The knuckle, which is left after cutting off the fillet, makes excellent soup, or is very good boiled with rice. It should cook slowly on the top of the range, so that the rice will not burn, and be dished up with the meat in the center, and small pieces of butter placed at intervals round it, in the rice.

KNUCKLE OF VEAL WITH RICE.

Boil a knuckle of veal, two turnips, one onion, six pepper-corns, a head of celery, and a tea-cupful of rice, together, very gently on the top of the stove for about three hours, skimming occasionally, and mixing in a little salt. When done, send it to the table with rice around the veal. The stock in which the veal has boiled, will help to make good soup.

VEAL CUTLETS.

Take six neck cutlets of veal, trim them neatly, and cut off the bone; lard the cutlets, put them into a frying-pan with a little butter, and let them brown; shake a little flour over them, and then moisten them with a little stock; add a bunch of fine herbs, some carrots cut in forms, or scalloped, some small onions, mushrooms, salt, two cloves; when the cutlets are done enough, dish them and put the vegetables in the middle; skim the sauce, strain it, and pour it over the cutlets. They must be well seasoned.

MINCED VEAL WITH MACARONI.

Mince up cold veal with a slice of ham, a little grated rind of lemon, a little salt, and a few spoonsful of broth or gravy. Simmer gently, taking care that it does not boil. Serve it upon small squares of buttered toast, and surround it with a border of macaroni, cooked without cheese.

VEAL FRITTERS.

Cut cold boiled veal into small pieces, dip each in butter, fry them a light brown color, drain them well from the fat, pile them high in a dish and pour round them a thick, brown sauce, strongly flavored with fresh tomatoes when in season—when not in season, use tomato sauce.

BLANQUETTE OF VEAL.

Cut cold roast veal in small pieces, put half a pint of white sauce, and a little mushroom catsup in a sauce-pan; when it boils, put in the meat and let it remain until it is well heated; break in an egg slightly beaten; when the sauce thickens put in a little juice of lemon, and send to table.

VEAL ROLLS.

Cut some slices of veal very thin and divide them into neat pieces. Lay on each some good forcemeat, seasoned high; roll each up tight, and tie them with coarse thread; put them on a bird spit; after dipping each in the yolks of eggs, well beaten, flour them over, and baste them with butter; half an hour will do them. Have a good gravy ready, with truffles and mushrooms chopped; and after dishing the rolls, pour the gravy round them.

MOCK BEEFSTEAK.

Take a leg of veal and corn it slightly, by sprinkling salt over it; let it lay a week, then cut from it steaks, which fry in the fat from a few thin slices of browned salt pork, or broil and serve with butter and pepper; no salt will be needed.

LOUIS' FAVORITE DISH.

Take two pounds of veal from the leg or the neck, and cut into nice pieces, which fry a light brown, with a slice of ham or salt pork, which may afterward be cut in pieces; have ready a sauce, made by mixing cold gravy or soup stock with a table-spoonful of flour, a little thyme, pepper, salt, and some button mushrooms; pour this over the veal and ham, and let the whole simmer together for half an hour. Of course, the veal and ham should be removed from the grease in which they were fried, and placed in a clean pan before the sauce is poured over them.

MINCED VEAL.

Take the part that is rare done, of either roasted or boiled veal, and chop it very fine. Take beef gravy sufficient for the veal to be cooked in, dissolve cavear, of the quantity of an acorn, to one pound of meat; put into the gravy the minced veal, and let it boil one minute. Pour it into a soup dish, upon sippets of toasted bread. Garnish the dish with slices of bacon broiled.

VEAL OMELETS.

Three pounds of finely chopped veal, three eggs, six cracker rolls, one table-spoonful of salt, one of thyme, one of sage, and half a table-spoonful of pepper, half a teacup of milk, mix well, form into a loaf, baste with milk and butter while baking. Bake two hours.

VEAL OLIVES.

Cut two thin steaks from a fillet of veal, beat them and rub them over with the yolk of an egg; then cut them in strips from four to five inches in length; lay over every strip a very thin piece of fat bacon, and strew them over with bread crumbs, a little lemon peel, and parsley, chopped small; season with cayenne pepper and salt. Roll them up separately, and fasten them with a little wooden skewer in each. Dip them into egg, bread crumbs and parsley, chopped small. Put some clarified beef dripping into a frying pan, let it boil up, then throw in the veal olives and fry them a light brown color. Take a pint of good gravy, add to it a dessert-spoonful of lemon pickle, and same of walnut catsup, and one of browning; cayenne pepper and salt to taste; thicken this with flour and butter. Place the veal olives on a hot dish, strain the gravy hot upon them, garnish with lemon pickle and forcemeat balls, and strew over them a few pickled mushrooms.

VEAL CHEESE.

Take the hind quarter of veal, add three eggs, one pound of pork, half a loaf of bread; season with salt and pepper to taste; chop, and wet the whole with milk. Bake two hours, then turn it out and eat it cold.

A ROAST PIG.

About three or four weeks is the right age, to roast whole; cut off the toes, leaving the skin long to wrap around the ends of the legs, and put it in cold water. Make a stuffing, with about six powdered crackers, one table-spoonful of sage, two of summer-savory, one chopped onion, half a pint of cream, two eggs, with pepper, and salt. Mix these together, and stew about fifteen minutes. Take the pig from the water, fill it with the stuffing, and sew it up. Boil the liver, and heart, with five pepper-corns, chop fine for the gravy. Put the pig to roast, with a pint of water, and a table-spoonful of salt. When it begins to roast, flour it well and baste it with the drippings. Bake three hours.

ROAST PORK.

For roast pork, make a stuffing of crackers powdered fine, with half a pint of cream, two eggs, a small quantity of summer-savory, pepper, and salt; cook about ten minutes. Take the leg of pork, of seven or eight pounds in weight, and raise the skin off the knuckle, and put in the stuffing, then make deep cuts in the thick part of the leg, and fill them also. It must be floured over, and a pint of water put in the pan. While roasting, baste it often with the drippings. Cook about three hours and a half. Skim some of the fat from the gravy, add a little flour, and boil it well a few minutes. Serve with apple sauce, or any other that may be preferred.

SPARE RIB OF PORK.

Joint it down the middle; sprinkle it with fine sage, salt, and a little flour; put it in the oven and baste it well. Serve it with apple sauce, egg sauce, or white sauce.

PORK CUTLETS.

To broil or fry these, cut them half an inch thick, trim them into neat form, take off part of the fat. To broil them, sprinkle a little pepper on them, and broil them over a clear and moderate fire a quarter of an hour, or a few minutes more; and just before taking them off, sprinkle over a little fine salt. For frying, flour them well and season with pepper, and salt, and sage. They may also be dipped into an egg, and then into bread crumbs mixed with minced sage; if for broiling, add a little clarified butter to the egg, or sprinkle it on the cutlets.

BOSTON PORK AND APPLE PIE.

Boil one pound of nice, sweet, salt pork, and when it is cold chop it up fine. Peel half a peck of greening apples, chop them up also, and mix with the pork. Sweeten with sugar, and spice with cinnamon and ground cloves, or allspice, and bake in deep soup plates, slowly and thoroughly, with a crust on both sides.

ENGLISH PORK OR RAISED PIE.

These constitute a favorite luncheon dish in England. Take a pound of nice lard, and heat it until melted, in a little water. Use this hot melted lard to mix the flour into a paste, with a little salt. Work the paste very smooth, divide it, and form each piece into a round ball, gradually working a hollow in the centre, and raising a wall, two, three, or four inches high all round, according to the size required. Have ready the pork, fat and lean, cut into small square pieces; fill each pie, season highly, fit a lid neatly to the top, egg over, and bake a light brown, in a steady but not a quick oven.

PORK AND POTATO PIE.

Take some pork bones from which the meat has been removed for sausages or other use. Put them into a deep dish and place amid them slices of apples and potatoes, with chopped onions, salt and pepper; add a little water; cover it with a crust and bake slowly.

BACON OMELET.

Beat up some eggs (according to the quantity required,) then add salt, pepper, some finely cut parsely and green onions, and a slice or two of bacon cut into very fine mince meat; mix all well together, fry and scorch the top with a red hot poker.

BACON EGG-CAP.

Cut a quarter of a pound of bacon into thin slices and stew them slowly, turning them over and over. Take out the slices and put to the grease two spoonsful of any stock you happen to have, and break over it six or seven eggs. Now add your slices of bacon again, pepper and salt, cook over a slow fire, and scorch the top with a red hot poker.

PORK RELISH.

Fry some slices of salt pork till crisp, take them out, pour a little water to the fat and season it with pepper; sprinkle in a little flour, then cut up the pork into small pieces and put it into this thickened gravy.

TO CURE HAMS.—1

Weigh your hams, and make a brine of one ounce of salt to every pound of meat, and one ounce of saltpetre to every twenty pounds. Cover the bottom of the tub with salt; pack the hams close, and fill the chinks with stones. Let the brine cover them well. After they have lain three or four weeks, take them up, dry and smoke them. Then wrap them in papers and lay them in ashes in a cool, dry cellar. This keeps the flies from them, and prevents them from getting dry and hard. Hams cured in this way, keep the year round.

TO CURE HAMS.—2.

For every one hundred lbs. of ham, take seven lbs. of salt, three ounces of saltpetre, two ounces of pearlash, one quart of molasses, five gallons of water. Re-pack the hams at the end of the first week, and put the same pickle on them again.

BOILED HAM.

A ham, if dry, may be soaked over night; if moist, this may be omitted. Put it in warm water, and boil it for five or six hours. If it is salt, the water may be changed once, though it should not be put into cold water. Soft water is best; if the water is hard, a little soda may be added to it. If it is desired to give the flavor of ham to vegetables, they may be boiled in some of the liquor the ham was boiled in, but the vegetables should not be put in with the ham. When done take off the skin, which should be kept as whole as possible, (to put over the ham when cold, which will prevent its drying,) and grate toasted bread over it. Boiled ham is best eaten cold. When served, remove the skin, stick cloves at intervals with a ring of pepper around them, and garnish with parsley, or put fringed paper around the small end.

SUGARED HAM.

After boiling the ham three hours, remove the skin, sprinkle sugar over it and bake one hour. It will be delicious.

POTTED HAM.

Take the remains of a boiled ham, cut in small pieces, and pound it, little by little, in a mortar; softening it during the process, with a little melted butter. Add Cayenne pepper to taste, and put it in small bowls, glasses, or potting jars, pressing it down very smooth. Over the surface pour a little more melted butter; cover tight, and set away. It will keep for weeks. This is a nice supper dish.

BROILED HAM.

Cut the ham in thin slices, and broil quick, on a gridiron set over lively hot coals. If the ham is too salt, soak it in hot water before broiling, and dry it with a cloth before putting it on the fire. Fry some eggs in an equal quantity of lard and butter, put an egg on each slice of ham, and serve.

WESTPHALIA LOAVES.

Mix a quarter of a pound of grated ham, with one pound of

mealy potatoes, well beaten until quite light, and add a little butter, cream, and two eggs; but do not get it too moist. Make into small balls, and fry with a little lard, a light brown. Serve with a brown thick gravy. Garnish with fried parsley.

HAM OR TONGUE TOAST.

Toast a thick slice of bread, and butter it on both sides. Take a small quantity of remains of ham, or tongue, and grate it, and put it in a stew-pan with two hard boiled eggs chopped fine, mixed with a little butter, salt, and cayenne; make it quite hot, then spread thickly upon the buttered toast. Serve while hot.

SECONDARY MEATS.

YALE BOAT PIE.

Lay three or four pounds of steak from the undercut of a round of beef, in a middling sized dish, having seasoned it with pepper and salt. Have a couple of chickens at hand, cut in pieces and seasoned; place them upon the steak, and over them one dozen and a half of fresh fat oysters, without the liquor. Add half a dozen fresh, hard boiled eggs, and after damping the bottom of the dish with half a pint of strong ale, cover the whole with fresh mushrooms, adding to these half a pound of glaze or plain neats-foot-jelly; lay over the dish a substantial paste, and bake in a brisk oven. This pie is excellent for a picnic or water excursion.

IRISH STEW.—1.

Take off the under bone from the best end of a neck of mutton, and cut it into chops; season them with pepper and salt, some mushroom powder, and beaten mace. Put the meat into a stew-pan, slice a large onion, and tie up a bunch of parsley and thyme, and add these and a pint of veal broth to the meat. Let this simmer until the chops are about three parts done, then add some onions, and whole potatoes peeled, and let all stew together until thoroughly cooked. Take out the parsley and thyme, and serve up in a deep dish.

IRISH STEW.—2.

Take as much of mutton as is required; the scrag end is the best for the purpose. Cut the meat into small chops, pare all the fat off the piece, chop it fine, and set it aside for dumplings; let the meat stew till perfectly tender, strain the liquor, and set the meat aside. The following day remove the fat, put the liquor in a sauce pan, roll each piece of mutton in flour, add the meat to the liquor, and sufficient potatoes and onions to thicken it. Before serving, add a layer of potatoes, boiled in a separate sauce-pan, also dumplings, about the size of an egg. The dumplings will take about twenty minutes to boil. No seasoning is required except pepper and salt.

BAKED IRISH STEW.

Fill a dish with alternate layers of mutton or beef, sliced potatoes and onions; season with pepper and salt, pour in plenty of water for gravy, and cover the top closely with potatoes; cook in a moderate oven, and let the potatoes on top be browned before it is served; the onion can be omitted if desired.

BOILED TONGUE.

Saltpetered tongue requires five or six hours to boil. When done, lay it in cold water three minutes, peel off the skin, beginning at the tip of the tongue, as it comes off much easier.

SWEETBREAD.

Add to a pint of water, or veal stock, a little grated lemon peel, mace, and pepper and salt; in this put your sweetbreads,—two good sized ones; stew them an hour or more; then take them out, mix a teaspoonful of flour with a little milk, mushrooms, and catsup, and add to the liquor when it boils; put in the sweetbread for a moment. Serve with the sauce poured over them.

TO FRY SWEETBREAD.

Scald them first; fry them in butter, with a little sweet marjoram and parsley chopped fine, and served with a gravy, flavored with mushroom catsup.

MEAT OMNIUM.

Take all the pieces of cooked meat you have, no matter whether boiled or roast, butcher's meat, poultry or game, and mince very fine. Put the whole into a stew-pan, with a little parsley, a few green onions, and mushrooms, if you can get them, one or two eggs beaten up, and a little gravy or stock. Simmer for a quarter of an hour; then take a meat dish, pour upon it a layer of your stew, a layer of bread in slices, another layer of stew, and so on, and heat in an oven. When hot, pour it over the rest of the stew hot, and serve.

SAUSAGE MEAT.

Take one pound of fresh pork, two pounds of lean beef, and chop them very fine; mix this with three tea-spoonfuls of black pepper, the same quantity of salt, five of powdered sage, and five of summer-savory; make this into small cakes and place them upon a plate. When needed, fry them in the same manner as sausages.

GOOD SAUSAGES.

First chop separately, and then together, a pound and a quarter of veal, free from fat, skin, and sinew, and an equal weight of lean pork, and of the inside fat of the pig. Mix them well, and sprinkle on an ounce and a quarter of salt, half an ounce of pepper, one nutmeg grated, and a large tea-spoonful of pounded mace. Turn and chop all together until equally seasoned throughout; press the sausages into a clean pan, and keep them in a very cool place. When wanted, form them into cakes an inch thick or less flour and fry them about ten minutes, in a little butter.

RISSABLES.

Chop veal and ham together finely, add a few bread crumbs, salt, pepper, nutmeg, and a little parsley and lemon peel, or shallot; mix all together with the yolks of eggs well beaten; either roll them into shape like a flat sausage, or into the shape of pears, sticking a bit of horseradish in the ends, to resemble the stalks; egg each over, and grate bread crumbs; fry them brown and serve on crisp fried parsley.

GRANDMOTHER'S BREAKFAST BALLS.

A little cold beef, or mutton, or both; a slice of ham, or salt pork; a small quantity of bread crumbs, a little parsley, a little sage, or thyme, all chopped together, and mixed with an egg, a little melted butter, and seasoning. Take a table spoonful of the mixture, dredge it with the flour, and make into a ball, which fry a quick brown.

This constitutes an elegant breakfast dish, and is a good way of getting rid of cold meat, particularly if hash is not liked.

TURKISH DALMA.

Chop the lean of any cold meat, with a quarter pound of beef wet, very fine; mix with quarter pound of scalded rice; season with salt, pepper, and add the yolks of two eggs. Take cabbage leaves, dip them in water, make the meat into shape of cucumbers, and fold the leaves round them, tying each with a thread; put them into a stewpan with gravy, an anchovy, and an onion: stew a long time gently. The thread is taken off when served, and the gravy browned with flour and a little butter.

TO COOK COLD MEATS.

Put the cold meat into a chopping bowl, cut them fine, season with salt, pepper, a little onion or else tomato catsup. Fill a tin bread pan two thirds full; cover it over with mashed potato which has been salted and has milk in it; lay bits of butter over the top, and set it into an oven for fifteen or twenty minutes.

SAVORY WINTER HASH.

Any kind of cold meat, a few cold potatoes, an onion, pepper and salt, a little dried parsley, sage, and summer savory. Chop all together. Put it in a sauce-pan, with a little gravy, or hot water, and a small piece of butter. Let it simmer gently for fifteen minutes. Turn out over thin slices of toast. It is palatable to persons who do not usually like hash.

TOAD IN THE HOLE.

Make a batter of six ounces of flour, one pint of milk, two or three eggs, a little lard, salt and pepper; put into it a pound of beef sausages, and bake for an hour. Instead of beef sausages, slices of any meat you have, or half a pound of pork sausages, or a few oysters with meat trimmings, may be used.

COW HEEL.

Boil in water a split cow heel (one already used for stock will do) four or five hours; then add a pint of milk, and boil for two hours more, adding an onion or two, and if you like, a little chopped parsley.

FRIED COW HEEL.

Cut a stewed cow heel into pieces about two inches long, and put the pieces into a frying pan with bread crumbs, salt, pepper, and a little minced parsley. You will require to have grease in the pan, and it should be boiling before you put your cow heel in. About a quarter of an hour will suffice for frying. It would be a great improvement if you were to beat up an egg and dip each piece into it, before you put it into the hot frying pan.

SHEEP'S TROTTERS.

Into a stewpan put a little suet with sliced onions and carrots, thyme, salt and pepper; let these simmer for about five minutes. Next add two spoonsful of flour and water, and keep stirring till it boils; when it boils, put in the trotters and simmer for three hours or more. Now mix in two eggs, beaten up in milk, but do not let your stewpan boil again. Pour into a deep dish, and garnish with toasted bread.

SWEET BREAD, LIVER AND HEART.

Parboil the sweet bread, and let them get cold. Cut them in pieces about an inch thick; put on salt, and pepper and sage; then dip them in the yolk of an egg and fine bread crumbs. Fry them a light brown. Another way is, to fry slices of salt pork until brown, take out the pork and fry the sweet bread in the fat. When done, make a gravy by stirring a little flour and water mixed smooth, into the fat; add spices, and wine, if you like. The liver and heart are cooked in the same manner, or broiled.

CALF'S HEAD CAKE.

Parboil half a calf's head, with a little sage; cut off the meat, put the bones back into the broth, and boil them until the broth is much reduced. Cut up the meat and put it into the jar with the tongue, mace, pepper, &c., add a few small slices of ham; put the jar into the oven covered, and let it stand some hours until the contents are thoroughly done; then mix it with the brains beaten up with an egg. Put pieces of hard boiled egg in a mold, pour the mixture from the jar into it, and let it get entirely cold, then turn it out. This dish can be made also with sheep's head, carefully scalded and soaked.

CALF'S HEAD HASH.

Take a calf's head or half a one, as you desire; parboil it, cut off the best parts in slices, and set these aside for the hash. Put the rest, bones and all, with any other bones you may have, especially a ham bone, each into the liquor with a bunch of sweet herbs, a sliced carrot, a fried onion, half head of celery, mace, salt, and peppercorns, according to taste. Let these ingredients stew gently together, until the liquor is so strong that, when it is cold, it will form a jelly. Strain it through a hair sieve, and afterwards through a cloth, and when cold, remove all the fat which may rise to the top. Take of this jelly the quantity that may be required for gravy, put it into a sauce-pan, and add to it mushroom catsup, Worcester sauce, a little lemon peel, and Chili wine. Now put in the slices of meat, and let them warm gently, but do not let them boil. Before serving to table add, if you desire, a wine-glass of sherry, and a table-spoonful of brandy, and garnish with brain cakes and slices of lemon. Butter may be added to the gravy to make it thicker.

LAMB'S HEAD AND HINGE.

Soak the head well in cold water and boil it a quarter of an hour. Parboil the heart, liver, and if desired, the lights; mince them quite small, mix them with gravy, season them, pour them on sippets of toasted bread in a soup dish, broil the bread and lay it upon the mince. It can be garnished with sliced pickled cucumbers and slices of bacon.

BRAIN CAKES.

Wash the brains thoroughly, first in cold and afterwards in hot water; remove the skin and fibers, and then boil the brains in water with a little salt, for two or three minutes. Take them up and beat them in a basin with some very finely chopped parsley, sifted sage, salt, mace, cayenne pepper, the well-beaten yolk of an egg, and a gill of cream. Drop them in small cakes into the frying pan, and fry them in butter a light brown color. A little flour and grated lemon peel are sometimes added.

TRIPE.

The tripe, after being corned, should be soaked in salt and water five or six days, changing the water every day; then cut it in pieces, scrape it and rinse it. Boil it until quite tender, which will take half a day or more, and it will then be fit for broiling, frying or pickling. Drop it into a jar of spiced vinegar.

FRIED TRIPE.

After being boiled, let it be quite cold; cut it in pieces, roll them cornerwise, tie them with a thread, sprinkle a little salt and mace over them, roll them in eggs and crumbs, fry in fat a nice brown; serve with onion sauce, with a little lemon and tomato catsup boiled in.

STEWED TRIPE.

Choose the thickest and whitest tripe, cut the white part into thin slices, and put them into a stewpan with a little white gravy, a spoonful of vinegar, a little lemon juice, and a little grated lemon peel. Add the yolk of an egg well beaten, with a little cream and chopped parsley, and two or three chives. Shake them together over a slow fire until the gravy is as thick as cream, but do not let it boil. Serve it with sippets, and garnish, if desired, with sliced lemon.

BRAWN.

Take the lower half of a pig's face, the feet and ears, rub them well with salt, let them remain so a week or ten days. Salt a beef tongue the same way, for the same time. Then let the face, ears, and feet boil half an hour in water enough to cover them; take them out and clean them thoroughly, then put them back with the tongue also, and boil for three hours, or until the meat will slip from the bones. Then take it off, remove the bone, cut the meat in small pieces, the tongue into thin slices; mix all together and season with plenty of pepper, a little ground allspice, &c. Then put it into a mold in layers of fat and lean, press it down with a spoon, add a little liquor from the saucepan, put a heavy weight on the top, and let it stand till next morning, when it is ready to turn out and send to table. It can be sent with a piece of white paper fastened round and served, if desired, with a little sauce of mustard vinegar, and brown sugar. The beef tongue makes it much nicer, though some omit it, merely chopping the pig's tongue with the face, ears and feet.

FISH.

TO BOIL FISH.

Clean and rinse the fish, wrap it in a cloth, and place it in the kettle with cold water, adding a little salt; boil slowly but constantly; let the water always cover the fish, remove the scum that rises, add a little vinegar when nearly done. The fish is done when the flesh can be separated from the back bone by running a thin sharp knife in; be careful not to let the fish be overdone. Drain it dry on a sieve, keeping it hot; lay it on the fish platter carefully, so as not to break it. Serve with sauces composed of drawn butter. If a fish kettle with strainer is used, the fish need not be wrapped in cloth.

Fresh cod, haddock, whiting and shad, are better for being salted the night before cooking them. The muddy smell that is sometimes noticed in fresh water fish, is obviated by soaking it, after cleaning, in strong salt and water; after which, dry it on a napkin, and dress it.

TO FRY FISH.

Cleanse them thoroughly, dry them well, dip them in flour, or first in the beaten yolks of eggs, and then in grated bread crumbs; fry in lard or beef drippings, or equal parts of lard and butter. Butter alone takes out the sweetness, and gives a bad color. Turn on both sides, and cook a rich yellow brown. Fried parsley, grated horse-radish, or slices of lemon are used as garnish. The fat fried from salt pork is good to fry fish in. Some fish can be dipped in Indian meal instead of flour, if preferred. Trout and perch should not be dipped in Indian meal.

WHITE FISH BROILED. (*Lake Superior style.*)

This is one of the most delicious of lake fish. Cut it in two pieces down through the centre of the back, lay in a pan, and cover with cold water, into which you have put a table-spoonful of salt. Let it lay for two hours, this makes it firm. Then take it out, wrap it in a dry cloth, and let it remain until ready for cooking. Have a nice bed of coals, grease your gridiron well, put on a little salt, and some pepper. Broil for twenty minutes, or half an hour, according to size, turning it to brown on both sides. It will not break in pieces. Serve with white sauce.

WHITE FISH BOILED. (*Lake Superior style.*)

This is a very delicate, and highly esteemed dish. Place the fish *whole*, in a fish kettle; cover with cold water, add a tablespoonful or more of salt, and let it come to a boil. Ten minutes after it boils, will cook it. Take it out carefully, serve with egg sauce, which is white sauce, with a hard boiled egg chopped up in it.

BOILED SALMON.

Draw the fish into the form of the letter S, by running a thread through the tail, centre of the body and head; or if it is part of a fish, fold it in a clean cloth. When bent, cut two or three slanting gashes on each side, to prevent the skin breaking and disfiguring the fish. Plunge it in boiling water in which a handful of salt to four quarts of water has been mixed, and the scum arising from it skimmed off. Put in with the fish, a little horse radish. Boil until very well done, about quarter of an hour to every pound of fish; and serve with lobster, or white parsley sauce; garnish with sliced lemon. For vegetables, mashed potatoes, and cucumbers sliced in vinegar, can be served. A salmon should be chosen for its brightness of color, complete covering of scales, firmness of flesh, whitness of the belly, brightness of the eye, and redness of the scales. Artificial means, it is said, are sometimes adopted to give redness to the gills of salmon and other fish, to deceive inexperienced buyers.

BROILED SALMON.

About an inch, is the proper thickness to cut the slices; dry them with a cloth, put salt on them, and lay them skin side down, on a gridiron over hot coals. Before laying on the fish, rub the bars with lard, to prevent them sticking. When broiled sufficiently on one side, turn the fish, by laying a plate upon it and turning the gridiron over; then slip the salmon from the plate on to the gridiron. This prevents its breaking.

SALMON AND SALAD.

The remains of boiled salmon, instead of being pickled, as is usually done; are very good sent to table cold, to be eaten with salad. Trim the fish neatly, ornament it with sprigs of parsley, and serve with a bowl of salad, made as follows: Boil a cauliflower till about two thirds done; let it get cold, break it in bunches, lay them in a dish, and put to it salt, pepper, oil, and vinegar. This is an excellent dish in hot weather.

TO KIPPER SALMON.

Lay the fish on its side and cut it from tail to head, taking care not to injure the belly by inserting the knife too far; wash the fish well, take out the eyes, and put a pinch of salt in their place; then sprinkle a handful or two of brown sugar over the inside, and above the sugar the same quantity, or rather more, of common salt; lay the salmon on a flat board, the inside up; cover with a cloth and let it remain twenty-four hours (or if wished saltish, thirty-six) in a dry place, neither too hot nor too cold. If the weather is fine, an hour or two of exposure to the sun and air will accelerate the curing process. The kipper is in perfection after it has been dried twenty-four hours, but it will keep a considerable time. To cook it, cut it in slices, wrap each in a piece of paper and fry it; send it to the table in paper.

PICKLED SALMON.

Scald, clean, and split the salmon; then cut into pieces and lay them on the bottom of the kettle, with an equal quantity of water and vinegar, enough to cover them; put in salt, pepper, six blades of mace, twelve bay leaves. When the salmon has boiled enough, drain and lay it on a cloth, put more salmon into the kettle and boil; continue doing this till all is done. When all is cold, pack the fish, and cover with pickle; place something heavy upon the fish to keep it down, that it may be covered entirely with the pickle, which must be occasionally poured off and scalded. Cover it closely to keep it from the air.

BROILED SHAD.

Shad should be baked, fried or broiled. For broiling, remove the roes, clean and dry thoroughly, cut into straight halves, and lay with the roes on a well-heated and well-greased gridiron, over a moderate fire; put the cover on so that it will cook through while it is browning, and only turn once; when it is done remove it to a warm dish, spread over a piece of butter the size of a walnut, a little pepper and salt, and put it, for a moment, in the oven; garnish with sprigs of fresh parsley before serving.

FRIED SHAD.

Divide the two halves in pieces two or three inches wide, salt and pepper them and put them in a pan, in which the fat, to keep them from sticking, has already been made boiling hot; fry a rich brown on both sides, cooking the inside first, and serve hot. The roes may be fried in the same way.

BAKED SHAD

Baked shad does not require to be cut down the back; only cleaned, the roes removed, and the inside filled with a stuffing made of bread crumbs, salt pork, an onion, sage, thyme, parsley, and pepper and salt; chop all together fine, fill and sew up the shad, and place in a pan with three or four slices of the pork over it, and the roes at the side; bake one hour, and you will have a dish fit for an editor.

SHAD MAITRE D'HOTEL.

Butter a pan and lay the shad in it, with an onion sliced, a bay leaf, five cloves, the juice of half a lemon, a spoonful of vinegar, and two of gravy; make four or five incisions on both sides of the shad, cutting down to the bone, cover with buttered paper, and put into a rather slow oven; let it bake twenty minutes, then take it out, remove the paper, baste thoroughly and put it back; let it remain in the oven altogether about three quarters of an hour, or an hour if the fish is a large one, basting frequently with the liquor in the pan; then take it out, fill the incisions with chopped parsley and butter, and put back, while making a sauce of a little butter, flour, broth, and lemon juice, into which pour all the liquid surrounding the shad; boil up once, dish the fish, and pour the sauce over it.

FRESH MACKEREL.

This is a Spring luxury. Purchased in the city they are already cleaned, and require only to be rolled in a clean cloth, put in cold water, and cooked for five minutes, after coming to a boil; serve with parsley sauce, made with a table-spoonful of flour, mixed smooth with cold milk, and a piece of butter the size of a small egg; garnish with green parsley, and eat with stewed gooseberries.

SOUSED MACKEREL.

Take fresh mackerel, well cleaned, and boil them for a few minutes, or until tender, in salt and water. Take of the water in which they were boiled, half as much as will cover them; add the same amount of good vinegar, some whole pepper, cloves, and a blade or two of mace. Pour over hot. In twelve hours it will be ready for use. Shad is very nice soused in the same way.

BOILED BASS, ROCK FISH, ETC.

These should be boiled plain, leaving on the head and tail. Let them boil steadily half an hour, serve with drawn butter mixed with finely chopped eggs, which have been boiled three quarters of an hour.

PICKED UP CODFISH AND POTATOES.

This is as old and esteemed a dish as pork and beans. Put your salted codfish in soak the night before; pick it off in shreds the next morning, and scald it in a saucepan, pouring off the water just before it comes to a boil; this will freshen it sufficiently.

Put in then a little more water, a small piece of butter, and a few shakes of pepper, and let it cook till it is tender. When it is done, thicken it with a beaten egg, but don't allow it to boil; and mix it with double its bulk in potatoes, mashed finely with milk, and season with pepper and a little salt. Pile up as near like a haystack as possible, pour over the whole some good egg sauce, and garnish with parsley and egg rings.

BAKED COD, BLACK FISH, HADDOCK, ETC.

Spread little slices of bread with butter; pepper and salt them and lay them inside the fish. Then take a needle and thread and sew it up. Put a small skewer through the lip and tail, and fasten them together with a piece of twine. Lay it into a dish, in which it it may be served; put two or three thin slices of salt pork upon it, sprinkle salt over it, and flour it well. Baste it several times with the liquor which cooks out of it. A fish weighing four pounds will cook in an hour.

BROILED WHITINGS.

Make a brine with salt and water, sprigs of parsley, shallots and onions, and let the whole boil together for half an hour; strain it and boil the whitings in it, adding a third part of milk. Drain them when done, and make the following sauce for them: A piece of butter, some flour, two whole green shallots, pepper, and salt. Thicken this with cream; take out the shallots, and pour the sauce over the whitings.

WATER SOUCHY, OR SOODJEE.

This mode of dressing fish may be used for soles, flounders, and also fresh water fish of almost any description. The fish should be thoroughly cleansed and put into a stew-pan, with sufficient cold water for broth, a very small quantity of white wine vinegar, and some salt. While boiling they must be carefully skimmed; and when thoroughly done, served in the liquor in which they were boiled; to which should be added some roots of parsley, cut, trimmed, and boiled. A few parsley leaves, boiled to a nice green, should be strewed over the fish, and bread and butter sent up to eat with the souchy.

FRIED COD AND HADDOCK.

Cut the fish in pieces about the size as to help at table; wash and wipe them dry, roll them in Indian meal. Fry some pieces of salt pork; take out the pork, and put into the frying-pan some lard; when it is quite hot put in the fish and fry it a light brown; dish it with the fried pork, serve with drawn butter.

COD OR SALMON CUTLETS.

To one and a half pounds of cold boiled fish, put half a pound of cold potatoes, half a pound of butter; pepper, salt, and a little mace, and some anchovy sauce. Pound all these together in a mortar, thoroughly. When well beaten, make the mixture into the shape of small cutlets, dip them in egg and bread crumbs, and fry them until they are of a light brown color. They are excellent as a side dish or *entree*.

FISH ROES IN CASES.

Put the soft roes from half a dozen broiled mackerel or shad into paper cases, with shred parsley, a little rasped bread, butter, salt, and pepper. Bake them, and serve them up with lemon juice squeezed over them.

SMALL FISH FRICASSEED.

Fry the fish a nice brown color, and drain them. Take another small fish, remove all the meat from it, and chop it fine, mixing with it a little grated bread, some lemon peel, chopped parsley, pepper, salt, nutmeg, the yolks of an egg, and a little butter; make this up into small balls and fry them. Into some good gravy thickened with flour, put some red wine, and boil it up adding cayenne pepper, catsup, and lemon juice; place the fish and balls in it, simmer them a few moments, and serve, garnished with lemon.

TRENTON FALLS FRY.

Let some small fish soak in the juice of two lemons, with salt, pepper, and chopped sweet herbs. After taking them out, drain them, and stuff them with crumbs of bread, boiled in milk, and beat up with the yolks of two eggs; then sprinkle them with flour, and fry them of a good color. Serve them up on fried parsley. They should be very dry and crisp.

FISH AND MACARONI

Rub the inside of a mold with fresh butter, and strew grated cheese at the bottom of it to the thickness of about an inch; then put in a layer of macaroni of about the same thickness. Upon this lay some fish of whatever kind preferred, boned, cut in pieces, and strewed with parsley, thyme, and shallots finely chopped; also some pounded spices and cayenne pepper, adding another layer of macaroni and cheese. Bake it for an hour in a moderate oven, carefully turn it out into a dish, and serve it up with a little good stock gravy round it.

FISH AND MACARONI.

Boil the macaroni in water until tender, drain it, and cut it into short pieces. Remove the bones and skin from any kind of white boiled fish, tear it into small pieces, and mix it with the macaroni. Then make a sauce of two ounces of butter, the yolks of one or two eggs, salt, pepper and a little lemon juice. Heat this in a sauce-pan, pouring in half a pint of good melted butter, stir it, and put in the fish and macaroni. When hot, pour it out in a dish, heaping it in the centre; sprinkle fine bread crumbs over it and bake the top a light brown color in the oven.

FRIED SMELTS.

Split them just far enough to clean them; lay them in salt and water, and let them remain an hour; then wash and wipe them, have ready two eggs beat up in a plate, and some cracker crumbs in another plate; put about two pounds of lard into the frying pan; set it on the fire until it is very hot; dip the smelts into the eggs, roll them in the crumbs, and put them into the boiling fat; fry them a light brown; serve them hot, with drawn butter.

FRESH HERRINGS

These can be broiled or fried. After scaling and cleaning them nicely, split them quite open, wash the insides with care, dry them in a cloth, remove the head, tail and back bones, rub the insides with pepper, salt, and a little pounded mace; stick small bits of butter on them; skewer two of the fish together as flat as possible, the skin of both outside; flour and boil them in twenty to twenty-five minutes, or fry them about ten minutes, until brown; and serve with melted butter mixed with a tea-spoonful of mustard, some salt, and a little vinegar or lemon juice.

TO DRESS FISH A SECOND TIME.

Put four table spoonsful of bread crumbs to a small quantity of fish; add two eggs, two ounces of butter, a little essence of anchovy, and a little pepper, salt and cayenne. Mix these all well with the fish, which should previously be taken from the bones, and steam it until it is heated through. Any cold boiled fish may be dressed this way.

FISH PUDDING.

Take cold boiled fish, the part that is white, and mashed potatoes, an equal quantity; mix well together, breaking the fish very fine; add two ounces of melted butter, or cream instead of the butter; season with salt and pepper. Butter a pudding dish, put the mixture in, keeping the top rough, and put it in the oven till heated through, and the top nicely browned.

CHOWDER.

For a capital Spring chowder, put a layer of fresh fish, cod, or haddock; then a layer of split crackers, sliced onions, and raw potatoes sliced very thin; strew a little salt and pepper over this layer; then put in more pork and fish, crackers, onions, and potatoes, and so on, until the ingredients are exhausted; over this mixture pour a bowl of liquid, composed of two table-spoons of flour, mixed smooth with milk and water; add milk and water to the flour until there is sufficient to just cover the contents of the pot; cover down tight, and cook slowly two or three hours.

FISH CHOWDER.

Pare, and cut into slices, seven or eight potatoes, and put them in a basin of cold water; cut a fresh cod into slices, then fry a few slices of fat salt pork; lay the pork in the bottom of the stew kettle; place two or three slices of fish on it, then a layer of split crackers, then some potatoes, and so on, with alternate layers, until the kettle is full; put in a little pepper and salt. Put in a quart of water; mix one table-spoonful of flour, in half a pint of water, and pour in, after it begins to stew. Cover very tight, and stew three hours.

FISH CAKES.

Mix together a pound and a half of mashed potatoes, a pound of cold boiled fish, either salt or fresh; add a little milk and butter, one egg if desired; pepper, onions, and a little chopped thyme, and salt if the fish requires it; sprinkle on a little flour, and fry them a light brown in small, thick cakes.

STEWED SALT COD.

Soak and scald the fish until sufficiently freshened; pick it into shreds, and stew it with milk to moisten it, a little butter rolled in flour, and pepper to taste. Stew gently a few minutes, and serve hot.

CAPE COD CHOWDER.

Fry some slices of sweet, salt pork till they are crisp; pour off part of the fat; take out the rashers and set them aside, where they will keep hot. Put in a layer of potatoes first, with a little onion, then pepper, then a layer of butter crackers, then a layer of fish, then a little more fat, more potatoes, more onion, more pepper, more butter crackers, more fish, and so on until the kettle is two thirds full; then put on top whatever fat may be left; fill up with water, cover close, and let it cook an hour or an hour and a half, according to quantity. A little salt may be required. Serve with the rashers placed round the dish on toast and pickle.

CLAM CHOWDER.

This is made in the same way, only they require a great deal of pork, and be careful to get soft shell clams.

SALT CODFISH AND POTATOES.

Soak a thick piece of fish over night, pour out the water and cover it with fresh, lukewarm water, and let it stand a short time; then put it in lukewarm water over the fire and let it simmer, but not boil, for an hour and a half or two hours, until it is done; remove the skin; serve with drawn butter or egg sauce, with whole boiled potatoes to be mashed or cut by each person with the fish, on their own plate. Serve also, if convenient, cucumbers in vinegar, pickles or nasturtiums. The fish can be garnished with hard boiled eggs. The cold fish left, will make a fine hash, or may be prepared in fish cakes.

SHELL FISH, EELS, Etc.

OYSTERS ETIQUETTE.

Procure two dozen oysters. Have them opened, and throw them into a clean basin or soup plate. Take a small bunch of parsley, chopped quite small, a little raw lemon rind ditto, half a nutmeg grated, and the crumb of a stale French roll, also grated. Let the latter be well mixed together, adding one drachm of cayenne pepper. Have at hand the yolks of three fresh eggs, beaten up into a fluid; dip the oysters separately into the eggs, and roll them in the crumb of the loaf until they are all encased in a bread coating or covering. Put a quarter of a pound of good butter into the oven, with a brisk fire, until the former is fully melted, arranging your oysters on the tray of the oven at your convenience. Keep the oysters continually turned until they assume a perfectly brown, crusty appearance. When fully baked, serve them up with a plate of bread and butter, cut thin, and use salt at discretion. A stick of celery eaten with them, adds greatly to the relish which the fish impart when served in this way.

STEWED OYSTERS.

Boil up the oysters in their own liquor, with a piece of butter the size of a walnut, and pepper and salt to taste. Have ready a pint or more of rich boiled milk, the quantity according to the number of oysters. Pour it hot into the soup tureen, and as the oysters come to a boil, skim them, let them boil up once, and then pour them into the milk.

SCALLOPED OYSTERS.

Wash out of the liquor two quarts of oysters; pound very fine eight soft crackers, or grate a stale loaf of bread; butter a deep dish, sprinkle in a layer of crumbs, then a layer of oysters, a little mace, pepper, and bits of butter; another layer of crumbs, another of oysters, then seasoning as before, and so on until the dish is filled; cover the dish over with bread crumbs, seasoning as before; turn over it a cup of the oyster liquor. Set it in the oven for thirty or forty minutes to brown. This is an excellent way to prepare oysters for a family dinner.

FRIED OYSTERS.

Select fine, large oysters, dry them out of their own liquor. Have ready a plate of egg, and a plate of bread crumbs. Let them lay in the egg a few minutes, and then roll them in the bread crumbs, allowing them to remain in these also, for a minute or two; this will make them adhere, and not come off as a skin, when in the pan. Fry in half butter and half lard, in order to give them a rich brown. Make it very hot before putting the oysters in.

OYSTER PIES.

Take a deep dish, cover it with puff paste, lay an extra layer around the edge of the dish, put in the oven and bake nicely. When done, fill the pie with oysters; season with butter, salt, and pepper, sprinkle a little flour over them and cover with a thin crust of puff paste; bake quickly; when the top crust is done, the oysters should be. Serve immediately.

OYSTER PATTIES.

Beard the oysters, and, if large, halve them; put them into a saucepan with a piece of butter rolled in flour, some finely shred lemon rind, and a little white pepper, and milk, and a portion of the liquor from the fish; stir all well together, let it simmer for a few minutes, and put it in your patty pans, which should be already prepared with a puff paste in the usual way. Serve hot or cold.

OYSTER LOAVES.

Cut out a piece of the size of a quarter of a dollar from the top of half a dozen buns, scoop out most of the crumb, put a portion of the latter with a good bit of butter, and about two dozen fresh oysters into a frying pan and fry all together for five minutes, add a little cream or milk and seasoning. Then fill the loaves, allowing four oysters to each; replace the pieces of crust on the tops, butter the outsides, and place them for a short time in an oven to get crisp. Serve them hot or cold.

OYSTERS AND MACARONI.

Slowly stew some macaroni in good gravy till quite tender; then lay it in a pie dish, put in a good layer of fresh oysters, bearded; add pepper, salt, a little grated lemon rind, and a tea-spoonful of cream, or olive oil if preferred. Strew bread crumbs over, and just brown it in a tolerably brisk oven. Serve with plenty of lemon juice, or a *sauce piquante*.

OYSTERS FOR LUNCH.

Take a fine oyster, wrap it thinly with bacon, fastening it with a little skewer. Lay it on a piece of toast, and put into a Dutch oven or a hot stove oven, a very little time. Prepare as many in this way as desired.

PICKLED OYSTERS.—No 1.

Wash fifty large oysters in their own liquor; wipe them dry, strain the liquor off, add to it a dessert-spoonful of pepper, the same of mace, the same of salt, the same of whole cloves, and a pint of vinegar. Let the oysters come to a boil in the liquor, then drain them off with a skimmer; put them into a jar; boil the pickle up, skim it, and when it is cold, pour over the oysters. They will be ready for use in twenty-four hours.

PICKLED OYSTERS.—No. 2.

Put the oysters, say two hundred, with their juice, into a large saucepan on the fire; let them simmer, but not boil, until the edges curl, and they become solid, but not shriveled. Be careful about this. Strain off the juice, and wipe the oysters with a nice, clean cloth. Let the juice settle, then pour off about a quart, leaving the sediment undisturbed; to this clear juice add one pint white wine, or other vinegar, a little mace, two dozen cloves, and a handful of black peppers. Heat it over the fire, but don't let it boil; pour it while hot, over the oysters. Put them in a stone jar, and in two days they will be very nice for use.

STEWED MUSCLES.

Open the muscles in their own liquor. When ready for use drain off the liquor and wash them in clear water. Then add to the liquor, or as much of it as is needed, an equal amount of water and of white wine, a blade of mace and a little whole pepper; boil them, and after awhile drop in the muscles, letting them just boil up, and thicken them with a piece of butter and flour. They can be served with sippets of bread and the liquor.

FRIED EELS.

After the eels have been skinned and cleaned, split them open and cut them in short pieces. Then make a pickle of vinegar, lemon juice, sliced onion, salt and pepper; place the eels in it and let them lie two or three hours. Roll them in flour and fry in lard or clarified butter. Place them on the table dry, with fried parsley, using plain butter for sauce.

SPATCHED EELS.

Take two pounds of eels, scour their skins with sand and salt, wipe them dry with flannel, gut them, cut them into short pieces, saturate them with the beaten yolk of an egg, and then roll into a plate containing crumbs of the inside of stale bread, chopped parsley, a sprig of sweet marjoram, a sprig of bruised anchovy, half a nutmeg grated, and some cayenne pepper, and salt all mixed. When well rubbed in these, baste them before a clear bright fire, with plenty of butter, until they are covered with a brown crust. Serve them with plain or melted butter for sauce.

COLLARED EELS.

Select a large eel, gut it and bone it without skinning it, and rub the inside with salt, pepper, mace, allspice, powdered cloves, chopped sage. Parsley, thyme, savory and knotted marjoram also improve the taste. Roll it tight, tie it, and boil it well in salt water. Then add vinegar, and when cold keep it in pickle.

STEWED EELS.

Wash the eels well, and cut into pieces two or three inches long. Place them in the pan with an onion, cloves, a bundle of sweet herbs, a blade of mace, some whole pepper in a muslin rag, and add enough water for sauce. Let them stew softly, and add the juice of half a lemon, and a piece of butter rolled in flour. When they are tender, take out the onion, cloves, herbs, mace, and pepper, put in sufficient salt to season, and serve it with the sauce.

BOILED EELS.

Boil them in a little water with some parsley until tender, season them properly, and serve them with the liquor and the parsley. Use chopped parsley and butter for sauce.

EEL PIE.

Cut up the eels in one or two inch lengths, line the dish with potato paste, such as used for meat pies; put in the eels, season with pepper, salt, parsley, and a little butter. Pour over a little stock, or a few spoonsful of gravy, a spoonful of mushroom catsup, and dredge with flour. Cover with potato paste, and bake an hour and a quarter. This is for family use; if company is expected, a richer paste may be used.

LOBSTERS.

To choose lobsters that are boiled, select those that are heaviest, and of a middling size; if they are fresh the tail will flap back with a springy motion, when raised up.

TO BOIL A FRESH LOBSTER.

Put it into a fish kettle of boiling water, into which a handful of salt has been thrown; boil it briskly for half an hour, then wipe off the skum, and rub over it a little sweet oil. When cold, break off the claws, and crack the shell, but do not disturb the meat; set the body upright in the dish, with the claws and tail around it.

MRS. MAJOR D.'S LOBSTER SALAD.

Boil the lobster about half an hour. When it is cold, take it from the shell, being careful to take out the vein in the back. To six lbs of lobster, take two heads of salad, one cup of melted butter; two table-spoons of mustard, mixed with a little vinegar. Salt and pepper to taste. Chop these together, and spread on a flat dish. Then beat six eggs, and mix with half a pint of vinegar. Put this on the stove to thicken, stirring constantly; when cold spread it over the lobster.

For another receipt, see " Salads."

CRABS AND CRAYFISH.

These are boiled in the same manner as lobsters.

LOBSTER SAUCE.

Mash the fresh eggs of a hen lobster; strain, and reserve; divide the flesh into small pieces, dust it with flour to prevent it adhering together, and put it into a white sauce, allowing it to simmer for a minute, before putting in the eggs; when these have been added, it will assume a brilliant red, and should be removed from the fire instantly, before it has time to darken. Such flavor as anchovy, or lemon, may be added at the table.

CRAB AND LOBSTER CUTLETS.

Take out the meat of either a large lobster, or crab, mince it, and add two ounces of butter browned with two spoonfuls of flour, and seasoned with a little pepper, salt, and cayenne; add again about half a pint of strong stock, stir the mixture over the fire until quite hot, lay it in separate table-spoonsful on a large dish. When they are cold, form them into the shape of cutlets, brush them over with the beaten yolk of an egg; dip them into grated bread crumbs, fry them of a light brown color in clarified beef dripping, and place them round a dish, with a little fried parsley in the centre.

LOBSTER BALLS.

Mince the meat with the coral, season, make it in balls mixed with bread crumbs and butter, dip them with the yolk of an egg and flour if desired, and fry them brown in hot lard; for lobster patties, place minced lobster in the shell in puff paste, and bake.

LOBSTER CURRY.

Put the meat of a large lobster into a stew-pan with a blade of mace, a large cup of veal stock or gravy, and a table-spoonful of corn starch, mixed smooth with a little milk, or cream. Add salt, a small piece of butter, a dessert-spoonful of curry powder, and the juice of half a lemon; simmer for an hour, and serve.

MUSHROOMS.

HOW TO KNOW MUSHROOMS.

To know the mushroom from the poisonous toadstool, observe the mushroom has no bad smell, that its top skin will readily peel off; there is a thick meat between the skin and the red gills or plates; the gills are of a pinkish or rosy hue, though turning brownish by age, but are never of the lurid brown of the toadstool; when sprinkled with salt and allowed to stand, the mushroom gives out juice, the toadstool becomes dry and leathery.

MUSHROOM FRICASSEE.

Put a quart of fresh mushrooms, cleaned, into a saucepan, with three spoonsful of water, three of milk, and a little salt, and set them on a quick fire. Let them boil up three times, after which take them off and mix in half a pint of milk, a piece of butter rolled in flour, and a little grated nutmeg. Put them into the saucepan, shaking it well occasionally, and when the liquor is thick, stirring them carefully in the saucepan with a spoon, all the time, and seeing that they do not curdle.

MUSHROOM POWDER.

Wash half a peck of large mushrooms quite clean from grit, and cut off the stalks. Put them in a saucepan, without water, containing a quarter of an ounce of mace, two spoonsful of pounded pepper, two onions stuck with cloves, a handful of salt, some allspice and nutmeg, if liked, and a quarter of a pound of butter. Let this stew till the liquor is dried up, then place them on sieves until they are sufficiently dry to be beaten to a powder. Bottle this and closely cork it. To give a good flavor to soup or gravy, a tea-spoonful of the powder must be added a minute or two before it is taken from the fire.

MUSHROOM POWDER.—2.

Wipe the mushrooms clean and pare the skin from the large ones. Put them on paper, and place them in a cool oven to dry. Lay them before the fire until crisp, then grind and sift them through a fine sieve, and keep the powder in small closely corked bottles.

MUSHROOM LOAVES.

Well wash some small button mushrooms, such as are generally used for pickling, and boil them for a few minutes in a very little water. Add to them a small quantity of cream, a piece of butter rolled in some flour, salt and pepper, then boil up all together again. Cut off a piece from the end of some rolls, scoop out the crumb; in its place put the prepared mushrooms, and replace the end of each roll.

MUSHROOM TOAST.

Remove the stems, and red inside, and skins, from a pint of freshly gathered mushrooms. Dissolve a little butter in a stew-pan, throw in the mushrooms, season with cayenne pepper, and toss them over the fire for about ten minutes; add a tea-spoonful of flour, and stir until all is slightly browned. Cut a crust about an inch thick from the under part of a loaf: scoop it out in the centre; butter it, and boil it over a brisk fire; then place it upon a hot dish before the fire. Pour in by degrees a tea-cupful of cream or new milk to the mushrooms; flavor with a few drops of catsup; stew gently for two minutes, and pour them into the crust. Serve hot.

STEWED MUSHROOMS.

Choose large button mushrooms, wipe them with a wet flannel, and put them into a stew-pan with a little water. Let them stew gently for a quarter of an hour; then put in a pinch of salt, work a little flour and butter to make it as thick as cream. Let it boil for five minutes, and before dishing it up, add two large table-spoonsful of cream mixed with the yolk of one egg. Shake the sauce-pan over the fire for a minute or so, to warm the contents, but do not allow them to boil, for fear they might curdle. Put some sippets around the inside of the dish, and serve hot. [For pickled mushrooms, see Pickles.]

FOWLS AND GAME.

ROAST TURKEY.

Have a stuffing prepared of bread crumbs, sausage meat, or sweet salt pork, chopped fine, thyme, summer savory, and one onion; with pepper, and salt in about equal proportions. If the liver and heart are not used with the gizzard, to make the gravy, they also may be chopped, and mixed with the stuffing. Fill the body, sew up the opening, truss it, and if you choose, place a ring of sausages round the neck of the turkey. Put in the pan with a cup of hot water; roast slowly at first, and baste frequently; if there is danger of scorching, cover the breast with white paper. It will require, if of good size, two and a half to three hours to roast; and should be served with a rich brown gravy, and with the sausages browned and lying on the breast. If sausages are not liked, thin slices of sweet salt pork should be laid over the breast, and round the neck.

BOILED FOWL.

Boil the liver, gizzard, heart and lower part of the legs, in a very little water, chop them fine, mix them with drawn butter and bread crumbs, and season with salt, summer savory, and a little pepper. Stuff the fowl with this; put it in sufficient water to cover it well, and stew it gently until tender; serve with drawn butter.

ROAST DUCKS.

Clean and truss them nicely, and fill their bodies with a stuffing made of half mashed potatoes, and half sage, and onions, well seasoned with pepper and salt. Baste them with slices of sweet fat pork in the pan, and baste frequently. Make a rich gravy, into which put a table-spoonsful of Worcestershire sauce. Serve with apple sauce.

For a change one of a pair of duck's may be stuffed with prunes.

ROAST FOWL.

The fowl being drawn, and prepared, fill the body with a dressing of bread and butter, seasoned with pepper, salt, and summer savory; sew up the opening, truss it, oil it with butter, roast it rather fast without scorching, the first half hour, heating all sides evenly; baste it all over every five minutes, and after that, roast rather slowly three quarters of an hour or more, until the fowl is done through. If not sufficiently browned, wet it over with a little yolk of egg, sprinkle it with flour, and let it stand a little longer, till browned evenly.

BOILED FOWL.

Divide the fowl at the back, lay the sides open, and skewer the wings as for roasting. Boil over a clear fire, seasoning with pepper, salt, and a little butter. Serve them immediately, on a hot dish.

MR. DEMOREST'S CHICKEN FRICASSEE.

Prepare a couple of nice plump chickens; joint them, dividing the wings, side, breast, and backbones, and let them lie in clear water half an hour; remove them then to a stew-pan, with half a pound of good, sweet salt pork cut up in pieces; barely cover with water, and *simmer* on the top of the stove or range for three hours; when sufficiently tender, take out the chicken, mix a table-spoonful of flour smoothly with cold milk, and add a little fine dried or chopped parsley, sage, and thyme, or summer savory, and stir gradually into the liquor; keep stirring till it boils; season with pepper and salt to taste; and then put back the chicken and let it boil up for a few moments in the gravy; garnish with the green tops of celery.

BOILED GOOSE.

Dress and singe it, put it into a deep dish, cover it with boiling milk and leave it all night. In the morning wash off the milk and put the goose into cold water on the fire; when boiling hot take it off, wash it in warm water, and dry it with a cloth. This process takes out the taste of oil. Fill the body with a dressing of bread crumbs seasoned with pepper, salt, and butter, two chopped onions, if relished, and a little sage, and close it. Put it into cold water and boil gently until tender, about an hour. Serve with giblet sauce, and with pickles, or acid jellies. For vegetables have beets, turnips and cauliflower.

ROAST GOOSE.

Make a dressing of two ounces of onion, an ounce of green sage chopped fine, a coffee cup of bread crumbs, a little pepper, and salt; do not quite fill the goose, but leave room to swell. The yolks of two eggs can be added to the dressing, if desired. Roast two hours or less, and serve with gravy and apple sauce.

DUCK, WITH GREEN PEAS.

Roast a duck until about half done. Place it into a stew-pan, with a pint of good gravy, and a very little sage; cover it close, and let the duck continue to simmer in the pan, for half an hour; then put in a pint of boiled green peas; the peas are put in the pan to thicken the gravy. Place the duck on a dish, and pour the gravy and peas over it.

NEW YORK MOCK DUCK.

Procure a good rump steak, fill it with duck stuffing, bread, a little sweet salt pork, sage, chopped onions, and pepper, and salt; roll it up, skewer the ends tight; tie a string round the middle, and simmer with a little stock, in a covered pan, for two hours; take it out, put in the oven, and bake for another hour without cover.

TURKEY STEWED WITH CELERY.

Choose a fine hen-turkey, and stuff it with some force meat as for veal, viz: four ounces of bread crumbs, the grated rind of half a lemon, a quarter of an ounce of savory herbs, minced fine, salt and pepper, two ounces of butter, and the yolk of an egg. All these ingredients to be well mixed together. Skewer the turkey as for boiling, and put it into a large sauce-pan filled with water, and let it boil until tender. Take up the turkey and put it into another sauce-pan, with sufficient of the water in which it has been boiled, to keep it hot. Wash well about four good sized heads of celery, put these into the sauce-pan with the rest of the water in which the turkey has been boiled, and stew them until tender. Take them out and put in the turkey, breast downward, and let it stew for a quarter of an hour; place it on a hot dish before the fire, thicken the sauce with butter and flour, and a breakfast-cup of cream; put it in the celery to warm, and pour the sauce and celery hot over the turkey.

STEWED CHICKEN.

Divide a chicken into pieces by the joints, and put into a stew-pan, with salt, pepper, some parsley, and thyme; pour in a quart of water, with a piece of butter; and when it has stewed an hour and a half, take the chicken out of the pan. If there is no gravy, put in another piece of butter, add some water, and flour, and let it boil a few minutes. When done, it should be not quite as thick as drawn butter.

COLD CHICKEN FRIED.

Place the cold chicken, divided into small joints, into a deep dish, and cover then with salt, pepper, a little melted butter, the juice of a lemon, and some chopped parsley and onion. Let the meat soak three or four hours in this, turning it once in a while. Then take them out, sprinkle flour over them, and fry them. When done, pile them high on a dish, and pour a good gravy sauce, seasoned and flavored with sweet herbs, round them.

VOL-AU-VENT OF CHICKEN.

Make a case of puff paste, and fill it, when baked, with minced chicken, prepared as follows. Take the meat of a cold chicken, and mince it small. Take half a pint of stock, thicken it with a little flour, flavor with salt, and nutmeg, and let it boil well; then add two or three mushrooms chopped small, a teacupful of milk, and the minced chicken. As soon as the mushrooms are cooked the mince is done. This may be served on a dish alone. Or put into vol-au-vent cases, and ornamented with a few button mushrooms, stewed in white sauce, on the top.

CHICKEN WITH CHEESE. (*A French dish*).

Braise a couple of chickens, and when nearly done, add to them some good stock, vegetables, white wine and butter, seasoning according to taste. When done, strain some of the liquor into a dish, and grate into it some parmesan cheese; place the chickens in this, pour over them the remainder of the gravy, grate more parmesan over them, and bake the whole.

CHICKEN PUFFS.

Mince up together the breast of a chicken, some lean ham, half an anchovy, a little parsley, some shallot and lemon peel, and season these with pepper, salt, cayenne, and beaten mace. Let this be on the fire for a few moments, in a little good white sauce. Cut some thinly rolled out puff paste into squares, putting on each some of the mince; turn the paste over, fry them in boiling lard, and serve them. These puffs are very good cold.

CHICKEN LOAF.

Bone a chicken carefully, and fill it with chopped sweetbread well seasoned; make it as nearly as possible into its original form, tie it up in bacon, and having wrapped a cloth round it, boil it in some white wine, good stock, and sweet herbs. When done, untie it, use the bacon as garnish, cut in narrow strips, and serve up with some rich sauce.

CHICKEN POT PIE.

Divide the chicken into pieces at the joints; boil until part done, or about twenty minutes, then take it out. Fry two or three slices of fat salt pork, and put in the bottom, then place the chicken on it with three pints of water, two ounces of butter, a tea-spoonful of pepper, and cover over the top with a light crust, made the same as for biscuit. Cook one hour.

MRS. MAJOR D.'S CHICKEN PIE, FLAVORED WITH OYSTERS.

Cut up a good sized chicken and stew until tender; meanwhile seasoning it. After lining the sides of your pan with paste, put in it a quart of oysters, seasoning them. Then throw in the chicken. Take the water in which the chicken was stewed, and thicken it with flour. Fill the pan with the thickened liquor, cover it all with paste; ornament with pastry, and bake till the crust is a nice brown, or about twenty minutes in a quick oven.

PLAIN CHICKEN PIE.

Take a chicken and cut it in pieces. Stew it in water enough to cover it. When tender, line a deep dish with pie crust, take the chicken out of the liquor, put it in the dish with three or four slices of pork, and two ounces of butter, the latter cut in small pieces; add some of the liquor, flavor with mushroom catsup, and thicken with flour. Cover it with pie crust, and bake it in a quick oven about an hour.

THANKSGIVING CHICKEN PIE.

Cut two chickens into small members as for fricassee; cover the bottom of the pie-dish with layers of veal and ham placed alternately; season with chopped mushrooms and parsley, pepper and salt, then add a little gravy; next place in the dish the pieces of chicken in neat order, and round these put slices of hard boiled egg in each cavity; repeat the seasoning and the sauce, lay a few thin slices of dressed ham neatly trimmed, on the top; cover the pie with puff-paste, ornament this with pieces of the same cut into the form of leaves, &c.; egg the pie over with a paste-brush, and bake it for one hour and a half.

AUNT ABBY'S CHICKEN PIE.

Joint two plump, tender chickens, stew them half an hour in barely enough water to cover them, take them from the liquor, and lay them in a deep dish, with some thin slices of very sweet, nice salt pork, and a few halves of small butter crackers. Season the liquor highly, and pour over the chicken. Have ready a nice top crust, and put a rim of it first round the edge of the dish, wet it slightly, so that the other edge will stick close, and ornament the top with pastry.

For family use, or to eat cold, for breakfast, or for lunch, put a layer of cooked potatoes in the bottom of the dish. The gravy will form a thick jelly round them. Omit the crackers.

PRAIRIE CHICKENS.

Skin the chickens, which makes them sweeter; cut them open on the back and through the breast. Fry them in butter, with salt and pepper to the taste. Cook them to a nice brown.

ROAST PRAIRIE CHICKENS.

When they are nicely prepared, fill them with a stuffing of bread crumbs, a slice of salt pork chopped fine; sage and onion and pepper and salt to season sufficiently. Roast slowly for the first half hour, briskly the last half hour. Serve with mushroom sauce.

STEWED PRAIRIE CHICKENS.

Prepare the chickens the same as for roasting. Put them in a stew-pan with some stock or water, and a cup of cold gravy, a little lemon, a clove or two, and some pepper and salt. Add after awhile a few spoonsful of tomato sauce. Stew slowly for a couple of hours, serve with a little tomato catsup added to the sauce, and a light thickening of butter and flour.

DEVILLED TURKEY'S LEGS.

Score the legs of a roasted turkey; sprinkle them with cayenne, black pepper and salt; boil them well, and pour over them the following sauce, quite hot: Three spoonsful of gravy, one of butter rubbed in a little flour, one of lemon juice, a glass of port wine, a spoonful of mustard, some vinegar, two or three chopped green chillis, a spoonful of mushroom catsup, and Harvey sauce.

ALICE CAREY'S MINCED CHICKEN.

Mince all that is left of cold roast, or boiled chickens. Warm it with half a cup of cold gravy and a table-spoonful of mushroom sauce. Pile it in the centre of a dish, and place round it alternately small and very thin slices of broiled ham, and poached eggs on toast.

HASHED FOWL.

Take the meat from a cold fowl, and cut it in small pieces. Put half a pint of well-flavored stock into a stew-pan, add a little salt, pepper and nutmeg, and thicken with some flour and butter; let it boil, then put in the pieces of fowl to warm; after stewing sufficiently, serve with some poached eggs laid on the hash, with a sprig of parsley in the centre, and garnish round the plate with pieces of fried bread.

BROILED PARTRIDGE.

Split the partridge, wipe it inside and out, but do not wash it; broil it delicately over a clear fire, sprinkling it with a little salt and cayenne; rub a bit of fresh butter over it the moment it is taken from the fire. Serve immediately with a sauce made of a slice of butter, browned with flour; a little water, cayenne, salt, and mushroom catsup poured over it. Another way is to dip it, after being dressed, flattened and seasoned, into clarified butter, and then into bread crumbs; broil gently twenty or thirty minutes, and serve with brown mushroom sauce.

PARTRIDGE SALAD.

Place the remains of roast partridge in a deep dish, with oil, tarragon vinegar, shallot minced, salt and pepper. At the time of serving, place the partridge in a dish, surround it with the hearts of lettuce cut in halves or in quarters according to the size; garnish the partridge with hard boiled eggs, cut in quarters, minced gherkins, pickled onions and capers, and stir it in thoroughly with the mixture remaining in the deep dish.

PARTRIDGE PIE.

Take two brace of partridges, pluck and draw them; carve three of them into six pieces each, viz., wings, legs, breast, neck and head, and back. One of the birds should be kept whole, trussed in the usual form. Let the pieces be seasoned with pepper, salt, and a little ground mace, and laid in a deep dish. Stuff the body of the bird left entire, and put it into the middle of the dish, breast upwards. Pour over the game half a pint of cold strong beef gravy well strained, in which two well roasted shallots and a few corns of allspice have been boiled; add the yolk of six hard boiled eggs, and half a gill of good catsup. Cover your dish with a light puff paste, and bake in a moderately heated oven.

PIGEON PIE.

Make a fine puff paste, lay a border of it around a large dish, and cover the bottom with a veal cutlet, or a tender rump steak free from fat and bone, and seasoned with salt, cayenne, and nutmeg or pounded mace; then prepare as many freshly killed young pigeons as the dish will contain in one layer; put into each a slice of butter seasoned with a little cayenne and mace; lay them into the dish breast downwards, and between and over them put the yolks of half dozen or more boiled eggs; stick plenty of butter on them, season the whole with salt and spice; pour in cold water or veal broth for the gravy, roll out the cover three quarters of an inch thick, secure it round the edge, ornament it and bake the pie an hour or more. The livers of the birds may be put in them, or they may be filled with small mushrooms.

CROQUETTES OF FOWL.

Mince very fine some meat from a cold fowl; put it in a pan with a little stock, a table-spoonful of cream, a little salt, and nutmeg, and make it of the right thickness with flour; let it boil well, then pour it out on a deep dish, and put it aside to get cold and set; then divide it into parts, form them into small balls, or egg shapes; roll each in fine bread crumbs, then egg over with the yolk of egg beaten; roll again in bread crumbs and fry, not too brown. Serve, ornamented with parsley.

GAME PATTIES.

Make as many patties of a small size as you require, of good light puff paste; egg them over, and bake them a nice light brown. Fill the centre with minced venison, or hare, or a mince of any kind of game; dish them on a nappy, and send them to table quite hot.

IMITATION CRAB.

Mince the white meat of a roast or boiled fowl very fine with the liver so as to make about six table-spoonsful in all. To this put two table-spoonsful of pounded cheese, two moderate sized onions, four or five green chillies (or if these cannot be procured, some cayenne peppers,) chopped very small. Mix these thoroughly together, and afterwards add one spoonful of anchovy, and one of Harvey sauce, a large spoonful of mustard, two of mushroom catsup, black pepper, and salt, and three spoonsful of sweet oil. Well mix the whole. This makes a nice relish to eat with bread and butter.

SMALL BIRDS.

Dress them nicely, split them down the back and open them out flat, cleaning them well. Broil them gently over a clear fire, season them with butter, salt and pepper; serve them on buttered toast with pickles.

ROAST GROUSE.

Dress and singe them. Fill the bodies with a stuffing of bread crumbs, seasoned only with pepper, salt and butter. Put some cold stock or gravy into the pan, and baste frequently; three quarters of an hour will cook them. Serve with gravy, enriched with Harvey, or some other good game sauce, with mashed potatoes and jelly.

FORCEMEAT FOR ROAST VEAL, TURKEY, ETC.

Mix thoroughly four ounces of the crumb of stale bread very finely grated; the grated rind, pared thin, of half a fresh lemon; quarter of an ounce of minced parsley and thyme, one part thyme, two parts parsley; pepper or cayenne sufficient to season. Add to these the unbeaten yolk of an egg, and two ounces of butter in small bits; work all smoothly together with the fingers. Other savory herbs than parsley or thyme may be used if preferred, and a little minced onion may be added, if desired. The proportions given here may be increased when more is required. The above will be sufficient for a middling sized turkey. Forcemeat for Ducks or Geese. Two parts of chopped onions, two parts of bread crumbs, two of butter, one of pounded sage, and a seasoning of pepper and salt.

VENISON PASTRY.

Cut the venison into pieces; line a dish with pie crust, place a layer of beef suet cut up finely, in the bottom of the dish, then put in the venison. Season it with salt and pepper, lay on butter, cover it with crust and bake it.

VENISON PUFFS.

Shave some cold venison very thin, and cut into small pieces; to to this add a little currant jelly and some rich brown gravy well mixed. Roll out some light puff paste very thin, cut it in pieces and in each piece put some of the meat, and make them into puffs. Place them all ready to bake, and brush them over with white of egg. Put them in a quick oven and bake a nice brown color.

VENISON STEAK.

Broil rare, and prepare a gravy with butter, pepper, salt, a teaspoon of flour, and some mushroom catsup. Cut the steak up into small pieces, and when the gravy is hot put it in, and cover tight. Set it back from the fire, or in the oven ten minutes, and serve with toast, and jelly.

STEWED HARE OR RABBIT.

Wash and soak it thoroughly, wipe it quite dry, cut it into joints, flour and brown it slightly in four or five ounces of butter, with some bits of lean ham, then pour on by degrees a pint and a half of gravy, and stew the meat very gently an hour and a half, or two hours; add salt if needed. When it has stewed a half hour or more, put in half the rind of a lemon, cut thin, and ten minutes before serving stir in a large dessert-spoonful of rice flour, mixed smoothly with two table-spoonsful of mushroon catsup, quarter of a teaspoonful of mace and less of cayenne.

RABBIT IN SLICES.

Take a fresh rabbit, cut it in slices, and fry it brown with some slices of pickled pork and some onions chopped fine. When nice and brown, take it out of the frying pan and put it in a stewpan with water sufficient to cover it; pepper and salt to taste; thicken with some flour and butter; and add force-meat balls, but be sure not to put the fat out of the frying pan. Let the gravy be the thickness of a very rich cream.

ROAST RABBIT.

Dress the rabbit, parboil the liver with a slice of fat ham, or sweet salt pork, and chop it up fine with bread crumbs, thyme, a small onion, and pepper and salt. Fill the body, and sew it up. Rub it over with sweet oil, or a little butter, and put a little butter in the pan with the water to baste it. Baste frequently, roast an hour and a half, and serve with mashed potatoes, and black, or red currant jelly.

Hare is prepared, and roasted in precisely the same way.

MEAT SAUCES.

WHITE SAUCE.

Boil well over the fire half a pint of milk, quarter of a pint of stock of a light color, season with salt, and thicken with some flour and butter. Mix the flour with milk instead of water, for white sauce.

BREAD SAUCE.—1.

Boil thin slices of white bread without the crust, in milk, with some whole white pepper, and a sliced onion; rub all through a coarse colander, put it back into the stewpan with a small piece of butter, a cup of veal stock or gravy, salt and a little cream, if you have it; warm, and serve it.

BREAD SAUCE.—2.

Pour quite boiling, on half a pint of the finest bread crumbs, an equal measure of new milk; cover them closely with a plate, and let the sauce remain for twenty or thirty minutes; put it then into a saucepan with a small salt-spoonful of salt, half as much pounded mace, a little cayenne, and about an ounce of fresh butter; keep it stirred constantly over a clear fire, for a few minutes, then mix it with a cup of milk, give it a boil, and serve it immediately.

RICE SAUCE.

Soak a quarter of a pound of rice in a pint of milk, with onion, pepper etc., as for bread sauce. When it is quite tender, remove the spice, rub it through a sieve into a stewpan, and boil it. If too thick, add a small quantity of cream or milk. This is good for game or chicken, as a change from bread sauce.

WHITE SAUCE.

Knead a large table-spoonful of butter in a little flour, melt it in a tea-cupful of milk; beat the yolk of an egg with a tea-spoonful of milk or cream, stir it into the butter, and place it over the fire, stirring it constantly. Chopped parsley may be added.

EGG SAUCE.

Mince two or three hard-boiled eggs, and mix in white sauce.

CAPER SAUCE.

Add one or two spoonsful of capers to white sauce.

OYSTER SAUCE.

Boil up oysters in their own liquor, then beard them; mix some butter with flour, and put into the strained liquor; when it is hot, stir the oysters into it; add some melted butter, and a little cayenne pepper; let it boil up once; put in a little lemon juice and it is ready for serving.

BROWN ONION SAUCE.—1.

Brown some sliced onions, in a stew pan, in a little butter; add a little good gravy, and stew them till quite tender. With the round steak of beef, this sauce is much admired.

TOMATO SAUCE.—1.

Take about one hundred and fifty good tomatoes, cut them into thin slices, place them in a dish with a pound of salt strewn over them, let them remain in the salt two days. Boil a quart of distilled vinegar with half ounce of mace, half ounce of cloves, half ounce of ginger and mustard seed, and twenty-five ripe capsicums, or long pepper pods, for half an hour; then add the tomatoes, having first poured away all the water and juice extracted by the salt from them, and boil all together for half hour; rub them through a clean, fine sieve, and when cold, bottle and cork tightly. If the tomatoes are gathered in dry weather, and carefully done, this sauce will keep for two years.

TOMATO SAUCE.—2.

Put tomatoes perfectly ripe, into an earthen jar, and set into an oven till they are quite soft; then separate the skins from the pulp, and mix this with capsicum vinegar and a few shalots finely chopped, which will be proportioned to the quantity of fruit. Add powdered ginger and salt to your taste. Some white wine vinegar and cayenne may be used instead of capsicum vinegar. Keep the mixture in small wide-mouthed bottles, well corked, and in a dry, cool place.

TOMATO SAUCE.—3.

Remove the skin and seeds from about a dozen tomatoes, slice them and put them in the stew pan with pepper and salt to taste, and three pounded crackers. Stew slowly one hour.

HORSERADISH SAUCE.—1.

Wash a good stick of horseradish, scrape off the outside, then grate to a powder. Then take one table-spoonful of the grated horseradish, one salt spoonful of mustard, a pinch of salt, four table-spoonsful of cream, and two table-spoonsful of vinegar, and mix them well together. Add the vinegar last, stirring rapidly as it is added.

HORSERADISH SAUCE.—2.

Stir together until well mixed one dessert spoon of sweet cream, the same quantity of powdered mustard, a table-spoonful of vinegar, and two table-spoonsful of scraped horseradish, with a little salt to taste. Serve the sauce separately in a sauce tureen. It will keep for two or three days or longer if olive oil is used instead of cream.

CRANBERRY SAUCE.

Wash, and pick over one quart of cranberries, put them to stew with a little water, and a pound of sugar, in a porcelain-lined saucepan. Let them stew slowly, and closely covered for an hour, or more. They can then be set away ready for use, or they can be put into a mould and turned out in form the next day.

Another, and nicer way is to stew them soft, then strain off the skins, add pound of sugar to quart of fruit, and boil all up together again for fifteen minutes. This will make a fine jelly for game, if put into a mould.

MINT SAUCE.

Choose fresh and young mint, strip the leaves from the stems, wash and drain, chop them finely, and add two table-spoonsful of pounded sugar to three heaped table-spoonsful of mint. Mix thoroughly, and pour in gradually, six table-spoonsful of good vinegar. The proportions can be varied according to taste.

CELERY SAUCE.

Cut the celery into inch lengths, fry it in butter until it begins to be tender, add a spoonful of flour which may be allowed to brown a little, and half a pint of good broth or beef gravy, with a seasoning of pepper or cayenne.

ASPARAGUS SAUCE.

Wash and drain half inch lengths of asparagus tops, about a half pint of them, throw them into plenty of boiling salt and water, and boil quarter of an hour or less until tender, then turn them into a strainer to drain. When ready to serve put them into thickened veal gravy, mixed with the yolks of two eggs, with seasoning of salt and cayenne; or into melted butter into which a little lemon juice has been squeezed.

SAUCE OF TURKEY'S EGGS.

Turkey's eggs are superior to others for sauce. Boil three eggs gently in plenty of water twenty minutes. Break the shells by rolling them on the table; separate the whites from the yolks, divide all the yolks into quarter inch dice pieces, mince one and a half of the whites rather small, mix them lightly and stir them into a pint of white sauce, and serve hot. The eggs of common fowl may be prepared for sauce according to these directions, using four yolks and two whites, and boiling four or five minutes less. The eggs of guinea fowl also make a good sauce after ten minutes boiling.

MILD MUSTARD.

For immediate use mustard may be mixed with milk to which a spoonful of very thin cream may be added.

FRENCH BATTER.

For frying vegetables and for apple, peach, or orange fritters, pour a gill of boiling water on a couple of ounces of bits of butter. When dissolved, add three gills of cold water to make it lukewarm; mix in smoothly twelve ounces of dry flour and a small pinch of salt if for fruit fritters, but more salt if for meat. If it is too thick, add more water. Just before using, add the whites of two eggs beaten to a solid froth.

BERKSHIRE SAUCE.

One full pint of nasturtium flowers must be placed in a stone jar, with five shallots bruised, two tea-spoonsful of salt, and the same quantity of cayenne pepper. Upon these, one quart of boiling vinegar should be poured, and the jar closely stopped down for a month or more. At the end of this time the liquid must be strained, and three ounces of soy added for each pint, after which the sauce may be bottled, and is fit for use. This is excellent for either hot or cold meat, and easily made when nasturtium flowers are plentiful.

A SAUCE FOR MADE DISHES.

One quart of vinegar, one ounce of cayenne pepper, six table-spoonsful of walnut catsup, two table-spoonsful of soy, two cloves of garlic, and the same quantity of shallots (both the garlic and shallots must be well bruised). Mix all the ingredients well together, bottle them, and keep the bottles closely corked. It will be fit or use in six weeks.

SAUCE FOR BOILED TURKEY OR CAPON.

When the turkey is plucked clean, singed and neatly trussed, stuff it inside with raw oysters, adding a lump of fresh butter and some stale bread crumbs. Place the turkey or capon in a clean cloth, fold it up carefully, put it in a saucepan of cold water, and let it boil over a moderately heated fire until it is done. Have a stick of white blanched celery at hand, and chop it up very small, place it in a quart of new milk in a saucepan and let it boil, gently, with a few black pepper corns, till the quantity is reduced to one pint; keep stirring the esculent up with the milk until it assumes the character of a consistent pulp. Thicken the whole with the yolk of a fresh egg, well beaten up, with half a tea-cup of fresh cream. Have upon the table a sauce boat of strong veal gravy.

SAUCE FOR ROASTED CHICKEN.

Cut up some carrots and parsnips into any shape preferred, and let them boil with some little onions in a small quantity of stock. Add mushroom catsup, a little ham cut into small pieces, and let all stew in butter, with sweet herbs, adding two cloves, some thyme and a bay leaf. When these are colored, put in some veal gravy. Let the whole boil slowly until sufficiently done. Skim it and add it with a little good veal broth to the carrots and parsnips. Roast two chickens (nicely stuffed) rolled in bacon and wrapped in pepper, and pour the mixture upon them.

SAUCE FOR BOILED FISH.

Pick and wash some fennel, parsley, mint, thyme and small green onions, using only a small quantity of each. Boil them until tender in a little veal stock; after which chop them up, add to them some fresh butter, the liquor they were boiled in, some grated nutmeg, the juice of half a lemon, a little cayenne pepper and salt. Let it boil; thicken it with flour and send it up in a sauce boat.

FISH SAUCE TO KEEP A YEAR.

Chop up forty anchovies, bones and all, put to them ten shallots cut small, a handful of scraped horseradish, a quarter of an ounce of mace, a quart of white wine, a pint of water, one lemon cut in slices, half a pint of anchovy liquor, a pint of red wine, twelve cloves, and twelve peppercorns. Boil together until reduced to a quart; strain it, put it into a bottle and cork it closely. It must be kept in a cold, dry place. When required for use, one tea-spoonful should be heated and put to half a pound of butter and a little flour.

SAUCE FOR VENISON.

Two spoons of currant jelly, one stick of cinnamon, one blade of mace, grated white bread, ten table-spoons of water, let it stew with a little water, serve in the dish with venison steaks.

DRAWN BUTTER.

Rub two tea-spoonsful of flour into a quarter of a pound of butter, add five table-spoons of cold water; set it into boiling water and heat till it begins to simmer, then it is done. For fish, chopped boiled eggs and capers can be put in. For boiled fowl, oysters can be put in while it is melting, and cooked through while it is simmering.

BROWNING FOR SAUCES.

Put half a pound of brown sugar into an iron saucepan, melt it over a moderate fire for about twenty minutes, stirring it continually until quite black; but it must become so by degrees, or too sudden a heat will make it bitter; then add two quarts of water, and in ten minutes the sugar will be dissolved. Bottle for use.

SAUCE FOR ROAST BEEF.

One quart of grated horseradish, two tea-spoons black pepper, two of mustard, one of allspice, two of salt, and a pint of best vinegar. Mix well, and bottle immediately.

MUSHROOM CATSUP.—1.

Break up the mushrooms and add to them a little salt, a handful to a peck, let them lie over night, and in the morning strain them through a coarse cloth; add to the liquor an ounce each of cloves, black pepper, Jamaica pepper, and ginger; two or three anchovies, and a glass of port wine for each quart, or in that proportion. Boil it gently then until the liquor is reduced to one half; take it off, let it cool, and bottle it air tight.

MUSHROOM CATSUP.—2.

Put in an earthen vessel layers of mushrooms, and thin layers of salt, and allow them remain half a day, or until the salt has penetrated them somewhat. Then mash them, and keep them standing another whole day, frequently stirring them up from the bottom. To each gallon of mushrooms add an ounce of peppercorns, an ounce of cloves, and one of allspice. Set the jar in cold water, and let it come to boiling heat. Simmer gently for two hours, then strain, and reduce one half, skimming carefully as it comes to a boil; strain it off, when it has settled, into small bottles for use, adding a teaspoon of brandy to each bottle, and seal. Keep in a dry place.

TOMATO CATSUP.

One gallon skinned tomatoes, three heaping table-spoonsful of salt, same of black pepper, two of allspice, three of ground mustard, half a dozen pods of red pepper. Stew all slowly together in a quart of vinegar for three hours; strain the liquor, simmer down to half a gallon. Bottle hot, and cork tight.

WALNUT CATSUP.

Boil or simmer a gallon of the expressed juice of walnuts when they are tender, and skim it well; then put in two pounds of anchovies, bones and liquor, two pounds of shallots, one ounce each of cloves, mace, and pepper, and one clove of garlic. Let all simmer till the shallots sink; then put the liquor into a pan till cold; bottle and divide the spice to each. Cork closely, tie the bladder over, and put it in small bottles. It will keep twenty years in the greatest perfection, but is not fit for use the first year.

VINEGAR PLANT.

To make vinegar from the vinegar plant, pour one gallon of boiling water on one and a half pounds of strong, clean, brown sugar, keep stirring it until it is the warmth of new milk, then put it into a large pickle jar, or any other convenient vehicle, and place the plant on it. If at the end of two or three days the plant does not float, take it out, put in a cork, and lay the plant on it. The vinegar will take making from six weeks to three months, and the above will make about three quarts. The jar must be placed in a warm—not a hot place.

EASY CIDER VINEGAR.

Take the water in which dried apples have been soaked and washed, strain it well and add a pound of sugar.

VINEGAR OF MARJORAM.

Pick sweet marjoram leaves before the plant flowers, wilt them a little and steep in strong vinegar two weeks; bottle and cork tightly.

VINEGAR FOR SOUSE.

Steep black peppercorns and mustard seed in strong vinegar for four weeks, strain and pour it over the souse after it is boiled tender.

VINEGAR FOR SOUSED FISH.

Steep in strong vinegar a few cloves, some peppercorns, mustard seed, and young walnuts bruised, until the vinegar is thoroughly spiced; strain, and pour it over the fish. The fish must be boiled before it is soused.

CLOVE VINEGAR.

Steep two ounces of bruised cloves in one pint of strong vinegar, for six weeks; then filter it until it is clear, bottle and cork closely, in half pint bottles.

TARRAGON VINEGAR.

Pick tarragon leaves from the stalk before the plant flowers, fill a large, wide-mouthed bottle with them, steep them in strong vinegar for two weeks or longer, strain clear; bottle and cork closely, in half pint bottles. This is used to flavor mustards and salads.

SAVORY VINEGAR.

Steep summer savory in strong vinegar until it is thoroughly flavored; strain, and bottle it tightly.

CELERY VINEGAR.

Into a pint and a half of boiling vinegar, throw a pint of fresh celery roots and stems, sliced fine, a large salt-spoonful of salt, a few grain of cayenne, and half an ounce of peppercorns; let it boil two or three minutes, turn it into a stone jar, and secure it from the air when it is cold. It will keep two or three months in the jar, or it may be strained off and bottled in three or four weeks.

GREEN MINT VINEGAR.

Put freshly gathered mint, chopped or bruised, into bottles until they are nearly full; pour in pale vinegar, and in six weeks strain it off and bottle it for use. Young leaves of mint stripped from the stalk and minced for sauce will keep in vinegar, though the color may not be very good.

RASPBERRY VINEGAR.

Put three or four quarts of raspberries in a stone jar, and cover them with vinegar. Let them stand twenty-four hours. Then strain this juice through a jelly bag, and pour it on fresh berries, letting this stand another day. Repeat this process until you have the quantity you desire. Add to each pint of juice one pound of sugar. Put it into a preserving kettle, and allow it to heat sufficiently to melt the sugar. When it is cold, put it into sealed bottles. It will keep two years.

BLACK CURRANT VINEGAR.

Well bruise the currants, pour the vinegar over them, putting in a little sugar to draw the juice. Let it stand three or four days, stirring it well each day. Strain the juice from the fruit, and putting one pound of sugar to one pint of juice; boil it gently three quarters of an hour; skim, and when cold, bottle it.

CHILI VINEGAR.

Let fifty small, ripe cayenne peppers chopped fine, remain in strong vinegar for a fortnight, then strain and bottle.

RELISHES.

SANDWICHES.

Make some nice biscuit which will be three-quarters of an inch thick, when baked. Split them, butter them lightly, and lay in a slice of tongue, or ham, touched with French mustard or anchovy sauce.

DRESSING FOR SANDWICHES.

Take three spoonsful of sweet oil, three table-spoonsful of mixed mustard, half-a-pound of good butter, a little red pepper, a little salt, the yolk of one egg, beat them together smoothly, and keep them cool; then chop together finely some tongue and ham, and if convenient, a little cold chicken. Spread the sliced bread with the dressing, then with the meat; add the second slice, press closely together and trim off the edges.

A COLD RELISH.

Cut odd scraps of meat into small pieces. If there is veal and ham among it, so much the better. Add three table-spoonsful of farina, some parsley, green or dried, a little sage, a little celery, parsnip, or carrot, or all three, chopped fine, and pepper and salt. Cover with water, and stew for two hours, very gently. Pour into a dish, and when cold it will be solid; and should be cut in thin slices, for the table.

A GERMAN ENTREMET.

Boil eight eggs quite hard, and when cold cut them in two lengthwise. Take the yolks out very carefully, pass them through a fine sieve, and mix them well with half a pint of cream (or more if required) and then add pepper, salt, and herbs. Pour this sauce into a very flat pie dish that will stand heat, and place the white half eggs carefully in it, arranging them in the form of a star, or any pattern preferred. Fill up the vacancy left in them by the yolks having been removed, with the same mixture, and strew a few bread crumbs over them. Bake this very slightly, just enough to give it a bright yellow color, and serve it up in the dish in which it has been baked.

SAVORY CUSTARD.

Beat two eggs into one and a half gills of cream; season to taste with pepper, salt, cayenne, chopped parsley, sweet herbs and shallot; add to these some chopped ham and tongue. Pour it into small round cups and steam ten minutes.

TOMATO TOAST.

Pare, slice, and cook green tomatoes until very tender. Add sweet cream, sweet milk will do, but it will need more butter to make plenty of gravy; season with pepper, salt, and butter. Have the bread nicely toasted and placed in a deep dish, and pour the contents of the frying-pan over it. This is an excellent way to use up dry slices of bread.

TOMATO OMELET.

Peel and chop a quart of tomatoes, simmer them for twenty minutes with as much water as will cover them; chop a few onions very fine, throw them in with crumbled bread and a lump of butter; when nearly done beat up four eggs, and stir them in a few minutes; salt and pepper to your taste.

SAVORY TOAST.

Put a piece of butter the size of a walnut into a saucepan, a dessert-spoonful of mustard, a wine glass of vinegar (that in which walnuts have been pickled is superior to all others), a dessert-spoonful of anchovy sauce, some pepper and cayenne, quarter pound of cheese broken into pieces. Stir it well until dissolved, then spread on toasted bread and serve.

TOASTED CHEESE.—1.

Grate three ounces of fat cheese, mix it with the yolk of one egg, four ounces of grated bread and three ounces of butter, beat the whole well in a mortar, with a dessert-spoonful of mustard, and a little salt and pepper. Toast some slices of bread, lay the paste thick upon it, put it for a minute before the fire and send to table very hot.

TOASTED CHEESE.—2.

Put into a clean sauce-pan a table-spoonful of either ale (not bitter) or cold water; add some slices of toasting cheese, and let it simmer until it is melted, stirring it all the time. Have ready in a bowl some good ale, sweeten it to the taste with moist sugar and add some grated nutmeg. Toast slices of bread without either burn or crust, put them hot into the bowl, to take the chill off the ale, then put a slice of the toast on a hot plate for each person, and pour upon it as much of the cooked cheese as may be agreeable. Take out of the bowl any remaining toast there may be left; stir well the sugar from the bottom, and drink the ale after eating the cheese.

ANCHOVY CHEESE.

Put a piece of cheese into a stewpan, and, when soft, mash it with butter or any other grease. Now add half a pint of water, hot or cold, a little salt, and an anchovy cut small. Boil the whole together, adding as much flour from time to time as the liquid will absorb. When you have got a thick paste, pour over it some eggs beaten up, and mix the whole well together. Lastly, pull your paste into small lumps, and bake in an oven.

CHEESE OMELET.

Butter the sides of a deep dish, cover the bottom with thin slices of cheese, place upon this very thin slices of bread, well buttered, a little red pepper and mustard, another layer of cheese, and, just before putting in the oven, beat the yolk of an egg in a cup of cream and pour into the dish. Bake half an hour or until nicely browned.

CHEESE FONDU.

A quarter of a pound of butter, one ounce and half of flour

four eggs, three ounces cheese grated, not quite half a pint of milk. Place the butter and flour in a saucepan on the hot plate, stir together: next add the grated cheese; stir on for twenty minutes, when remove it, and let it get cold. Beat the eggs, yolks and whites separately, add the yolks to the mixture cold, but the whites must be beaten and added just before baking. Bake in a brisk oven on a silver fondu dish, or a round cake tin concealed with a frilled paper, about three quarters of an hour. Serve hot, as it will fall in cooling.

FONDU STRAWS.

Quarter of a pound of puff paste and quarter of an ounce of good cheese grated very fine, a little salt and cayenne pepper mixed; sprinkle the cheese, salt, and pepper over the paste, and roll it two or three times; cut it into narrow strips about five inches long; bake them in a slow oven and serve very hot.

POTTED CHEESE.

One pound of cheese beaten in a mortar; two ounces of liquid butter, one glass of sherry, and a very small quantity of cayenne pepper, mace, and salt. All should be well beaten together and put into a pretty shaped glass potting-jar, with a layer of butter at the top. It makes a delicious relish for bread or toast.

POT CHEESE.

Scald a pint of sour milk till it curdles, strain off the whey and form the curd into round cakes an inch thick, adding salt to taste. The milk should not be old; if very sour, a little sweet milk scalded with it improves the flavor.

MACARONI.

Put four or five ounces of macaroni in water, and boil for twenty minutes, until tender. Mix into half a pint of milk a little flour, and a small piece of butter, half a tea-cup of cream, half a tea-spoonful of mustard, salt, pepper, and cayenne, and four ounces of good fat cheese grated very fine; stir all together and boil for ten minutes. Pour this over the macaroni, after draining it from the water; boil five or six minutes and serve.

TIMBALL OF MACARONI.

Roll some puff paste very thin, and cut it into narrow bands, and twist each into a kind of cord, which coil around the insides of small butter moulds. Then fill each mould with macaroni, cover the top with equal quantities of grated bread and good fat cheese; put them into a warm oven, and let them bake three quarters of an hour, turn them out on a dish and serve them.

PICKLES.

CUCUMBERS.—1.

To pickle cucumbers for market cut them from the vines without bruising the stems, take them carefully to the cellar, pack in barrels putting different sizes in separate barrels; spread a layer of salt between each layer of cucumbers, sufficient to entirely cover the pickles. Pack the cucumbers daily as they are picked, discarding the crooked or those of slow growth. The brine will be formed without the addition of water, by the juice extracted by the salt. Keep boards over the pickles, with weights to press them under the brine. Pickles packed in this way can be preserved for years with pure salt; but if the salt is mixed with lime they will soften and spoil. In two months after the barrel is filled, take them from the brine, freshen and green. To green them, prepare alum water, put the pickles in a vat or boiler lined with tinned copper; heat the alum water, and pour it over them. Pickle makers usually employ this process except that they throw steam into the vats to heat the alum water, and if managed properly the pickles may be greened with less action of copper than when scalded in the usual method in bright brass kettles. Take the pickles from the vat when a little green, and pour over them water boiling hot. If not greened sufficiently, repeat the hot water until they are the desired color, and when cold put them in good vinegar. Let them remain until quite soured; then change to pretty strong vinegar, which will keep the pickles hard and sour. Add six large peppers, without bruising, to each barrel, and keep the pickles under the vinegar with weights.

CUCUMBERS.—2.

A simpler method is, pick the cucumbers with a bit of the stem on, wipe them clean and put them into the following pickle, at the rate of one part vinegar, two parts water, and three salt, with a good sized root of horseradish. When the tub is full, put a cloth over the cucumbers and a clean flat stone over the cloth, cover the tub and set it in the cellar. In the spring soak them and pickle them in vinegar.

TOMATOES.

Wipe the tomatoes clean; slice them, if large, twice in two; if small, only once. Sprinkle a thin layer of sugar on the bottom of a stone jar, then a layer of tomatoes, and then a sprinkling of sugar, and so on. When the jar is full, add vinegar and set it in a warm place. In a few weeks they will be good pickles. The tomatoes must be kept under the vinegar, and the jar tightly covered.

BEETS

Boil the beets till tender, then drop them whole or sliced into spiced vinegar.

GREEN TOMATOES.

Let green tomatoes stand in salt and water for twelve hours. Then stick four or five cloves in each one, and pour boiling vinegar over them. Place them in a jar and set them in a cool place.

MUSTARD PICKLE.

Half peck of small cucumbers, half peck of green string beans, one quart of green peppers, two quarts of small onions. Cut all in small pieces; put cucumbers and beans in a strong brine for twenty-four hours. Remove from brine and pour on two pounds of ground mustard mixed with one pint of sweet oil, and three quarts of vinegar.

GREEN PICKLE.

In two quarts of good vinegar, boil quarter of a pound of salt, two ounces of shallots, two large tea-spoonsful of cayenne pepper, one ounce of ginger, and one ounce of white pepper; when well boiled, cool and pour it in a jar upon any freshly gathered green fruits and vegetables desired to be pickled.

ONIONS.—1.

Peel small onions and lay them for one day in salt and water, changing their position once during the time. Boil together good vinegar, cloves, mace, and a little pepper, dry the onions, pour the pickle over them in a jar, and cover them closely.

ONIONS—2.

To prevent watery eyes while peeling, put them in a pot of boiling water. Let them stand a few moments to drain, then peel them, put them into milk and water, with a little salt; when it boils, strain off the onions, wipe dry, and put them in wide-mouthed bottles. Have very old white wine vinegar, in which whole white pepper, ginger, mace, and horseradish have been boiled. Pour it over the onions, and cover down close with bladders.

PORTUGAL ONIONS.

The Portugal onion makes an excellent pickle prepared in the following way: one large onion and one large baking apple, cut up into small pieces, mixed well together, and put into a pickle jar, into which enough boiling vinegar must be poured to cover the mixture and fill up the jar.

FRENCH BEANS.

Make a strong brine of salt and water, gather the beans before they have strings, lay them in the brine till yellow, drain them dry and put boiling hot vinegar over them. Close them tightly for a day and night. Boil the vinegar and pour it on again for several days till they turn green. To one peck of beans put half an ounce each of pepper, mace and cloves.

CABBAGE.

Cut a firm cabbage into thin slices, spread it on an open dish, sprinkle it over with salt for two or three days, then strain it through a sieve or colander, so as to take all water from it; place it in your jar, and pour as much boiling vinegar as will cover it; lay over the jar a cloth to keep in all the steam until quite cold, then tie it down air tight. It will keep for a very long time. A few slices of beet root gives a good color.

CABBAGE WITH SWEET PICKLE.

Cut the heads into quarters, let them stand in cold water a short time. Chop them fine, together with nice fine celery sufficient to season it. Fill small jars or cans, make a sweet pickle of molasses and vinegar, season with plenty of red pepper and cinnamon, and other spices to the taste; boil altogether a few moments and pour over the cabbage while hot. Cork the cans and place in the cellar. This should not be eaten under three or four weeks. It is a nice relish with cold meats, etc.

RED CABBAGE.

Put a quarter of an ounce of cochineal into a small bag, and boil it with the quantity of vinegar considered sufficient for the cabbage you wish to pickle, adding a little salt, and bay salt. When it boils, scald the cabbage with it, having previously cut it into slices; boil the vinegar up again, this time adding ginger and pepper. Let it cool, and when quite cold, having put the cabbage into jars, pour the pickle upon it, and tie it down closely. The cochineal preserves the color; beet root may be used instead. Both are quite harmless.

MELONS, MANGOES AND CUCUMBERS.

Melons should not be much more than half grown, but cucumbers full grown. Cut off the top, but leave it hanging by a bit of rind, which is to serve as a hinge to a box lid; scoop out all the seeds with a spoon, and fill the fruit with equal parts of mustard seed, ground pepper and ginger, or flour of mustard instead of the seed, and two or three cloves of garlic. The lid which incloses the spice may be sewed down or tied, by running a white thread through the ends. The pickle may be prepared with the spices, or, if preferred, with the following ingredients: To each quart of vinegar put salt, flour of mustard, curry powder, bruised ginger, tumeric, half ounce of each; of cayenne pepper, one drachm; rub all these together with a large glassful of salad oil; eschalots, two ounces, garlic, half ounce, sliced. Steep the spice in the vinegar as before directed, and put the vegetables into it hot.

GHERKINS.

A quick mode of pickling gherkins, or prickly cucumbers, is to prick them with a needle in several places, and put them in a pan of cold water, adding as much salt as will make a strong brine. Let them soak for three hours. Take them out, wipe them dry in a clean cloth; put in a saucepan, over a gentle fire, add some strong, brown pickling vinegar, with allspice, half the quantity of whole black pepper, a little brown ginger and some cayenne pepper. Let them simmer quarter of an hour; take them up, and when cold, pour them over the gherkins in a jar, and stop them tightly down. They will be fit for use in the course of three or four days. One or two eschalots will be found an improvement.

PICCALILLI.

Use all kinds of vegetables that may be pickled. Slice cabbages, and pull cauliflowers in bunches, put them on earthen dishes, sprinkled over with salt, and let them stand three days to dry. Sliced cucumbers, green tomatoes, gherkins, radish pods, onions, beans, nasturtiums and anything you like that may be pickled, put it into salt and water one day. The next day dry them; take a few at a time and scald in brown vinegar, and when all are scalded, set the vinegar away. To four quarts of brown vinegar, put a quarter of a pound of ginger, two ounces of allspice, quarter of a pound of shallots, two ounces of tumeric, and boil slowly half an hour. Take some boiling vinegar, and mix eight ounces of flour of mustard and pour it into the vinegar and spices; it must not boil after the mustard is put in. Put the prepared vegetables and spices in a large jar, scatter some brown mustard seed among the mixture, and stir it up well in the jar. If at any time it should become too dry, add cold boiled vinegar; for the vegetable must be kept covered with vinegar mixture. Cover the jar air tight and set in a cool place.

LEMON PICKLE.

The fruit should be small with thick rinds. Rub them with a piece of flannel; then slit them down in quarters, but not quite through the pulp, fill the slits with salt hard pressed in; set them upright in a pan for four or five days until the salt melts; turn them three days until they become tender in their liquor. Then make enough pickle to cover them, of ripe vinegar, the brine of the lemons, Jamaica pepper and ginger; boil and skim it. When cold, put it over the lemons.

TO PICKLE ROOTS.

Roots, such as carrots, salsify, and beet roots, may be pickled by being sliced, or cut into small pieces, and slightly boiled in vinegar without destroying their crispness, and adding the common spices; with beet roots put button onions, or cut some Spanish onions in slices, lay them alternately in a jar; boil one quart of vinegar, with one ounce of mixed pepper, half an ounce of ginger, some salt, and pour it cold over the beet root and onions.

BARBERRIES.—1.

Gather when not over ripe, pick off the leaves and dead stalks. Place them in jars, pour over them cold boiled salt and water, and close them tightly. They must be looked at occasionally, and as soon as a scum is seen to rise on them, they should be put into fresh salt and water.

BARBERRIES.—2.

Another method is to place them in a wide-mouthed bottle and pour over them cold distilled vinegar that has been previously boiled with a little spice, and keep them well corked. They are delicious when eaten with fish, and look very pretty round the dish.

BARBERRIES, (*Sweet.*)—1.

Add half a pound of sugar and a pint of molasses to each pound of the berries, simmer them together half an hour or more, until they become soft.

BARBERRIES, (*Sweet.*)—2

With every half pound of moist sugar mix one pint of water, and one pint of white wine vinegar: put the worst of the barberries in this and boil till the liquor is a bright deep color. Put the rest of the berries in glasses, let the liquor stand till cold, then strain it, wringing the cloth to get all the color from the barberries. Let it settle, then pour it into the glasses. Cover tightly with a bladder and leather.

WALNUTS.

Put them into strong salt, and water, for nine days; stir them frequently, and change the salt and water, every three days. Let them stand in a hair sieve till they turn black. Put them into strong stone jars, and pour boiling vinegar over them. Cover them, and let them stand till they are cold. Scald the vinegar three times more, pour it each time upon the walnuts, and let them stand till cold between each boiling; cover them closely, and let them stand two months. Make for them a pickle of two quarts of vinegar, half an ounce of olives, the same of mace, one ounce of ginger, the same of long-pepper, and two ounces of salt. Boil it ten minutes, pour it hot on the walnuts, and cover them tight.

ASPARAGUS.

Fill a stone pot with asparagus, make a pickle of water and have it salt enough to bear an egg; pour it on hot and keep it covered tight. Before using, put the asparagus in cold water for two hours. Then boil and butter and send to table. If they are used for pickles take them out of the brine, boil them and cover them with vinegar.

BLACKBERRIES.

To six wooden quarts of blackberries add three pounds of sugar and one quart of good vinegar. Let them stand covered until a syrup is formed, then pour it off, boil, and skim it off clear; put in the fruit and let it just come to a boil. Take it out carefully. Let the syrup boil up once more, then pour over and seal or tie down.

MUSHROOMS.

Button mushrooms, to preserve their flavor, should be rubbed with a piece of flannel dipped in salt. To preserve their color, keep them in spring water both before and after rubbing. From the larger mushrooms remove the red inside; when this is turned black they are too old. Throw a little salt over them and put them into a stewpan with some mace and red pepper; as the liquor comes out, shake them well and simmer them over a gentle fire till all of it is dried into them again. Put as much vinegar into the pan as will cover them; make it warm, and then pour all into glass jars or bottles, and tie down tightly, with a bladder. They will keep two years.

SALADS.

SPRING SALADS.

Use salads on the table as early as possible in the Spring; they are pleasant and very healthful. Water-cresses should be a standing dish upon the breakfast table; and lettuce, with chives, peppergrass, and whatever else is available, at dinner. Never mind the regular salad mixture of sweet oil and the like, if it is not convenient or agreeable. Pepper, salt and vinegar, are very good condiments alone, and we must even confess a weakness for an old-fashioned sprinkling of white sugar and vinegar on our lettuce, occasionally; but eat it at any rate, if only with salt.

CHICKEN SALAD.

Mince all the tender meat, white and dark, of a pair of chickens, fine. They should have been previously boiled or roasted. Chop all the white part of a large head of celery, with one or two young heads of lettuce, if they can be had, and mix with the chicken. Make a dressing of the yolks of eggs, boiled twenty minutes, and rubbed smooth with a spoon, two tea-spoonsful of made English mustard, a tea-spoonful of salt, two table-spoonsful of salad oil, a dessert-spoonful of white sugar, and half a pint of strong vinegar. Pour the dressing over the chicken and celery, in a salad bowl, and garnish with rings cut from the boiled whites of the eggs.

CARROT SALAD.

Boil your carrots tender, chop them fine, with the whites of hard boiled eggs. Pour over them a sauce made of the yolks of the eggs beaten smooth, with a small piece of butter, a little pepper and salt, a table-spoonful of vinegar, and a tea-spoonful of made mustard.

FISH SALAD.

Cold fish may be made into a very excellent salad in this way: Cut it as neatly as possible into pieces about one or two inches square; put them into a deep dish, add a little salt, and a small quantity of very finely chopped onions; squeeze the juice of a lemon over it; cover the dish with a plate, and set it away for two hours. Then take fresh lettuce, well drained from the water, cut it into pieces and pile it up high in the centre of a dish; drain the fish from the lemon juice, and place in a circle round the pile of lettuce as you would cutlets; pour some salad sauce over the lettuce, only keeping the fish white. Place parsley leaves between the pieces of fish, or a small piece of red beet-root, to garnish.

LOBSTER SALAD.

Mince the meat from the body and claws fine, mash the coral, and mix it with scalded lettuce chopped fine. Make a sauce of a little pepper, a very little cayenne, a tea-spoonful of French mustard, four table-spoonsful of salad oil, and four table-spoonsful of strong vinegar. Mash the yolks of three boiled eggs, mix them with the coral and the sauce, and add it before serving. [For another receipt, see Lobsters.]

AN EAST INDIAN SALAD.

Take a large boiled crab, pick the meat clean from the shell, and chop it up finely. Place it in a deep salad dish, adding one gill of tarragon, and one tea-spoonful of Chili vinegar, one table-spoonful of pure Lucca or Florence oil, with an anchovy bruised in a mortar. Let these be well mixed together. Chop one blanched endive, one stick of celery, and a small bunch of green chives, with salt to taste, and arrange the ingredients with a spoon in your salid dish. This is a good relish eaten with toasted cheese, or cold fowl, and other choice meats.

SALAD FOR COLD LAMB.

Wash and chop finely three large lettuces. Have ready a bunch of *barbe de capuchin* a bunch of water cresses, half a dozen young radishes, a little punnet and cress, two or there sprigs of tarragon leaves, a handful of corn-salad, twelve young chives, and a boiled beet root. Pour into a salad bowl two table-spoonsful of Lucca or Florence oil, a tea-spoonful of sweet anchovy sauce, a teaspoonful of Chili vinegar, the yolks of three hard-boiled eggs beaten up with cream, with salt to taste. Mix all together, adding a gill of vinegar. Cut up the roots and esculents, and stir them in till the salad is evenly mixed.

TOMATO SALAD.

Take ripe tomatoes and cut them in thin slices; sprinkle over them a small quantity of finely chopped green onions, add salt, pepper, vinegar, and oil if liked. The oil should be in the proportion of three table-spoonsful to one of vinegar. Serve with any roast meats.

POTATO SALAD.

When materials for a salad are scarce, this is a good way of disposing of cold potatoes. Slice them, and dress them with oil, vinegar, salt, and pepper, precisely like any other salad; adding a little chives, or an onion, and parsley chopped fine. If oil is not agreeable, use cream or a little melted butter.

THE POET'S SALAD.

Pass two well boiled potatoes through a sieve, add a tea-spoonful of mustard, two tea-spoonsful of salt, one of essence of anchovy, quarter of a tea-spoonful of very finely chopped onions, well-bruised into the mixture, three table-spoonsful of oil, one of vinegar, the pounded yolks of two hard boiled eggs. Stir it up thoroughly before serving.

LETTUCE SALAD.

Chop lettuces small and mix in a little of young onions if liked, make a sauce for them in the proportion of a table-spoonful of sugar to two of vinegar, and a little black pepper.

HOTCH POTCH.

Green tomatoes, cabbage, and cucumbers, one pint of each,

half-a-pint of onions; chop all very fine, salt well, let them stand one night, after which strain through a sieve, and add pepper, horseradish, white mustard seed, and half pint of sugar; mix well, lightly, fill your jar, and cover with good vinegar.

CHOW CHOW.

One peck of green tomatoes, six onions, four green peppers; chop fine, mix salt with them, let them stand one night, then squeeze through a cloth all moisture; after which add one table-spoonful of allspice, one of cloves, one of black pepper, four table-spoonsful of horseradish, one half pound of white mustard seed, mix it well, pack it in your jar, and cover with good vinegar.

CABBAGE AND VINEGAR.

Take half a cup of vinegar and a tea-spoonful of butter heated well. Beat an egg and stir into it, but after it is cool enough, so as not to cook the egg. Then cut up your cabbage, add salt and pepper; pour the mixture warm over it and set aside for dinner.

COLE SLAW.

Take the small head of a cabbage after removing six or seven outside leaves and cutting off the stalk as close as possible, chop fine, and mix with plenty of vinegar, salting it to taste.

AN EXCELLENT CHOW CHOW PICKLE.

Take one large head of slaw cabbage, two large bunches of celery, and twelve onions; slice all fine and salt well. After twenty-four hours, drain well and cover with vinegar, to remain twelve hours; then drain from the vinegar; add four red peppers and two green ones, finely cut up; one ounce of tumeric, quarter of a pound of mustard-seed, two table-spoonsful of mixed mustard, one spoonful of allspice, half the quantity of cloves, one table-spoonful of black pepper, half a cup of sweet oil, one cup of brown sugar; mix all together and cover with vinegar. More celery may be used if desired.

TOMATO SOY.

To a peck of green tomatoes, put a tea-cup of fine salt and a dozen green peppers. Chop tomatoes and peppers fine, work the salt well through the whole. Let stand twenty-four hours; then drain the brine off, spice to taste with cinnamon and cloves, pack down in a jar, and just cover with vinegar, in which the spice has been boiled, while it is hot.

HANDY CHOW CHOW.

Chop together very finely a head of cabbage, six green peppers, six green tomatoes, add two tea-spoonsful of mustard, sufficient salt, vinegar to wet it, and if desired a little cloves and allspice. It is ready then for use, and will keep a long time. No better appetizer can be made.

EGGS.

BOILED.

Put the required number of eggs into a saucepan containing *boiling* water sufficient to cover them, and put it in a place on the range where it will keep boiling hot, but not boil. Let them stand seven minutes. When taken up, they will be found thickly and deliciously jellied throughout, and perfectly digestible. It is a much better and more certain way, than boiling them.

Another method is to let them boil gently for thirty minutes. This is an excellent plan for persons who like hard boiled eggs, or for invalids, as eggs cooked for this length of time can be easily digested, by the most delicate stomach.

SCRAMBLED.

Beat up a dozen eggs and turn them into a pan in which a little butter has been allowed to melt; throw in finely chopped boiled ham or parsley, and a little pepper and salt, and toss about rapidly, to prevent sticking. Serve upon buttered toast.

POACHED.

Carefully break fresh eggs into a shallow pan of boiling water; have ready slices of buttered toast, and when the white part has set round the yolks, take them up with a skimmer and lay each one upon a slice of bread. They are seasoned at table.

BUTTERED EGGS.

Warm a piece of butter in a saucepan, add pepper and salt, or other seasoning. Break in the eggs, stirring them very quickly with a fork over the fire, and take them off instantly they begin to set. Continue the stirring for a minute, and serve on buttered toast.

FRIED (*with ham.*)

Break eggs one by one, into a saucer, and slip them into a pan in which ham has been lightly and quickly browned, (not dried up,) and fry them a light brown on the underside; by this time they will have assumed consistency on the top, and must be taken up carefully with a fish-slice or skimmer, without turning, and placed round the edge of the dish, the ham occupying the centre.

OMELET.

The proper way to make an omelet is to take three tea-spoonsful of milk for each egg, and a pinch of salt to each one also; beat the eggs lightly for three or four minutes, and pour them into a hot pan in which a piece of butter the size of a walnut has been melted a moment before; the mass will begin to bubble and rise immediately, and the bottom must be lifted incessantly with a clean knife so that the softer parts run in. An omelet should be cooked three or four minutes, and, made in this way, will melt in the mouth. If desired, beat with the eggs finely chopped ham or parsley. In sliding the omelet from the pan to the dish, fold it double.

PUFF OMELET.

Beat the yolks of six eggs light, mix with a small tea-cup of milk, and little salt. Beat together of sweet butter and flour each a table-spoonful until smooth; add the mixture to the custard, and beat the whole well together. Pour into a buttered pan, and when it appears to thicken add the whites, well beaten; dust over a trifle of salt, and when the whole is stiff, remove carefully to the dish.

OMELET WITH KIDNEYS.

Take a calf's kidney roasted, chop it finely and beat it with the eggs; cook them as directed for plain omelet.

OMELET WITH HERBS.

Beat half a dozen eggs as for plain omelet, chop fine parsley and cives, take two table-spoonsful of parsley; and one of cives beat with the eggs, and put all in a pan in which three or four ounces of butter are melted; fry, dropping a piece of butter the size of a nutmeg under it when half done, so that it will not adhere to the pan, and serve hot.

ASPARAGUS AND EGGS.

Boil the good part of the asparagus in water and a little salt, drain it and chop it fine, beat it with the eggs as for omelet; put it in a pan with hot butter in it, fry and serve hot. Sorrel may be cooked with eggs in the same manner.

EGGS AND APPLES.

Beat up the eggs as for omelet, pare and slice the apples, fry them in a little butter, take them out, and stir them in with the eggs. Melt a little butter in the pan, put in the eggs and apples; fry, turning over once and serve it hot.

EGGS AND MUSHROOMS.

Dress and chop the mushrooms, beat them with the eggs as for omelets, melt a little butter in the pan, and put them in; fry them, and serve hot.

FANCY OMELET.

Make four omelets of three or four eggs each, one plain, one with herbs, one with apples, one with asparagus or sorrel. Serve on the same dish, one lapping over the other.

EGGS AND HERRINGS.

Beat up three or four eggs, according to the quantity required, with pepper, a little parsley, a green onion cut very fine. Also open a red herring at the back, broil it and mince it fine. Add all together, and fry in a frying-pan with a little grease. No salt is required, as the herring is salt enough.

EGGS AND CHEESE.

Into a pie dish put four or five spoonsful of cream, or milk thickened with flour; break into it some six or eight eggs without breaking the yolks; sprinkle over the whole some grated cheese, and a little pepper. Bake in an oven, without allowing the yolks to harden.

PICKLED EGGS.

Take as many eggs as you wish to pickle, cover them with cold water, let them come to a boil, and boil *five* minutes. Take off and put into cold water; remove the shells carefully, and put the eggs in a jar. Take as much strong vinegar as will cover them, with cloves, allspice, black pepper, and a little red pepper; when it comes to a boil, pour it upon the eggs, with a little salt. Cover down when cold. They will be ready for use in three days, but are best when about a week old.

TO PRESERVE EGGS.—1.

Make a pickle of quick lime and salt strong enough to bear up an egg. Put in your eggs point downward, and they will keep perfectly for a year. Another method is to rub the outside of each egg with a piece of fried fat, and then put them in a jar, small end downward, in which has been placed a layer of coarse salt. Alternate a layer of salt with a layer of eggs until the jar is filled, rubbing each egg with grease, and placing always the small end down. Cover down tight and keep in a cool, dry place, and they will keep from June to June again.

TO PRESERVE EGGS.—2.

Store them away before they are twenty-four hours old. Pack them in a cask with plenty of bran, taking care that they do not touch each other. Another method is to place them in a box, small end downwards, in salt which entirely covers them.

VEGETABLES.

BOILED POTATOES.

New potatoes are scraped instead of peeled. In peeling, the thinner the portion taken off, the better. The nutriment of a potato is contained within half an inch of its surface, and careless hacking with a large knife will waste half of it. Late in the season, when potatoes are old, they may be pared and put to soak in cold water four or five hours before cooking. In boiling put a small handful of salt in the water, and let it boil before putting in the potatoes. Pour the water off, and let them stand uncovered near the fire to dry. To steam them, the pot may be returned to the fire covered with a coarse cloth. The water should be poured off the moment they show a tendency to crack, or a fork will pass easily through them. The potatoes for each mess should be of as equal size as possible.

MASHED POTATOES.

After being boiled break them to a paste and season with a little butter, salt and cream or milk. If any are left over press them down in a dish, and the next morning cut in slices and fry brown, with butter and pepper and a little chopped parsley.

FRIED POTATOES.

Peel half a dozen medium potatoes, cut them up small, and put them into cold water for about half an hour; take them out, dry with a towel, and put them in a frying-pan, with two ounces of butter and a little salt; cover down, and every little while, shake and turn them; when they are tender, and of a clear, light, rich brown, they are done; the grease should be drained off from them, and they are ready to send to table.

POTATO SHAVINGS.

Wash and peel three or four large potatoes, then continue cutting them into thin wide ribbons, as evenly as possible. Have ready boiling fat, drop them into it; when they are done a light brown drain them well over the stove and send them to table immediately, before they lose their crispness.

STEWED POTATOES.

Pare the potatoes, cut them in slices, throw them into hot water to rinse, then put them in the sauce pan with boiling water enough for gravy. When nearly done season with pepper, salt, and a little butter; and thicken with flour batter. Let it boil up two or three times, and send to the table.

BAKED POTATOES.

The most wholesome method of preparing potatoes is to bake them in hot ashes, and eat them with butter. To bake them in a stove, wash and rinse them, place them on a tin, and let them remain in the oven about two hours. Send them to the table with the skins on, or mash them with a little salt and gravy or cream. They are very good served with cold meat.

POTATO PIE.

Make a thin pie-crust in the usual way, and line with it a basin or deep pie-dish. Fill to the top with finely-shred potatoes, among which mix an onion or two, sliced very thin, pepper and salt, and a little butter, dripping, or lard. Pour over all as much good milk or cream as the dish or basin will hold. Either cover with a crust or not, according to option, and bake in a slow oven.

POTATO CAKES.

Take two pounds of very mealy boiled potatoes, mash them very fine with a little salt, mix them with two pounds of flour, add milk enough to beat this into dough, beating it up with a spoon, and put in a little yeast. Set it before the fire to rise, and when it has risen, divide it into cakes the size of a muffin, and bake them. These may be cut open and buttered hot.

POTATO PUDDING.

Mash up well all your cold potatoes with a fork, moisten with milk, add two table-spoonsful of flour, two table-spoonsful of minced onions, and one ounce of grease to every pound of mashed potatoes. Put into a basin, bake till brown, which will be about half an hour, and serve hot.

POTATOES A LA CREME.

Put into a saucepan about two ounces of butter, a dessert spoonful of flour, some parsley and scallions, both chopped small, salt and pepper; stir these up together, add a wine glass of cream, and set it on the fire, stirring continually until it boils. Cut some boiled potatoes into slices, and put them into the saucepan with the mixture, boil all together, and serve them very hot.

SCOLLOPED POTATOES.

Beat boiled potatoes fine with cream, a large piece of butter and some salt. Put it in scollop shells, smooth them on the top, score with a knife, lay thin slices of butter on them and brown them quickly before the fire, or in the oven.

TO BOIL VEGETABLES GREEN.

Dress them, and throw them into plenty of boiling water which has been salted and well skimmed; boil them fast until well done, keeping them uncovered, but being careful that they are not smoked. If the water is hard, a third of a tea-spoonful of carbonate of soda may be added with the salt to improve the color, but too much will injure them, and if green peas are being boiled, will reduce them to a mush.

GREEN CORN.

Take two dozen ears of green corn well cleaned from the silk, slightly cut off the edge of the kernels with a sharp knife, and scrape the remainder off. Place in a pot with two tea-cupsful of water. When cooked out so there is danger of burning, thin with sweet milk; when done, season with salt and pepper; add butter to your taste.

GREEN CORN ON THE EAR.

Select a dozen more or less, of nice, young ears, free them from every particle of silk, and throw them into boiling water with a table-spoonful of salt. If very young, fifteen minutes will cook them. As the corn grows older, it will require more time. Serve hot, with butter, pepper and salt.

CORN OYSTERS.

Take six ears of boiled corn, three eggs, one and a half table-spoonsful of flour. Beat the yolks very thick; cut the corn off the cob, season it with pepper and salt; mix it with the yolks, and add the flour. Whisk the whites to a stiff froth, stir them in with the corn and yolks; put a dessert-spoonful at a time in a pan of hot butter, and fry to a light brown on both sides.

SPRING GREENS.

Young beet and turnips tops make nice greens in the early spring. Pick, and wash them carefully from dust and insects, and boil with them a small piece of salt pork, bacon, ham or corned beef. Drain free from water, and serve with vinegar. They may be boiled plain, and served with gravy sauce.

SUCCOTASH.

Strip off the kernels from a dozen ears of nice sweet corn, very close to the ear, with a sharp, thin knife. Put them in a saucepan with a quart of Lima beans, a little veal stock or gravy or plain water, and let them simmer steadily, till the moisture is absorbed, and the corn and beans tender. Add then, a cup of milk, a small piece of butter, pepper and salt to taste, and let all simmer together until thoroughly amalgamated. Serve in covered dish. Succotash is very good made with string beans, cut small, and boiled with a slice of sweet salt pork; it then requires neither milk nor butter.

SQUASH FRITTERS.

One pint of cooked squash, one pint of milk, two eggs and a little salt, and sufficient flour to make them turn easily on the griddle.

BOILED SQUASH.

Peel a nice spring squash, take out the seeds and coarse part from the centre, cut it up in slices, and put it to stew with a little water, in a small covered saucepan. When it is quite tender, mash it, put to it a spoonful of cream or a little butter, pepper and salt to taste, and keep hot, till wanted for the table.

SEA KALE.

This should be boiled quite white, in milk, and may be served on toast like asparagus.

STEWED CUCUMBERS.

Cut them in quarters, peel and remove the seeds, boil until tender, and serve with toasted bread and sweet cream.

SALSIFY OR VEGETABLE OYSTER.

The roots look like horseradish; they must be well scraped, cut in two, and parboiled. The water is then drained off, the plant cut up fine and boiled up in milk, with a little butter, pepper and salt. Some persons think it acquires more the taste of the oyster, by having a little cod-fish stirred among it, but we prefer it without.

JERUSALEM ARTICHOKES.

They should be boiled, putting them at first into cold water, and must be taken up the moment they are done, or they will be too soft. They may be boiled plain, or served with white fricassee sauce. When boiled, if rubbed through a sieve with some fresh butter and cream, they form a splendid purre as a sauce for cutlets, or as a thickening for some sorts of white soup, or they may be sliced and fried.

ARTICHOKE FRACIS.

Having parboiled the artichokes, remove the middle leaves, pare it, stuff the centre with forcemeat and bake them until the meat is done. Serve with melted butter.

MASHED TURNIPS.

Pare the turnips, cut them in half, and boil in a pot with either beef, mutton, or lamb. When they become tender, press the liquor from them and mash them with pepper and salt. They may be served in this way, or they may be sent to the table whole, with white sauce.

EGG PLANT.

This is a delicious vegetable. Select a medium sized one. Peel, and cut it in round, thin slices. Sprinkle a little salt between each slice, and then cover them down with a bowl, and let them stand for an hour. Then rinse off the salt with clear, cold water; throw away the liquid at the bottom of the dish, which will be dark colored; wipe each slice dry, dip it in egg, and bread crumbs, and fry it in half lard, and half butter, a fine brown.

SPINACH.

Pick apart and wash carefully in three or four waters; put into the saucepan with a little salt. Press it down with a spoon and let it boil quickly about fifteen minutes. When tender turn it into a colander, and press out the water. Place it in the dish, raising it with a fork so that it may lie hollow; serve with melted butter or egg sauce, and garnish with hard boiled eggs cut in rings. It requires no water in boiling, the expressed juice being quite sufficient to keep it moist, and the spinach being much finer without, than with it.

DANDELIONS.

These are relished by many as well as spinach cooked in the same way. Take the young leaves before the plant blossoms or while in the bud, mash quite clean, boil tender in salted water, drain well and press them dry. They can be served plain with melted butter, or can be chopped and heated afresh with pepper, salt, and a little butter rolled in flour, and a spoonful or two of gravy or cream. A large quantity should be boiled, as they shrink very much. The dandelion is considered very healthy, and the slight bitterness is relished by most persons.

FRENCH BEANS.—1.

Well drain the beans; after scalding them, color some butter in a saucepan, toss up the beans in it over the fire, season them with salt and pepper, and when dishing up add a very little vinegar.

FRENCH BEANS.—2.

String the beans, cut them in two and then across, sprinkle them with salt, put them in boiling water and boil them up quickly.

YOUNG BEETS BOILED.

Beets are sweeter, and better when young, than when they have attained full size. Wash, and boil them, take off the skins after they are boiled, and put over them pepper, salt, and a little butter. When they have grown older, they require vinegar, and are indeed only fit for a pickle. Be careful never to prick beets in putting them in the pot, or while they are cooking, as that spoils the color, and injures the flavor.

ASPARAGUS.

Cut off the white ends, removing most of that which is hard; scrape the hard ends a little. Put them in cold water for a short time, then tie them up in small bundles. When the water boils, put them in with a little salt; boil until tender, about fifteen or twenty minutes. Toast a slice of bread brown on both sides. Take them up carefully, dip the toast in the asparagus water, and lay the heads on it with the white ends outwards. Pour melted butter over them, and if desired garnish with quarters of an orange.

STEWED TOMATOES.

Pour boiling water over ripe tomatoes to crack the skin, so that it can be removed; then cut them into small pieces, squeeze out some of the seeds without losing too much of the juice, then stew them without water, seasoning them with butter and salt. An onion, chopped fine may be stewed with them. Pepper may be added while stewing, or added at the table to each person's taste.

GREEN PEAS.

These should be fresh and newly shelled. Wash them and put them into enough boiling water to cover them, with a few leaves of mint, and a small piece of butter. Stir them occasionally and when tender drain the water from them, sprinkle on a little salt and serve them with melted butter.

ONIONS, BOILED.

Put them, after being peeled, in boiling water. Then when they are tender pour the water off, add butter, pepper, salt and a little milk, stew them up again and send them to the table hot.

FRICASSEED PARSNIPS.

Boil them in water until they are tender, then cut them into pieces two or three inches long, slice them and stew them in half a cupful of cream or milk, half a cupful of broth, a piece of floured butter, and pepper and salt.

FRIED PARSNIPS.

Boil them tender; when they are cool, slice them lengthwise, and fry them with some thin slices of boiled salt pork. Put in the parsnips when the fat is hot, pepper them, brown them on both sides; crisp the pork, and serve with them.

BOILED PARSNIPS.

Wash, scrape, cut out every speck or discoloration, and if large divide them. Put them in boiling water, skim it occasionally and let them boil from twenty to thirty minutes. Serve them mashed or plain, with melted butter.

PORTUGAL ONIONS STEWED.

Boil in water until they begin to soften, let them drain, put in a stewpan, cover with good thick brown gravy; let them remain until they are perfectly tender, and send them to table.

PORTUGAL ONIONS FRIED.

Peel and cut them in slices; fry in butter or lard, or fat from cooking meat; stir constantly while frying, and let them be of a dark brown color.

LIMA BEANS.

Shell the beans, put them in a considerable water, boiling with pickled parsley and sufficient salt; boil them quickly, and when done strain off the water; take them out, and season them with butter, pepper, and salt; garnish with boiled parsley.

BEST PORK AND BEANS.

Pick over a quart of small white beans, put them to soak over night. Set them to boil the next morning, throwing off the water, just before they reach boiling point. Cover with cold water again, put in a square pound of nice sweet salt pork and let both boil together till the beans are tender. When the beans are done, the water should have all become absorbed; they are then put in one pan to brown, and the pork in another, scoring the latter first, through the skin. Before serving set the pork in the centre of the beans. Serve with pickles and horseradish.

BOILED CARROTS.

To boil carrots in their own juice, wash clean and scrape them, cutting out discolored spots; cut them in rather thick slices and throw them into as much boiling salted water as will cover or barely float them, and no more. Boil gently till they are tolerably tender, then boil very quickly to evaporate the water, of which only a spoonful or so should be left in the saucepan. Sprinkle on them a little pepper, put in a small piece of butter rolled in flour, turn and toss them gently till their juice is thickened by them, and adheres to them; serve immediately. They are improved by adding a dessert spoonful of minced parsley, with the butter and a little thick cream mixed with a very little flour to prevent its curdling. Gravy may be used instead of cream.

CARROTS WITH PARSLEY.

Take boiled carrots, and divide them down the length once, if very large divide again; then cut them in slices the thickness of a silver quarter of a dollar. Take some sprigs of parsley, parboil and chop them small; then put the sliced carrots into a stewpan with the chopped parsley, a little bit of butter, some pepper, and salt, and a little cold gravy; toss them over the fire till hot, and serve.

BOILED CABBAGE.

Take off the outer leaves, cut the head in halves or quarters, and boil quickly in a large quantity of water, until done. Drain and press out the water, chop fine and season. Boil from half an hour to an hour. The water can be drained off when they are half done, and fresh water added if desired.

BROCCOLI.

Cut the heads with short stalks, peel off the hard outside skin, which is on the stalk and small branches, wash them, boil them fifteen minutes, tie the shoots into branches, add a little milk or cream, and stew gently for ten minutes more until the stalks are tender. It should be eaten, like asparagus, on toast with drawn butter.

BUTTERED CABBAGE.

Boil cabbage with a quanity of onions, then chop them together, season with pepper and salt, and fry them in butter. It is a rather homely but savory dish, and is frequently used with fried sausages laid over it, or as an accompaniment to roast beef

A CABBAGE RELISH.

Take the stalks of cabbage, scrape them, leave them in the water all night, and the next day cook them like vegetable marrow, and they will be found very good.

A RED CABBAGE RELISH.

Put the cabbage sliced into a stewpan, with sliced onion according to taste; add half a teacup of vinegar, and let it simmer four or five hours, stirring frequently. When dished, add a little flour and butter.

RED CABBAGE STEWED.

After slicing a small red cabbage, and well washing it, put it into a saucepan with pepper, salt, and butter, but no more water than will hang about it after the washing. Cover it closely, and let it stew two or three hours or until very tender, and shortly before serving add two or three spoonsful of vinegar, and give it one boil over the fire. It may be served with cold meat, or with sausages on it.

FRENCH CABBAGE

Boil together as many different vegetables as are convenient, but with them must be a pint of split peas, and a cabbage cut into quarters, and tied with thread. Add two spoonsful of nice olive oil, melted butter, or cream, pepper, and salt. When cooked enough, pour off the liquid, (which save for another time,) and leave the rest to stew.

VEGETABLE MARROWS.

Peel the marrow, then divide down the centre, and take the seeds out; cut the marrow in pieces, boil until quite soft, then drain in a colander until all the water is out; beat well with a fork and season with pepper, salt, and a lump of sugar. They are also very nice sliced and boiled, then laid upon toast, with melted butter poured over, like asparagus.

VEGETABLE MARROW TART.

Peel and core the marrow, cut into small pieces, boil until quite soft, drain the water well from it, and beat with a fork until all the lumps are out. Have ready three eggs, well beaten with a little milk, mix with the marrow until it is in the consistency of custard; sweeten it, and add a little grated nutmeg; pour into shallow dishes, lined with short paste, similar to baked custards.

CAULIFLOWER.

Break off the green leaves, cut the flower close at the bottom, from the stalk; if large, divide into four quarters. Put into cold water, let it lie not over an hour, then put into boiling milk and water, or water only—milk makes it white—skim while boiling. When the stalks are tender, take it up, which must be done before it loses its crispness. Lay it on a cloth or colander to drain, and serve with melted butter.

RAREBIT CAULIFLOWER

Put into a frying pan, amidst boiling grease, a few small mushrooms or mushroom buttons, and the flower part of a cauliflower or broccoli, broken into sprigs. Sprinkle over them some grated cheese, and baste the whole well from time to time with the hot grease. This is a delicious food, and very nutritious.

PASTRY.

PUDDINGS AND PIES.

A great deal has been said lately against puddings and pies, and desserts generally. People have been warned against them as unwholesome; long catalogues of diseases,— in fact, all the ills that flesh is heir to, have been laid to their charge; and all, we verily believe, without any more reason than could be given for stopping the use of fuel, because some people are careless enough to set fire to their dresses, or their houses.

The dessert is to many people the most important part of the dinner; it is always so to children, and there is no reason why it should not be just as healthy, just as digestible as the dinner. In fact, there are many persons, who neither eat puddings nor pies themselves, nor allow their children to eat them, who will yet compel them to swallow tough, ill-cooked meat, soggy potatoes, and bread, heavy, sour, and indigestible, as so much lead.

Eating is not merely a duty, it is one of the pleasures of life; and pains should be taken by every housekeeper to make it a source of as much enjoyment as possible. The dessert is the holiday part of the dinner; it is a subject of expectation and anticipation—it affords an opportunity of making up for a rather slim first course, and often drives away the unpleasant remembrance of a cold leg of mutton, or impenetrable beef-steak.

Of course, it requires a little time and judgment — every detail of housekeeping does, and should be adapted to the dinner which has preceded it.

When the meal is hot,— and hearty, a light, simple dessert is sufficient, but when it consists of cold meat, or some make-shift warmed up from the previous day, nice fruit puddings, and home-made pies, deep and good, are very welcome.

We always suspect a man who does not like pie or pudding, just as we would a woman that did not love children; he is sure to be cross, and hard to manage, difficult to please, and never feels good natured, not even after his dinner.

Solid flour puddings are always doubtful. They are too heavy for this climate, unless made a very important part of the dinner. Desserts require to be fruity,—fruity in substance, fruity in flavor. We do not condemn all pastry, but in puddings and pies, the more fruit and less paste, the better.

Fruit alone makes a very good dessert; and when in the season, and plentiful, a very cheap one. Apples, grapes, melons, pears, and peaches, are all fine for dessert, and can be used singly, or combined, according to means, and occasion.

Nuts, with apples, are excellent in winter; but nuts should never be put on the table alone,—they are not only indigestible, but without juicy fruit as an accompaniment, unpalatable. A dish of apples, or oranges, will be found a very welcome addition to a dessert composed of any kind of pie or pudding in which fresh fruit is not an ingredient, such as plain rice, corn starch, custard, and the like.

Bread and butter, apple-sauce, and a cup of tea, winds up a family dinner very nicely, on washing or any other day, when it is not convenient to have anything else.

But whatever your dessert is composed of, be careful to have it put upon the table with due ceremony. Children are great observers of small matters of etiquette, and quickly notice the difference between company, and family manners. Do not, because "there is no one present," allow it to be huddled upon the table, amidst a confusion of meat and vegetables, without changing the plates, or the knives and forks, and brushing off the table cloth. Go through "all the motions." A little ceremony in families is a good thing; it preserves the respect of the members for themselves and each other; it prevents the familiarity which breeds contempt, and teaches children how to behave away from home. If circumstances require a degree of hurry which compels you to waive ceremony, apologise as you would to friends, were they present, and request the other members of the family to proceed as usual.

But be sure, young housekeepers and young mothers, not to

relinquish your pies and puddings, it is one way of appealing to, and winning the hearts of husbands, and children. Moreover, acquire the practice, and as a general rule make them yourself. There are very few servants that can be trusted with the use of the materials required, or who can make the same article twice alike. It is also a privilege which a good wife and mother will not like to forego, to compound the particular dish of which husband and children are so fond, and which they will always remember in connection with her kind heart, and skillful hand, as long as they live. Who that has lived to man's or woman's estate, but remembers something which "mother" used to make, the like of which no one could make or ever will again, and in nineteen cases out of twenty it is some especial pie or pudding.

POTATO PIE CRUST.

Put a tea-cupful of rich sweet cream, to six good sized potatoes after they have been well boiled, and mash fine. Add salt to taste, and flour enough to roll out the crust. Handle it as little as possible. It is better not to put crust at the bottom of a pie if the fruit is very moist, for it will be clammy from the moisture, but let the under crust only cover the rim of the plate. Prick the upper crust to let out the steam, else the juice will run over. This paste is excellent for apple dumplings, or meat pies, and may be eaten by the most fastidious dyspeptic.

PUFF PASTE.

Take four ounces of the best wheat flour, four ounces of sweet butter; divide the butter into three parts; take one of the three pieces and rub it into the flour with the hand, till well mixed; then stir in a table-spoonful of water, and form with a spoon into a very stiff paste; put it on a marble table or a very smooth board, and roll it out once each way; fold the four ends inwards, and roll first lengthways, and then sideways; spread on half the remaining butter in little pieces, sprinkle with flour, fold and roll as before; spread on the rest of the butter and repeat the process; now fold and roll twice, and put it away to cool for ten minutes. Roll out the paste very thin, and it is ready for whatever use required.

CRUST FOR RAISED PIES.

Take two ounces of lard, two ounces of butter; put both together into a stewpan with a tea-cupful of water to boil; mix it with one pound of sifted flour while it is boiling hot, first with a spoon and then with the hand. Roll out as other crust for pies.

SUET CRUST FOR MEAT PIES.

Take the fibre from eight ounces of soft beef suet, and pound it to a soft mash; mix it with one pound of fine flour; then make the crust in the same way as for puff paste, using the pounded suet instead of butter. It may be used for a pie at once, without setting it aside to cool.

MINCE PIES.

Mince pies are not healthful, and one batch in a season is quite sufficient. A shin of beef boiled down till very tender, one pound of nice clear beef suet chopped very fine, a table-spoonful of salt, six pounds of greening apples peeled, cored and chopped, three pounds of raisins stoned, three of currants carefully cleaned, one pound of brown sugar, a cup of maple syrup, half a pound of citron, shredded, half a pound of candied lemon peel, a quart of the best cider. This mixture makes rich pies, but mince pies are nothing if not rich. These are also particularly fine in flavor. Instead of cider, some persons put in a quart of Madeira wine, and a little brandy; but it is better not to use alcohol in food when it can be avoided.

ENGLISH MINCE PIES.

Three and a half pounds of good chopped beef, three and a half pounds of suet, three and a half pounds of raisins, three and a half pounds of currants, seven pounds of apples chopped, one pound of candied citron, two pounds of sugar, one ounce of nutmegs, four quarts of good cider, one pint best vinegar, salt, a pint of golden syrup. Half the raisins should be stoned and chopped, the other half left whole.

The quantity, of course, may be reduced or increased; for example, by giving five, or seven pounds of beef, to fourteen pounds

GREEN APPLE PIE.—2.

Take ripe and rather tart apples such as pippins, russets or greenings; pare, core, and cut them into very thin slices, fill the under crust, throw over them slices of fresh lemon, cinnamon, and plenty of white sugar; lay on the upper crust and bake in a mild oven.

ENGLISH APPLE PIE.

Lay some paste crust round the sides of a deep dish; quarter the apples and take out the cores. Put in a thick layer of apples, cover with half the sugar you intend for your pie, some lemon peel grated fine and a few cloves; then put in the rest of the apples and sugar, and add a little lemon juice; boil the cores and peelings of the apples in water with a blade of mace, until they are soft, then press it through a colander; boil it with sugar, and pour it in the pie with a little quince or marmalade. Put on the upper crust and bake.

FRUIT PIES.

Fruit pies should be eaten fresh and baked in tolerably deep earthen platters. Their excellence consists in a small quantity of pastry and a large amount of fruit and sugar. Line the dish with good paste, leaving half an inch to project over the edge. Fill with fruit, and cover thickly with sugar; no spice is needed for fresh small fruit pies. Put on a lid of puff paste, and bring the outer edge of the under paste up and over it, moistening slightly with cold water, so that it will fasten down tight. This prevents the juice from boiling out. Notch the edge and center.

CHERRY, PLUM, OR GOOSEBERRY PIE. (*English method.*)

Make a good crust and lay a little around the sides of a deep dish. Cover the bottom with sugar, and lay in the cherries, plums, or gooseberries whole, sprinkle sugar over the top and bake in a moderate oven.

WHORTLEBERRY PIE.

Wash and pick over the berries, place them an inch thick on the under crust, cover them thickly with sugar, put on the upper crust and bake half an hour. Other berry pies, such as blackberry and raspberry, are made in the same way. They require no spice; but we think whortleberries are greatly improved by having a few red currants, or the juice of a lemon sprinkled among them. Sift powdered sugar over all fruit pies before serving.

PUMPKIN PIES.

Take a small pumpkin, or half of a large one, stew long and slowly, then strain it, after peeling, and cutting it in small pieces. Mix with this quantity of pulp, one quart of sweet milk, three eggs, and two table-spoonsful of corn starch mixed first smooth with a little of the milk. Salt, sugar, and ginger must be put in to taste. A large cup of sugar is about right; one nutmeg. The ginger is indispensable to a genuine pumpkin pie. If part cream can be used the pie is much richer, as well as more delicate in flavor. Bake with an under crust only.

COCOANUT PIE.

For three pies one quart of milk, five eggs, one grated cocoanut. Beat the eggs and sugar together to sweeten, and stir into the milk when hot; then add the cocoanut and spice. Put it in a rich paste, and bake twenty minutes.

GRAPE PIE.

Pop the pulps out of the skins into one vessel, and put the skins into another. Then simmer the pulp a little and run it through a colander to separate the seeds. Then put the skins and pulp together and they are ready for jugging, or for pies. Pies prepared in this way can hardly be distinguished from plum pies.

RHUBARB PIE.

Take off the thin skin, cut the stalks in small pieces, add a little flour, place it in the pie. When the paste is done remove the top crust and add sugar and butter, mixing it thoroughly with the rhubarb. Put the top crust on and serve warm. A little nutmeg may be grated over the top of the fruit before putting on the crust, if it is relished.

MOCK APPLE PIE.

Two soda crackers, one egg, one cup of sugar, and one of water, the juice and yellow rind grated of a lemon. This a good recipe for Spring use.

DRIED APPLE PIES.

Wash the apples in two or three waters, and put them to soak in rather more water than will cover them, as they absorb a great deal. After soaking an hour or two, put them into a preserving kettle with the same water, and with the thin peel of one or two lemons, chopped fine. Boil tender; when they rise, press them down, but do not stir them. When tender, add sugar, and boil fifteen or twenty minutes longer. Dried apples, soaked over night, are made tasteless, and are mashed up by being stirred. When cooked, stir in a little melted butter, some cinnamon, and powdered cloves. It is important that the apples should be of a tart kind.

DRIED PLUM PIES.

Soak the plums, and stew them gently; season them with spice and sugar to taste; put a puff paste on to the plate; then put a layer of the plums, stewed; roll out a piece of paste thin, cover them, add another layer of plums, and cover for the last time. You may have as many stories to your pie as you choose.

CORN MEAL PIES.

Stir a small tea-cupful of very fine ground Indian meal into two quarts of boiling milk; when nearly cool add four beaten eggs, and sweeten to taste, like a custard, adding spice and orange peel, if desired. Bake with a crust like custard pie.

PUDDINGS.

BUFFALO PUDDING.

A quart of flour, two tea-spoonsful of baking powder, a table-spoonful of maizena, a salt spoon of salt, a piece of butter the size of a small egg, and cold water; mix the baking powder with the flour thoroughly, put in the salt and maizena, and mix to the consistency of drop cake. Have the butter melted and stir into the mass. In berry time, drop a part of this mixture in a tin pail, or a steamer if you have one, which has been buttered, then put in a layer of berries doing up with batter. In the winter, chopped apples, dried currants, or any kind of dried fruit are an excellent substitute. Zante currants will not require previous soaking, but common garden fruits will. Steam the pudding for one hour and a half, and serve with liquid sauce. A pudding can be steamed in a tin pail, by inverting and old tin cup, and setting the pail upon it in the pot. Be sure that the water boils and keeps boiling, and that the pail is covered tight by its lid. This pudding contains neither milk nor eggs, yet, if properly made, it will be thought by the best judges to possess both. When mixed with milk however, it is whiter than when mixed with water.

ENGLISH APPLE PUDDING.

Make a paste of a pint of sifted flour, a quarter of a pound of finely chopped beef suet, a little salt, and cold water. Line a pudding bowl, fill with tart apples cut in quarters. Sprinkle a little sugar on the top, cover with paste, and boil an hour and a quarter. Turn out, and serve with a sweet liquid pudding sauce, spiced with lemon, and ginger.

APPLE PUDDING.—1.

Stew six large apples, pared and cored, in six table-spoonsful of water with the rind of a lemon. When they are tender, beat them to a pulp and stir with them four ounces of brown sugar, a cup of cream, two well-beaten eggs, and a tea-spoonful of lemon juice. Put it in a dish lined with puff paste, bake it, and when done stick chips of candied citron and lemon peel in the top.

APPLE PUDDING.—2.

Peel six apples, take out the core, leaving the apple whole, fill them with sugar, place them in a pudding-dish, pour over them a batter, prepared as for a batter pudding. Bake an hour in a moderate oven.

APPLE PUDDING.—3.

Prepare six apples as for sauce, and mix with them two ounces of melted butter, two well-beaten eggs, bread crumbs, a little cream, nutmeg, sugar. Bake in small cups, turn them out and serve with sifted sugar.

APPLE PUDDING.—4.

Pare and chop half a dozen good sour apples. Butter a pudding-dish and put in a layer of grated bread half an inch thick, add small bits of butter; put in a layer of chopped apples, with sugar and nutmeg, and repeat till the dish is full. Pour over the whole a tea-cup of cold water, and bake thirty minutes. No sauce.

POOR MAN'S PUDDING.

Take some stale pieces of bread, pour boiling water over them, and cover down tight. When they have absorbed the water, and become soft, mash them to a pulp. Mix in one table-spoonful of corn-starch, one egg, a cup of milk, a little salt, some sugar, and a few currants cleaned by rubbing in a colander with some flour. Bake in a dish with a few small pieces of butter on the top, and a little nutmeg grated over. It is good hot or cold, and when cold, will turn out, and cut like an English cheese-cake. It is also inexpensive.

VICTORIA PUDDING.

Take half a pound of mashed potatoes, half a pound of grated carrots, half a pound of grated bread, half a pound of sugar, quarter of a pound of suet, half a pound of currants or raisins, three well-beaten eggs, a little nutmeg, cinnamon, lemon peel and salt. Stir all well together; boil four hours and serve them with sauce.

SARATOGA PUDDING.

Take one pint and a half of milk, two eggs, and a small table-spoonful of flour; mix the flour with cold milk to the consistence of thick cream; boil the rest of the milk, and pour, boiling hot, upon the flour, stirring all the time; add a salt-spoonful of salt, sugar to your taste, and, when cool, two eggs well beaten; have ready a buttered dish, pour the whole into it, grate lemon-peel or nutmeg over it, and bake thirty-five or forty minutes. It should be out of the oven fifteen minutes before serving. It is delicious to eat cold with fruit.

INDIAN FRUIT PUDDING.

Make a batter of a pint of hot milk and enough corn meal to make it stiff, add a little molasses and a tea-spoonful of salt; then mix in a pint of sweet apples chopped, or a pint of huckleberries. Tie it in a wet cloth, leaving room for it to swell, put it in boiling water, boil three hours and serve with sweet sauce.

SNOW PUDDING.—1.

Take half a pound of the pulp of roasted apples, carefully separated from the skin and core, half a pound of powdered lump sugar, and the whites of two eggs. First beat the eggs to a very stiff froth, then add by degrees first the sugar and then the apples; beat all together for an hour, until, when taken up in the spoon, it stands quite stiff. With the yolks of the two eggs make a sweet custard for the bottom of the dish, and build the snow up by spoonsful to any height you please. Savoy cakes and sweetmeat likewise laid in the dish are an improvement.

SNOW PUDDING.—2.

The juice of three lemons, one cup of white sugar, whites of three eggs, half package gelatine. Let the gelatine stand half an hour in a pint of cold water, then throw off that, and add a pint of boiling water. Beat the eggs and sugar well, then add the lemon-juice and gelatine, and beat till it looks like snow.

BIRD'S NEST PUDDING

Peel and core eight tart apples; in each hollow stuff sugar and a blade of mace, or a little cinnamon; make a batter of a pint of flour, a spoonful of corn-starch, a large tea-spoonful of baking powder, milk, or water, and a table-spoonful of melted butter. Mix almost as thick as drop cake, pour over the apples, and bake three-quarters of an hour. Eat with sauce.

To make a richer pudding, stew the apples first, but gently, and hot so as to break them, stuff them with sugar, and citron. pour over a sweet custard, and bake. Boil it two or three hours and serve with wine sauce.

WASHINGTON PUDDING.

Scald and pulp the apples, add well-beaten eggs, one egg for each large-sized apple, an ounce of butter in pieces, a little cream, candied or grated lemon peel, sugar, and a table-spoonful or more of brandy; bake in a thin paste, in a mild oven.

FRUIT PUDDINGS.

One quart of flour, two tea-spoonsful of good baking powder, and a little salt. Mix to the consistency of drop biscuit, with cold milk or water, add two table-spoonsful of melted butter. Butter a mould or a small tin pail, and lay it in a layer of the batter, then a layer of any kind of fresh small fruit, alternating them until the vessel is filled. Cover tight and steam an hour and a half. Eat with sweet liquid sauce. This is excellent without either milk or eggs.

FIG PUDDING.

Half a pound of bread crumbs, half a pound of figs, six ounces of moist sugar, four ounces of suet, two eggs, a little nutmeg, and a tea-cupful of milk; the figs and suet to be chopped very fine, and all well mixed together; to be boiled in a mould for four hours, and served with sweet sauce; it is good fried in slices next day, with pounded sugar sifted over it.

ENGLISH ROLL PUDDING.

Roll out half an inch thick a paste made of suet chopped fine, flour, water, and a little salt. Spread over it preserves of any small kind—damsons, currants, berries, or the like. Dust a little flour over it, roll up, wet and pinch the ends tight, and tie in a cloth which has been wet with cold water and well floured. Boil or steam one or two hours, according to size, and eat hot with rich liquid sauce.

CITRON PUDDING.

Half a pound of butter, half pound of sugar, well beaten together, half pound of citron cut fine, five eggs, and grated orange peel to taste. Bake in puff paste half an hour.

MINNIE'S FRUIT PUDDING.

Mix a pound of red currants, stemmed, with an equal quantity of raspberries, have ready bread and butter in slices; place a layer of bread and butter in the bottom of a buttered pudding dish; then a layer of fruit, covered thickly with sugar, then another layer of bread and butter, and so on till the fruit is used up, and the dish is full. A thick layer of fruit and sugar should complete the top. Bake slowly for an hour, and serve in the same dish. It is delicious and wholesome.

LITTLE BREAD PUDDINGS. (*Birthday*).

Steep the crumb part of a baker's six cent loaf, in a pint of milk, until it is soft and warm. Beat up two eggs with some sugar, an ounce of butter warmed, a little essence of lemon, and a little cream, or table-spoonful of condensed milk. Add quarter of a pound of Zante currants, well cleaned and floured. Pour into buttered cups, grate nutmeg over them, and bake half or three quarers of an hour. Serve with pudding sauce.

CHERRY PUDDING.

One pint of bread crumbs, one cup of sugar, four eggs, a quart milk, grated lemon rind, a little powdered cinnamon, and salt. Mix thoroughly, butter a mould, and spread in a thick layer of the preparation, and then a layer of cherries, then another layer of bread, etc., and one of cherries, alternately until it is filled. Close tight, and steam for two hours. Eat with sweet liquid sauce. Blackberries may be used instead of cherries.

INDIAN HUCKLEBERRY PUDDING.

Take a quart of boiling milk and water, stir into it Indian meal enough to make a stiff batter. Add a little salt, a small cup of chopped suet, a little molasses, and a pint of huckleberries. Boil one hour and a half in a bag, leaving room to swell. Eat with sweet liquid sauce.

Two eggs and half a teaspoonful of soda may be used instead of suet, and the butter, in that case made a little thinner. This makes a more delicate pudding.

LITTLE BATTER PUDDINGS.

Make a smooth batter with four fresh eggs, four table-spoonsful of flour, and a quart of new milk. Fill little buttered cups, and stick in chips of candied citron, or lemon peel. Bake, and serve with wine sauce.

LEMON PUDDING.

Soak together the juice and peel of two lemons, the peel to be rubbed off with lumps of sugar, six ounces of loaf sugar pounded, except what has been used for the lemon peel, a good sized tea-cup ful of grated bread crumbs; beat up four eggs leaving out two of the whites, melt three ounces of fresh butter and mix all together. Edge, and trim a dish with puff paste, pour in the mixture, and bake in a quick oven three quarters of an hour.

ORANGE PUDDING.

Pound in a mortar three ounces of fresh butter and four ounces of lump sugar; grate in the rinds of two Seville oranges, also the whole of a large, or two small apples. When thoroughly mixed add three eggs well beaten. Spread it to the thickness of half an inch on puff paste. Bake quickly.

ARROWROOT PUDDING.

Mix four spoonsful of arrow root with a teacup of new milk, then boil nearly a quart of milk and stir in the arrowroot. When almost cold add two well-beaten eggs, two ounces of good butter in pieces, two ounces of pounded sugar, and a little grated nutmeg, stir all together and bake it a quarter of an hour or more, in a buttered dish.

LINNIE'S APPLE PUDDING.

One pint of bread crumbs, six tart-apples chopped fine, a little finely chopped suet, one egg, juice and rind of one lemon, and a little salt mixed to the consistency of drop cake, with milk or milk and water. Boil in a buttered bowl or well floured bag an hour and a quarter, and serve with sweet liquid sauce flavored with nutmeg.

AUNT MARY'S PLUM PUDDING.

Three quarters of a pound of grated bread, half a pound fresh beef suet, chopped fine, half a pound of apples chopped fine, half a pound of currants, same of chopped raisins, four eggs, one pint of milk, a table-spoonful of brandy, another of sherry, a small cup of sugar, a salt-spoon of salt. Boil in a bag four hours, eat with rich sweet sauce.

APPLE AND SAGO PUDDING.

Peel and core as many apples as will set into the dish in which the pudding is to be baked; fill the cavity in the cored apples with ground cinnamon and sugar. Take as many dessert spoonsful of sago as you have apples; mix it with a little cold water, and add as much boiling water as will be required to fill the pudding dish; stir it all the time till it begins to thicken; then cover it up and let it stand about two hours, until the sago swells. Turn it into the dish, set it into a rather hot oven, and bake it one hour. Serve with sugar and cream.

BAKED INDIAN PUDDING.

One quart of milk scalding hot, one cup of Indian meal, one half cup of molasses, a piece of butter the size of an egg, a small tea-spoonful of salt, a small tea-spoonful of ginger, a large tea-spoonful of cinnamon. Wet the meal with cold water, and pour the boiling milk on it to scald it. Add one egg when cold, before baking. Bake one hour and a half.

BOILED RICE PUDDING

Pick and wash very clean in cold water, four ounces of rice; add six ounces of raisins and mix them equally through the rice; place them in a pudding bag, leaving sufficient room for the rice to swell; boil two hours, and serve it with melted butter, sugar, and grated nutmeg upon it.

RICE PUDDING.

To one quart of milk put a cup of rice, and simmer slowly until it is thick and the rice perfectly tender. Then stir in a table-spoonful of butter, three of sugar, and three yolks of eggs while it is hot, with salt to tase. Pour it in a shallow pudding dish lined with rich paste, and bake a light brown. To the whites of the three eggs add six table-spoonsful of powdered sugar and the juice of a lemon, (the rind should have been grated into the rice before baking,) beat it up, cover the top of the pudding, and put it back in the oven five minutes.

PORTUGUESE RICE PUDDING

Boil half a pound of rice in water until it begins to open, then strain it from the water, and boil it slowly with a quart of boiled milk, half a pound of loaf sugar, and the peel of a lemon; when the rice is sufficiently boiled, remove it from the fire and take out all the lemon peel; stir it until it becomes cool, then add four eggs that have been well-beaten (stirring it all the while) and a wine-glassful of orange-flower water; when these ingredients have been properly mixed, pour the whole into a flat dish, and, when cold, cover it with cinnamon powder. This is a birthday dish in Portugal; as famous there as plum-pudding is in England.

FRENCH RICE PUDDING.

Put a pound of rice into a pint of milk and let them simmer over the fire until the milk is soaked up and the rice soft. Take it from the fire, and when somewhat cooled put into it two eggs, a table-spoonful of butter, a little loaf sugar, and the grated rind of a lemon, and stir them well together; then butter a pudding mould, sprinkle in a layer of grated bread crust, pour in the rice and bake about an hour.

APPLE AND RICE PUDDING.

Add to some clean rice, a sufficient quantity of milk to boil it soft; with a little sugar, lemon-peel, and cinnamon. Fill a large high mould with the rice; put in a sauce pan of water and let it stand in the oven thirty minutes. Have ready some fresh apple sauce sweetened, and of lemon peel flavor. When the rice is done, turn it out of the mould upon a dish, and fill in the hollow centre with the apple sauce; beat the whites of three eggs to a froth and put it upon the apples so as to make a top to the mould of rice; sift pounded sugar over the whole. Brown it a little over the top and it is ready for the table.

RICE FLOUR PUDDING.

Take a quart of milk, add a pint of the flour; boil them to a pulp; beat up four eggs, to which add six spoonsful of sugar and one spoonful of butter, which, well beaten together, add to the milk and flour; grate nutmeg over the mixture, and bake in a well-greased dish.

BADEN PUDDING.

Boil in a pint of milk, a teacupful of rice, when it is swelled add a quarter of a pound of raisins, two ounces of chopped suet, two eggs; stir well together and boil in a buttered mould. Serve with sweet sauce, flavored with lemon or vanilla.

SEVILLE PUDDING.

Boil in a quart of milk a teacupful of Carolina rice. When the rice is swelled and soft, mix in enough grated marmalade to color and flavor it; pour it in a buttered mould and boil it again to make it turn out; serve with wine sauce.

SAGO PUDDING.

Wash and pick five table-spoonsful of sago, and boil it in a quart of milk with a stick of cinnamon until soft. Mix in six table-spoonsful of powdered loaf sugar, one table-spoonful of butter; when cold add two well-beaten eggs and a little nutmeg. Stir well together and bake in a buttered dish three quarters of an hour.

TAPIOCA PUDDING.

Put a teacup of tapioca and a tea-spoon of salt into a pint and a half of water, and let it stand several hours where it will be quite warm, but not cook. Peel six tart apples, take out the cores, fill them with sugar, in which is grated a litttle nutmeg and lemon-peel, and put them in a pudding-dish; over these pour the tapioca, first mixing with it a table-spoon of melted butter and a little cold milk. Bake one hour. Eat with sauce.

ICE CORN STARCH PUDDING.

Take the cream from a quart and a pint of milk after it has stood a few hours, or long enough to "raise." Set it away in a cool place, and mix with a little of the cold skimmed milk four heaping table-spoonsful of corn starch, and two beaten eggs. Place on the fire meantime a quart of the skimmed milk, in a thick, lined saucepan, and when it comes to a boil, mix rapidly and smoothly with it the eggs and corn starch, allowing it to boil up once. Pour into a mould or small oval dishes which have been wet with cold water to prevent sticking. A little salt is an improvement. Set away in a cool place, and it will turn out clear and quivering. Eat with the cream taken from the milk and powdered sugar. This is a cheap, easily made, and delicious summer dessert.

BOILED YANKEE PLUM PUDDING

Three cups of flour, two thirds of a cup of molasses, an egg-size of lard, one cup of chopped raisins, a small tea-spoonful of salt, a coffee-cup of milk, a small tea-spoonful of soda. Boil in a form or a bag made of thick cloth, or steam three hours. To be eaten hot with a liquid sauce, or butter and sugar.

MRS. CROLY'S CHRISTMAS PLUM PUDDING.

One pound of raisins, one of currants, one of bread-crumbs, half-pound of suet chopped fine, eight eggs, one quart milk, one tea-cup sugar, one nutmeg, quarter pound candied citron, quarter candied lemon cut in strips, salt, and other spice to taste. Boil slowly four hours, and eat with rich sauce. This is delicious.

BAKED PLUM PUDDING.

Take two quarts of milk, ten soda crackers, eight eggs, one pound of stoned rasins, spice to suit, and sweeten with sugar; a little butter. Bake from two to three hours.

PRUNE OR DAMSON PUDDING.

Take two well beaten eggs, a quart of milk, sufficient flour to make a batter, a little salt, and three spoonsful of ginger. Mix the milk in gradually with a pound of prunes; put it in a pudding bag and boil it an hour or more. Serve with melted butter poured over it.

ENGLISH PLUM PUDDING.

One pound of the best raisins stoned, and chopped a little on a paste board; one pound of currants washed and picked, quarter of a pound of candied lemon peel; quarter of a pound of candied citron, cut up in strips; quarter pound of the best Jordan almonds blanched and chopped; one pound of beef suet picked and chopped fine; half pound of flour, and quarter pound of biscuit powder; half pound of moist sugar; nutmeg and mixed spices to taste; half a tea-spoonful of carbonate of soda, and half a teaspoonful of salt; eight eggs, well beaten, yolks and whites separately; and a gill of old ale. Then take a little milk in a saucepan, and put into it half a pod of vanilla. Let it simmer on the hob, with the lid closed until the pod is quite soft. Take out the pod and mince it small, put it in a mortar with a little of the milk, and bray it until it is reduced to a paste; return it to the milk and pour all into the pudding. Just before putting the pudding into the basin or mould, give it a very good stir and mix in a gill of good brandy. It will take eight hours to boil.

PLUM PUDDING WITH SNOW.

Mix together a pound and a quarter of flour, half a pint of sweet cream, a pound of stoned raisins, four ounces of currants, four ounces of mashed potatoes, five ounces of brown sugar, and a gill of milk. Work thoroughly together, season it, mix eight table-spoonsful of clear snow very quickly throughout the mass; put the pudding in a bag and boil four hours. Two table-spoonsful of snow are equal to an egg in any pudding.

SUET PUDDING.—1.

One small cup of chopped suet, one cup of molasses, one cup of chopped raisins, one cup of sour milk, half a tea-spoonful each of cloves, cinnamon and nutmeg, one tea-spoonful of soda. Stir this thick with flour; put in a pudding bag, leaving room for it to rise, and boil three hours. It will be quite light.

SUET PUDDING.—2.

Mix half a pound of finely chopped suet, two well-beaten eggs, salt, and half a pound of Zante currants in one pint of milk; make it a thick batter with flour, then mix in another pint of milk and boil it two hours. Serve with wine sauce.

EXHIBITION PUDDING.

Mix together a quarter of a pound of finely chopped suet, a quarter of a pound of stoned raisins, two table-spoonsful of flour, two table-spoonsful of sugar, three well-beaten eggs, the grated peel of a whole lemon, and a little nutmeg. Boil three hours.

LEICESTERSHIRE HUNTING PUDDING.

Mix together half a pound of chopped suet, three-quarters of a pound of currants, a quarter of a pound of raisins stoned and chopped, a pound of flour, a tumbler of milk, two gills of brandy, four beaten eggs, a cup of sugar, and some grated lemon peel. Boil it two or three hours, and serve with wine sauce.

BREAD PUDDING.—1.

Take the crumbs of stale bread, pour over it one pint of boiling milk, and set it by to cool. When quite cold, beat it up very fine with two ounces of butter, sifted sugar sufficient to sweeten it, grate in half a nutmeg, and add half a pound of well washed currants; beat up three eggs separately and mix them up with the rest, adding, if desired, a few strips of candied orange peel. All the ingredients must be beaten up together for about half an hour, as the lightness of the pudding depends upon that. Boil it an hour. Serve with wine sauce.

BREAD PUDDING.—2.

One pint of nice fine bread crumbs to one quart of milk, one cup of sugar, the yolks of four eggs beaten, the grated rind of a lemon, a piece of butter the size of an egg. Bake until done, but not watery. Whip the whites of the eggs stiff, and beat in a tea-cupful of sugar in which has been stirred the juice of the lemon. Spread over the pudding a layer of jelly, or any sweetmeat you prefer. Pour the whites of the eggs over this, and replace in the oven and bake lightly. Eat cold with cream.

CHESTER PUDDING.

Two ounces of butter, four ounces of white sugar, one and a half ounces of almonds, blanched and pounded, (six bitter, twelve sweet) the juice of one lemon, and the peel grated, the yolks of four eggs. Put all this in a stewpan over the fire, and stir it till it nearly boils, then pour it into a pie dish lined with light pastry, and bake it. The whites of the eggs to be beaten up into snow, and put over the pudding. Just before it is taken out of the oven, strew a little pounded sugar over it.

MRS. STOWE'S BREAD AND FRUIT PUDDING.

Take thin slices of white bread, nearly fill a buttered mould with layers of bread and layers of fruit alternately; beat four eggs, mix them in a pint of warm milk, and pour it over the bread and fruit. Boil it twenty minutes, and serve with white sauce.

AN EDITOR'S FAVORITE PUDDING.

Butter thinly sliced bread, and place it in a deep dish; between every layer sprinkle Zante currants, well cleaned, and, if you please, chipped citron. Beat three eggs well, add them to a pint and a half of milk, and a pinch of salt; pour over the bread, and bake slowly, with a cover on, three quarters of an hour; then take the cover off and brown. Eat with sauce. Instead of the currants and citron, marmalade may be spread thickly upon the bread, and the bread cut into small oblong pieces, to make marmalade bread and butter pudding. Bake half an hour.

SALLY LUNN PUDDING.

Scoop out a piece from the under side of a Sally Lunn cake without injuring the upper crust, and replace it. Put the cake into a basin that will just hold it, pour boiling milk over it, let it soak for three hours, and turn it out; mix one egg, well beaten, with a glass of white wine and a little spice and sugar, and having removed the piece previously cut out, stir in these ingredients, still taking care not to break the crust, and replace the piece. Butter the basin you boil it in, and if not full, fill it with bread and crumbs, and boil three quarters of an hour.

NURSERY PUDDING.

Stew four pounds of rhubarb with one pound of brown sugar, moisten quarter of a pound of arrowroot with cold water, then stir it into the boiling rhubarb. It is best eaten cold, with milk or cream. The children like this pudding.

DANDY PUDDING.

One quart of milk, yolks of four eggs, three table-spoonsful of corn-starch; sweeten to taste; scald the milk, and when very hot, stir in the starch, previously dissolved in cold milk. Add the eggs with the starch; stir until it thickens well. To be boiled in a pail, set in a kettle of boiling water. Pour, when done, into a pudding-dish. When quite cold, pour over it a frosting, made of the beaten whites, with a table-spoonful of white sugar to each egg. Flavor both the frosting and pudding with extract of lemon or vanilla. Set the pudding in the oven, and brown the frosting a delicate color. The colder when eaten, the better.

ICE PUDDING.

Boil one pint and a half of new milk with one tea-spoonful of isinglass. Beat five eggs and mix them with the milk as you would for custards. Take a tin mould with a cover, oiled, not buttered, and line it with candied fruits, such as plums, green gages, etc. Then pour the custard in very gradually, so that the fruit will remain at the bottom. Put on the cover and bury the mould in ice for the whole day, only turning out the pudding at the moment it is wanted.

THE DEACON'S APPLE INDIAN PUDDING.

One pint of scalded milk, one-half pint of Indian meal, one tea cup of molasses, tea-spoonful of salt, six sweet apples cut in thin slices; bake three hours.

CORN PUDDING.

Twelve ears of corn, one quart of milk, two eggs, table-spoonful of sugar, one of flour, two tea-spoonsful of salt. Bake four hours; serve with butter and sugar.

LITTLE CURRANT DUMPLINGS.

A pint of flour, quarter of a pound of fresh beef suet chopped fine, a salt spoon of salt, a quarter of picked and clean Zante currants, one egg, and milk, or water enough to mix to the consistency of drop biscuit. Boil in dumpling cloths, three quarters of an hour, a table-spoonful to a dumpling. Serve with sauce.

SMALL AND LIGHT PLUM PUDDING.

Soak three ounces of the grated crumb of a stale loaf in a gill of boiling milk, and mix in four ounces of finely minced suet, an ounce of dry bread crumbs, ten ounces of stoned raisins, a little salt, the grated rind of an orange and three eggs, leaving out one white; put no sugar in it. Boil the pudding two hours or more, and serve with very sweet sauce.

THE POET'S PUDDING.

Well sugar any summer fruit, and fill a deep tart dish with layers of it alternated with thin slices of the inside of a light stale loaf; let the upper layer be of fruit, and if it is a dry kind, sprinkle over it a dessert-spoonful of water or a little lemon juice. Raspberries, currants, or cherries will not require this. The sugar must be used according to the sweetness of the fruit. For a quart of ripe green gages, split and stoned, five ounces will be sufficient. Bake in a quick oven about half an hour.

THE PASTOR'S PUDDING.

Wash and pare some rhubarb stalks, cut them into short lengths and put a layer of them in a deep dish, with one or two spoonsful of sugar; cover evenly with thin slices of a roll, then add a thick layer of fruit and sugar, then one of bread, then one of rhubarb, and then cover with a thick layer of fine bread crumbs mixed with a table-spoonful of sugar. Pour over a little clarified butter, and bake thirty or forty minutes. Good apples sliced, sweetened and flavored with nutmeg and lemon rind, and covered with well buttered slices of bread, make an excellent pudding of this kind. Black currants may also be used, leaving out the butter.

BOILED INDIAN PUDDING.

A quart of sour milk, half a cup of molasses, a cup of raisins, a cup of chopped suet, a tea-spoonful of saleratus, and meal enough to make it stiff.

PLAIN INDIAN PUDDING.

Seven table-spoonsful of sifted Indian meal, scalded with boiling water until the quantity is thoroughly wet; add three pints of new or skimmed milk, cold, two thirds of a cup of molasses, little salt, four eggs. Some persons think a little chopped suet improves it. Place it in the oven, with a moderate heat, and bake it slowly three hours. After being in the oven a half hour stir it from the bottom, as that is apt to thicken at first. Eat with butter.

NANTUCKET CORN PUDDING.

Take two dozen ears of young corn, husk, and grate or pound

it fine; add three pints of new milk, cold, one half tea-cup of brown sugar, a little salt, two soda crackers pounded fine, six eggs; put it in the oven, with a moderate heat and bake three hours. Eat with butter.

MRS. HOWITT'S PUDDING.

Butter lightly on both sides, some evenly cut slices of roll, or of light bread freed from crust, and spread the tops thickly and evenly with orange marmalade. Prepare as much in this way as will cover the surface of the pudding without the edges of the bread overlaying each other, as this would make it sink to the bottom of the dish. Pour in a custard of two well-beaten eggs, new milk, a pinch of salt, and two ounces of sugar. Flavor with French brandy only. Let it stand an hour, then place it carefully in an oven and bake it until it is set, and no longer. Too fierce a heat will spoil it. The bread should be a light, clear brown, and the custard under it smooth and firm.

BOILED APPLE DUMPLINGS.

Select apples that will cook quickly, pare and core them, leaving the apple whole. Prepare a plain paste, roll the crust about quarter of an inch thick, cover each apple with it, and then steam them about an hour; if you boil them instead of steaming them, make the paste of suet, put them in boiling water, and boil an hour.

BAKED APPLE DUMPLINGS.

Select smooth, even-sized apples; peel, core them, and fill the cavities with sugar, and a little cinnamon. Divide your paste into as many parts as you have apples. Roll each one out square, and inclose the apple in it, slightly wetting the edge, to make it stick. Bake them in a shallow pan, and eat with a dry sauce made of butter and sugar beaten together.

APPLE FRITTERS.

Beat three eggs very light, then stir in one tea-spoonful of salt, one table-spoonful of sugar, the grated rind of half a lemon and the juice, one pint of milk, one half pound of chopped apples, one half pound of sifted flour; stir it well together, and fry in lard, or can be baked on a griddle as pancakes.

LEMON DUMPLINGS.

Mix with ten ounces of fine bread crumbs, half a pound of beef suet, chopped fine, a large table-spoonful of flour, the grated rinds of two small lemons, or one very large one, four ounces of pounded sugar, or if wished very sweet, more; three large or four small eggs beaten and strained. Divide these into four equal portions, tie in well-floured cloths, and boil an hour.

PUDDING SAUCES.

MAPLE SUGAR SAUCE.

Take half maple sugar and half light brown sugar, boil them together with a little water, clarify the syrup with an egg, strain it and melt a small piece of butter in it. All maple sugar, or all common sugar can be used. It is very good on puddings.

CHERRY SAUCE.

Take ripe cherries, mash them with the meat of the pits in their own juice until tender, pulp through a sieve all that will pass, add wine and sugar, and spice if desired, and boil until it is of the consistency of thick cream.

HARD SAUCE.

This is made simply by stirring together to a light cream two cups of pounded loaf sugar to half of a large cup of sweet butter. It may be flavored according to taste. For cream and plain batter pudding it may be thinned with a few spoonsful of boiling water and flavored with vanilla. Nutmeg is the best flavor for apple puddings. For rice puddings a little lemon juice or wine may be added.

SWEET LIQUID SAUCE.

One table-spoon of flour mixed smooth with cold water, a pinch of salt, piece of butter the size of a hickory-nut, half a cup of sugar, and a little maple or other syrup. Stir into this mixture hot water enough to make a pint bowl of sauce; boil all up, and grate in lastly a little nutmeg.

AN EXCELLENT PUDDING SAUCE.

Beat up, as for hard sauce, white sugar with butter, until very light, in the proportion of half a cup of butter to one of sugar; flavor with essence of lemon or bitter almonds. Fifteen minutes before serving, set the bowl in a pan of hot water on the range, and stir it till hot. It will raise in a white foam to the top of the bowl.

WINE SAUCE.

Take half a cup of butter and two cups of sugar, beat them together and mix in slowly a cup of wine; melt all over steam but do not stir it while melting.

BRANDY SAUCE.

This can be made the same as wine sauce, or as follows: Heat over steam in a covered saucepan half a pint of brandy, beat two eggs, and beat together to a cream two cups of sugar, and half a large cup of butter; stir the eggs into it, add also the brandy, mixing quickly and thoroughly. Keep it in hot water until needed.

ROSE HIP SAUCE.

Take rose hips, open them and take out the seeds, soak them and boil them to a paste, pulp them through a seive and stir them in boiling wine with sufficient sugar, until of the consistency of thick cream.

LEMON BRANDY.

This is used for flavoring sweet dishes. Fill a wide-necked bottle with very thin rinds of fresh lemons, cover with good brandy, and after two or three weeks strain off the spirit and cork it for use. A few apricot kernels are sometimes blanched and added with the lemon peel to give a good flavor.

DESSERT DISHES.

CREAM PUFFS.

For shells: a pint of boiling water; melt in it half a pound of lard, and stir, while boiling, into this, three-quarters of a pound of flour. Boil until a thick paste is formed. The best way to boil it, is to set one kettle in another, or a pail in a kettle of boiling water with the ingredients in the pail, as in boiling a custard. When thick, take from the fire, and when cool add ten eggs, and a little salt. Mix thoroughly, and bake in a quick oven for twenty-five minutes; oven about as hot as for pies. This makes five dozen cakes. Drop with a spoon, on buttered tins, some distance apart. When cool open carefully with a knife, and fill with mock cream, which is made as follows:

One quart of milk, four eggs, three-quarters of a pound of white sugar, five ounces of flour, extract of vanilla to taste. Make a smooth paste of flour, in some of the cold milk; put in a kettle of boiling water with all the milk; when thickened a little, add the eggs well beaten with the sugar. When creamy it is done. Take from the fire, and add a little extract of vanilla. Do not use until cold.

This is the only receipt for making cream puffs that we have used with success. But this never fails, if the directions are followed; and when done they are nice enough to set before a king.

PASTIES.

Rub a quarter of a pound of lard into two pounds of flour; beat the whites of two eggs light, and mix in two half-pints of water; wet the flour, leaving out some to work the crust with; take one pound of butter; roll out the crust four times, each time putting in with a knife a quarter of the butter; use flour freely, when rolling out; cut it round, lay in your preserve or apple, which must be dry; turn over the paste, to join a half circle; nip the edge with the thumb and finger, to confine the preserve; dip the hand in water, pass it lightly over the paste, then sift sugar thick upon them, and bake in a quick oven.

CUSTARD.

Use about four eggs to a pint of new rich milk. Flavor the milk by putting six young laurel leaves, or grated lemon peel into it, before beginning to make the custard, and leaving them in until it is done; sweeten the milk with an ounce or more of sugar according to taste. Beat up the eggs thoroughly with sugar and add the milk to it boiling hot. Place all in the saucepan, and stir it over a slow fire until it begins to thicken. Then remove it from the fire and continue stirring it until it is of exactly the right thickness. Turn it out immediately and keep stirring it until it is cool.

BOILED CUSTARD.

Put one quart of milk over the fire; when it steams up, add the yolks of nine eggs and four table-spoons of sugar, well beaten together. Stir the mixture well till it thickens. Remove it from the fire, and set away to cool. Add flavor and salt to taste. To make it extra nice, beat up the whites of the eggs with some extract of lemon and sufficient powdered sugar to make it stiff. Divide it over the custard cups.

APPLE CHARLOTTE.

Make a nice syrup; cut up your apples very fine, and boil them in the syrup with a peel of a lemon, till perfectly transparent; when done, put it into a large tumbler, or a mould, and the next day it will be solid; turn it into a glass dish and pour over it a rich soft custard; if you choose, put a whip and some bits of currant jelly on the top.

CHOCOLATE KISSES.

One pound of sugar, two ounces of chocolate, pounded together and finely sifted; then mix, with the whites of eggs, well beaten to a froth. Drop this on buttered paper, and bake slowly.

LEMON SPONGE.

Soak half an ounce of gelatine in a pint of water for an hour, then add a quarter of a pound of loaf sugar, the rind and juice of a large lemon; put in a pan and simmer on the fire until the gelatine is dissolved; strain it into a large pitcher, let it remain until it is quite a jelly, when the white of an egg must be added, and the whole whisked thoroughly well for an hour; put into moulds previously rinsed in cold water. When turned out it should look like snow.

CHOCOLATE CREAM CUSTARDS.

Scrape quarter of a pound of the best chocolate, pour on it a tea-cupful of boiling water and let it stand by the fire until entirely dissolved. Beat six or eight eggs light, leaving out the whites of one or two; stir them by degrees into a quart of sweet milk alternately with the chocolate, and three table-spoonsful of white sugar. Put the mixture into cups, and bake ten minutes.

APPLE CUSTARD.

Select half a dozen sour apples, peel and core them, and cook them in half a tea-cup of water. When they become a little tender, take them out, place them in the pudding dish, sugar them and pour over them a mixture of six or eight eggs, well-beaten with four spoonsful of sugar and three pints of milk. Bake them for about half an hour.

RASPBERRY CUSTARD.

Take three gills of raspberry juice, and dissolve in it a pound of white sugar, mix it with a pint of boiling cream, stir until quite thick, and serve in custard glasses.

RICE CUSTARDS.

In a pint and a half of sweet milk, boil two ounces of ground rice; mix with it four ounces of sugar, four ounces of cream, an ounce of grated cocoanut, and bake in a mild oven.

STRAWBERRY, OR APPLE SOUFFLE.

Stew the apples with a little lemon peel; sweeten them, and lay them pretty high round the inside of a dish. Make a custard of the yolks of two eggs, a little cinnamon, sugar and milk. Let it thicken over a slow fire, but not boil; when ready, pour it in the inside of the apple. Beat the whites of the eggs to a light froth, and cover the whole; throw over it a quantity of pounded sugar, and brown it of a fine brown. Any fruit made of a proper consistency will do for the walls. Strawberries when ripe, are delicious.

SWEET SOUFFLE.

Take a pint of milk and as much flour as will come to a thick paste, over the stove; keep stirring it all the time; add six yolks of eggs and a pinch of salt, as much sugar as you like. Beat six whites of eggs to a froth; stir them altogether. Put it into a quick oven a quarter of an hour before it is wanted. Glaze it with white sugar, and send quickly to table. It may be made with ground rice. The rind of a lemon, grated, or lemon juice, gives it a nice flavor.

SUPERIOR OMELETTE SOUFFLE.

Twelve eggs, four heaping table-spoonsful of sugar, six of flour, one quart of milk. Boil the milk, stir the yolks of eggs, sugar, and flour together, add them to the milk, and let it stand hot but not boil. One hour before it is to be eaten, beat the whites to a stiff froth, stir them into the mixture and bake in a quick oven. Flavor to taste.

ORANGE CREAM.

Pare and squeeze two oranges on a cup of finely powdered sugar, with half a cup of water. Add four well beaten eggs and beat all together some time. Strain the whole through flannel into a saucepan; set it over a gentle fire, and stir it one way until thick and scalding hot, not boiling, or it will curdle. If lumps of sugar are rubbed on the oranges before they are pared, the flavor may be extracted; or they may be grated. Serve as custard in jelly glasses.

LEMON CREAM.

Take a pint of thick cream; the yolks of two eggs well-beaten; a cup of white sugar, and the rind of a lemon cut thin; boil it up; then stir it until almost cold; put the juice of a lemon in a dish and pour the cream upon it stirring well until cold. Serve in a large glass dish, or in custard cups, either alone or with sweetmeats.

VANILLA CREAM.—1.

Boil a stick of vanilla in a pint and a half of rich new milk, until it is highly flavored, take out the vanilla and sweeten the milk to taste. Beat up thoroughly the yolks of six eggs, and the white of one, and gradually mix in the milk, stirring them all the while. Then cook the cream until it is thick enough. If the vanilla be carefully dried it will serve several times provided it is good.

VANILLA CREAM.—2.

Make a jelly of isinglass with the proportion of one ounce to a pint of water. Get a strong flavor of the vanilla in a little milk, with sugar enough to sweeten one quart to taste; mix the isinglass jelly, the flavored milk, and one pint of good cream, and pour them into a mould to set. The isinglass jelly should be made in time to get cold before it is wanted for the cream, in case there should be any sediment to cut from it.

ITALIAN CREAM.

Take one pint of cream, and half pint of milk; make it hot, sweetening it to taste, and flavoring it with lemon peel. Beat up the yolks of eight eggs; beat up all together, and set it over a slow fire to thicken. Have ready an ounce of isinglass, melted and strained, which add to the cream; whip it well, and pour it into the mould.

TEA CREAM.

Boil two drachms or more of green tea in a quart of milk, after several minutes strain it, add the well-beaten yolks of three eggs, quarter of a pound of powered sugar; boil it to reduce it to one half, strain it again and serve when cold.

DESSERT DISHES.

ROCK CREAM.

Boil a tea-cupful of good rice in sweet milk till soft, sweeten it with powdered loaf sugar, and pile it up high on a dish. Lay on it, here and there, square pieces of currant jelly, or any kind of preserved fruits; beat up very stiff the whites of four or five eggs, and a little powdered sugar, flavored with orange flower water or vanilla, then add to it a tea-spoonful of cream, and drop it over the rice, giving it the appearance of a rock of snow.

CHARLOTTE RUSSE.—1.

Make first a pint of custard—two eggs to the pint of milk—then dissolve a box of gelatine in a pint of water, and let it boil as in making jelly. Strain each into the same vessel—a tin pan is the best—and stir it gently all the while, until it gets cold. In the meantime, take a quart of cream, season with vanilla, sweeten with a pound of sugar and churn it to a froth. Skim the froth and stir it into the mixture as soon as it begins to thicken.

CHARLOTTE RUSSE.—2.

Boil one ounce of gelatine in two tumblers of milk, and boil hard. Beat the whites and yolks separately of six eggs, adding to the yolks half a pound of loaf sugar, and stir them into the boiling milk long enough for them to thicken like a rich custard; then stir in the whites, beaten to a stiff froth. Season with vanilla. Whip a pint of rich cream to a stiff froth, and stir into the custard. When cold, arrange your cake in the mould and pour in the mixture. Set it on ice.

EUGENIE RUSSE.

Whip a pint of cream to a sponge froth. Pound half a stick of vanilla with sufficient sugar to sweeten it; melt half an ounce of isinglass and add all together to the cream. Plums and strawberries, or other fruit are then laid round a plain mould, the vanilla cream poured into the middle, and when cold the whole turned out.

MERINGUES.

Beat the whites of five eggs to a strong froth, mix in by degrees a table-spoon and a half of sifted sugar, then drop the mixture with a spoon on floured or sugared writing paper, put them into a very cool oven and let them remain until the outside is firm to the touch; when cold scrape out any remaining moist parts from the inside, fill them with whipped and flavored cream or with preserve, and join two together putting the flat sides upon each other.

LUCY STONE'S BREAD MERINGUE.

To a pint of nice, fine bread crumbs put a quart of sweet milk, one cup of brown sugar, the yolks of four eggs beaten, the grated rind of a lemon, and a piece of butter the size of an egg. Bake until stiff, then take it out and pour over it the whites of the eggs, beaten to a froth, with a tea-cup of powdered sugar and the juice of the lemon. Return to the oven, brown it lightly, and you will have a delicious " company," pudding, which may be eaten cold, with or without fruit or cream.

ALMOND BLANC MANGE.

Break an ounce of isinglass in small pieces, wash well, pour on a pint of boiling water; the next morning add a quart of milk; boil till the isinglass is dissolved, and strain. Put in two ounces of blanched almonds powdered; sweeten with loaf sugar, turn into a mould, and stick thin slips of almonds all over it. Dress it with whipped cream.

TAPIOCA BLANC MANGE.

In a pint of milk soak half a pound of tapioca for an hour. Boil till tender, sweeten, and pour it into a mould. When cold turn it out, serve it in a dish with jam round it and a little cream, or flavored with lemon or bitter almond without jam or cream.

ARROWROOT BLANC MANGE.

Mix three well filled up table-spoonsful of arrowroot with a little milk. Boil one pint and a half of rich, new milk, sweeten and flavor to taste; pour it on the arrowroot, mixing them well, and stir the mixture over a slow fire until it is thoroughly cooked and thickened, taking care that it does not burn. Pour it into a jelly shape, and do not turn it out until the next day.

RICE FLOUR BLANC MANGE.

Boil one quart of milk, season it to your taste with sugar and rose-water, take a table-spoonful of the rice flour, mix it very smooth with cold milk; add this to the other milk while it is boiling, stirring it well. Let all boil together about fifteen minutes, stirring it occasionally; then pour it into moulds, and put it by to cool.

WHOLE RICE BLANC MANGE.

Put four ounces of whole rice in one quart of sweet milk. Boil it slowly for a long time, and flavor with lemon peel, cinnamon, and sweeten to taste. Put it into a mould, tie it down close, and boil half an hour in a saucepan of water, taking care that the water does not get into the mould. When cold, turn it out of the mould on to a dish; place any kind of jam you like around it, and serve with custards or cream.

GROUND RICE BLANC MANGE.

Put half a pound of ground rice into two quarts of new milk, with a little cinnamon and lemon peel, and boil all together till quite thick, stirring it well. When it is thoroughly boiled, take out the cinnamon and lemon peel, and pour into a wetted mould; when quite cold, turn out of the mould, pour some fruit syrup round it in the dish. Serve with cream and sugar.

RED ROBIN.

Put a pint of water into a stewpan, throw in one pound of lump sugar, and boil till it becomes thick, then add two pounds of tart apples peeled and cored, and the rind of a lemon cut thin, boil all together till it is quite stiff; stir it often. Pour it into a mould, and when cold turn out. Serve with a custard, or it is very good without.

LOVE APPLES.

Make some blanc mange of maizena, in the proportion of four table-spoonsful of maizena, to two eggs and a quart of milk. While still warm, pour it into semi-circular moulds, the size of half an egg, taking care first to dip the moulds in cold water, to prevent sticking. When cold, turn out, stick the halves together with a little gum and sugar water, so as to form shining balls. With a little brush and extract of cochineal then tinge one side carefully, and arrange on a dish, in a pyramid, with apple, quince, or currant jelly in the interstice, and white sugar sifted over the whole. Nicely managed, this makes a very pretty and inexpensive dish.

MASKED TARTS.

Line small tart-pans with puff-paste, and place in each half an apple which has been boiled tender, in a rich syrup. Bake a light brown and, when done, dilute quince jelly, or jam, with a little of the syrup, and mask the apple with a spoonful of it. Sift over white sugar.

FRUIT TARTS.

Line your pans as for masked tarts; fill with any kind of jelly, preserve, or jam, and cover with a lattice of pastry. Glaze with white of egg, bake a light brown, and sift over powdered sugar.

APPLE TART.

Scald eight or ten large apples; let them stand till they are cold, and then take off the skins. Beat the pulp as fine as possible, with a spoon; then mix the yolks of six eggs, and the whites of four; beat all together very fine, put in some grated nutmeg, and sweeten to your taste. Melt some good fresh butter, and beat it till it is of the consistency of fine thick cream; then make a puff-paste, and cover a tin patty-pan with it; pour in the ingredients, but do not cover it with the paste. When it has baked a quarter of an hour, slip it out of the patty-pan, on a dish, and strew over it some sugar, finely beaten.

APPLE MERINGUE.—1.

Prepare six large, tart apples, as for sauce. While hot, put in a piece of butter the size of an egg. When cold, add a cup of fine cracker crumbs, the yolks of three eggs well beaten, a cup of sweet milk or cream, a little salt, and nutmeg and sugar to taste. Bake in a large plate, with an under crust of rich paste and a rim of puff paste. When done, take the whites of the eggs, half a large tea-cup of white sugar, and a few drops of essence of lemon; beat to a stiff froth, pour over, and put back in the oven to brown lightly.

APPLE MERINGUES.—2.

Scoop out the core from six apples, and fill them with quince marmalade; stew them until tender in half a pint of water, with some sugar, some lemon-peel, and a little more marmalade. Lay the apples in a dish with the liquor. Beat up to a strong froth the whites of four eggs, flavoring them with orange flower water and sugar to taste. Cover the apples with this whip, and bake them half an hour.

APPLE SNOW.

Peel, core, and quarter a dozen Spitzenberg apples, and stew them gently, with a cup of water, white sugar sufficient to sweeten, and a little cinnamon; when reduced nearly to a pulp, turn into a dish. Make a soft custard of a quart of milk, the yolks of four eggs, a little sugar, and extract of lemon; when it is cold, lay it over the apples, and whip up the whites of the eggs with a quarter of a pound of powdered sugar, and heap lightly on the top.

APPLE MARMALADE.

Pare twenty pounds of pippin apples, make a syrup of ten pounds of sugar, boil the apples sufficiently in it to mash, take them out, beat them fine, put them back, cut six oranges into small pieces, and boil all together, stirring it till done.

BAKED APPLES.

There is nothing better for a simple ordinary dessert than plain baked apples. Wash the apples, and place them whole without peeling in the baking dish sprinkled with sugar, with a little water added for sauce and bake until quite soft. A good way is to cut out the stem, leaving a little cavity; fill this with sugar and place three layers in the dish, the stem end up. Sprinkle over some more sugar, add a little water and put a slice of lemon over each apple in the top layer; first, slightly squeezing the juice over the apples. Water enough may be used to supply a sauce, although they are delicious with cream if that can be obtained. Sweet apples are usually much preferred for baking instead of tart ones, though this is in some degree a matter of taste.

STEWED APPLES.

Make a clear syrup of half a pound of sugar to one pint of water. Skim it; peel and core the apples without injuring the shape. Let them be in cold water till the syrup is ready, to which add the juice of a lemon and the peel cut very fine. Quarters of oranges may be boiled in the syrup instead of apples.

APPLE CREAM.

Boil rich, well-flavored apples till soft, rub the pulp through a hair sieve, mix in sugar; when cold stir in sweet cream and serve cold.

DRIED APPLES STEWED.

Wash the pieces, soak several hours, boil in sufficient water to cover them, over a slow fire; when nearly done add sugar. They are better flavored with a few dried quinces or peaches. Orange peel or lemon is excellent for flavor.

STEWED PIPPINS.

Pare and quarter golden pippins, remove the core, stew them over a slow fire with sufficient sugar to sweeten, the juice and rind of a lemon and a little water, let them cook till very tender.

GINGER APPLES.

Take Newtown pippins, pare, core, and throw them into cold water to preserve their color. Take a pint of water, and half a pound of sugar to every pound of fruit. Place it on the fire in a stew pan and bring it to a boil before the fruit is put in. Now take the apples out of the cold water and put them in the syrup; and add one ounce and three quarters of cleaned ginger, for each pound of fruit. Let them boil till they become clear, an hour or less. If not used immediately, put them in a jar closely covered down, and set in a cool, dry place. They will keep some time.

FLOATING ISLAND OF APPLES.

Bake or scald eight or nine large apples; when cold, pare them and pulp them through a sieve. Beat this pulp with sugar, and add to the whites of four or five eggs previously beaten, with a small quantity of rose water, or essence of lemon; mix this into the pulp a little at a time, and beat it until quite light. Heap it up on a dish, with Savoy cakes, and jelly under, and around it.

APPLE SNOW BALLS.

Take six apples pare and quarter them and cut out the cores completely. Place the quarters together in the shape of the apple before, and in the cavity made by removing the core put a clove and a slice of lemon peel. Have six small pudding-cloths at hand, and half pound of rice, and cover the apples severally, one after the other in an upright position, with rice, tying them up tight. Then place them in a large saucepan of scalding water, and let them boil for one whole hour. On taking them up, open the tops, and intermix with the fruit a little grated nutmeg, with butter and sugar to your taste.

COMPOTE OF APPLES.

Boil a sauce pan of clarified sugar, half sugar and half water on the fire; skim it, have ready the apples pared, cut in halves, and cored, drop them in the syrup and let them boil very slowly. Take them off when done, and let them cool; if the syrup is too thin, give them another boil.

NINA'S APPLE CREAM.

Take two pounds of apples, pare and core them, slice them into a pan, add one pound of loaf sugar, the juice of three lemons, and the grated rind of one. Let these boil about two hours. Turn it in the mould and serve it with boiled custard, or cream.

MOTHER'S "SURPRISE."

Take a square loaf of baker's bread, cut into thin slices, (crust and all,) and butter them. Peel, core, and cut up sufficient of nice baking apples in proportion. Take a pie dish, line it with bread and butter. Next make a layer of apples at the bottom, then of sugar, then of bread and so on, till the dish is filled. Bake until the apple is perfectly soft, then before serving, turn it out into a dish. It ought to keep its shape, and eat almost like a sweetmeat, all the ingredients being thoroughly blended in baking.

APPLE CHEESE.

Take equal weights of apple and sugar; boil the sugar in water, take off the scum as it rises, and when it is clear, put in the apples with some lemon juice and peel, and boil until it is all of a proper thickness.

A cream for this cheese may be made by putting to a pint of cream or new milk, the yolks of two eggs, a stick of cinnamon, a spoonful of rose water, and the peel of a lemon; let it quite boil, and when it is cool, sweeten it to taste, and pour it over or around the cheese.

SARATOGA APPLE SAUCE.

Take two pounds of apples, boil them with as little water as possible, and make them into apple sauce, then add a pound and a half of sugar, and the juice of a lemon; boil all together till quite firm, and put it into a mould. Garnish it with almonds stuck over it. It will keep for many months, if allowed to remain in the mould.

BAKED PEARS.

Take any kind of pears, wash them, and place them whole and without peeling, in the baking tin, with merely the water that will hang on them after washing. Sprinkle sugar over them, and bake until quite soft. A syrup will be found in the bottom of the dish, which may be poured over them. They are better and more wholesome than any complicated pastry.

SCALDED PEARS.

Wash the pears, whole, and without pealing; boil them in just enough water to cover them, until they are soft, then pour in molasses, sufficient for a sauce, boil up until it is thick, and serve the pears in a dish, with the sauce poured over them.

TO MAKE A TRIFLE.

Make a boiled custard not very thick and let it cool. Break in pieces some Naples biscuits, some macaroons in halves, add ratifia cakes, cover the bottom of a dish with them, and wet with white wine; pour the custard over them, and put a syllabub over it. It can be garnished with currant jelly, and if convenient with flowers.

GOOSEBERRY OR APPLE TRIFLE.

Scald the fruit, pulp it through a sieve, and add sugar to taste. Make a thick layer of this at the bottom of the dish. Mix a pint of milk, a pint of cream, and the yolks of two eggs, scald it over the fire, stirring it well; add a small quantity of sugar, and let it get cold. Then lay it over the apples, or gooseberries, with a spoon, and put on the whole a whip made the day before. If you use apples, add the rind of a lemon grated.

RHUBARB TART.

Pare off the thin skin, and cut it in small lengths, stew them an hour very slowly; to one pint of rhubarb add, while simmering, a syrup of sugar, and a little water; when done let it cool, then make it into tarts.

ICING FOR TARTS.

Beat the white of an egg with a quarter of a pound of powdered sugar, and flavor with two spoonsful of almond, or lemon extract, stir them together one way till the mixture is quite thick, and then lay it on the tarts with a feather or a bunch of feathers, then let the tarts stand in a mild oven until hard, but not long enough to become discolored.

COMPOTE OF RHUBARB.

Take a pound of the stalks after they are pared, and cut them in short lengths, have ready a quarter of a pint of water boiled gently for ten minutes, with five ounces of good lump sugar, or six ounces if the fruit is very tart; put it in and let it simmer for about ten minutes.

COMPOTE OF RED CURRANTS.

Make a syrup of a pint of water and five or six ounces of lump sugar, boiled ten minutes. Simmer a pint of currants, freed from the stalks, from five to seven minutes. They are an excellent accompaniment to a pudding of batter, custard, bread or rice, or to boiled rice. A compote of raspberries may be made in this way, or raspberries may be mixed with the currants.

COMPOTE OF GREEN CURRANTS.

Make a syrup of half a pint of spring water and five ounces of lump sugar boiled together ten minutes. Strip a pint of green currants from the stalks, and simmer them in the syrup five minutes.

COMPOTE OF GREEN GOOSEBERRIES.

Make a syrup of half a pint of water, and five ounces of good lump sugar broken fine, boiled together gently for ten minutes, and skimmed. Simmer gently in this syrup for eight or ten minutes a pint of gooseberries freed from tops and stalks and well washed and drained; these compotes will only keep good two or three days; transparency of the fruit will be increased by using more sugar in the syrup.

COMPOTE OF PEACHES.

Pare them, and remove the stone, boil gently until tender, take them off and put them in cold water. Then put them in clarified sugar, add a little boiling water, set them again over the fire, and when done enough, pour them out into dishes.

CHERRY CHEESE.

Take the stones from twelve pounds of cherries, break the stones of part of the cherries and blanch the kernels; take these with the fruit and three pounds of loaf sugar, put into a kettle, and boil all gently till the jam becomes quite clear; pour into small and rather shallow pots, and keep in a dry place.

GOOSEBERRY FOOL.

Put into a deep dish some green gooseberries, a quart or more if desired, after baking them in the oven until quite soft, pulp them through a colander and add pounded sugar to taste. When it is cold, mix in a gill of cream to each quart of berries, and serve in a glass dish.

PINEAPPLE FRITTERS.

Take quarter of a pound of fine flour, one and a half pints of new milk, the yolks of four fresh eggs, and make the same into a light battter, adding the whites of two eggs, first beaten into a light froth. Bruise half a dozen slices of a round ripe pineapple into a pulp and stir it well up with the batter, adding at the same time a little nutmeg and cinnamon grated fine. Put the pan over a brisk fire, and ladle out the batter into the pan as it may be required, according to the size of the fritters. Fry them in fresh butter turning them only once, when they will assume a brown, crisp complexion. When quite done remove them into a dish, sprinkling over them a dessert-spoonful of powdered loaf sugar. Apple and currant fritters can be prepared after a like manner. The cinnamon can be dispensed with if objected to.

ORANGE FRITTERS.

Take three oranges, or more if desired, peel them, and pick off the white part without breaking the thin inner skin; then tear them into the natural divisions of the orange; each one will make from seven to eight pieces. Dip each into a light batter; fry them in hot fat, not too brown. Serve as soon as convenient with sifted sugar over them.

STEWED PRUNES.

Soak the prunes in cold water, if not very dry, for one hour; but if they are old a longer time is necessary. Stew them, closely covered with a thin syrup, with lemon peel chopped finely, for three hours.

GOOD COMMON PRESERVE.

Boil together in equal or unequal portions any kinds of early fruit until they can be pressed through a sieve, weigh the pulp and and boil it over a brisk fire half an hour, add half a pound of sugar for each pound of fruit, again boil it quickly, stirring and skimming, from fifteen to twenty minutes; cherries if used, should be stewed tender apart, as they require a longer time than other summer fruits.

A NICE AND CHEAP DESSERT.

Cook a teacup of rice very thóroughly, putting in water first, afterwards milk, and a little salt. When it is done to a jelly, add a table-spoonful of currant-jelly, or half a teacup of any fruit-juice, that is of a bright color; and put it over the fire a few minutes. Turn it into a mould, to cool; and eat with sweetened cream, or cream and dry white sugar.

ANOTHER.

Tie a cup and a half of rice, which has been well washed, in a bag with a few raisins. Allow plenty of room to swell, and boil an hour or more. Turn out, and pour over it some boilling syrup, in which a small piece of butter has been melted.

LOPPERED MILK.

A delicious summer dessert consists simply of milk which has *thickened*, take it out quivering, like custard, and eat with cream and white sugar. It must not be allowed to *whey*, as it is then not *loppered* but sour milk. It is a favorite dish in Germany.

STRAWBERRIES.

It is not necessary to urge upon any one the *eating* of this delicious fruit; everybody, man, woman, and child, anticipates the season with pleasure. But we should like to urge upon all who possess a few feet of ground the wisdom of cultivating a "strawberry patch." So great a gift, so profusely bestowed in return for a little labor, ought to be shared by the poorest. We hope the time will come when fruit will be so plentiful and so cheap that it can be picked by the weary, thirsty traveller on the roadside. Why should not apple-trees, cherry-trees, plum-trees, peach-trees, and pear-trees be planted along the unsightly fences, hiding them, and supplying God's good gifts, without money or price, to those who need them? The man who shall first endow his farm in this way will, at small cost, become a public benefactor, and establish a claim to immortality. But to return to strawberries: this is so perfect a fruit, so exquisite in flavor, so excellent in quality, that cooking, or manipulation of any kind, rather impairs than improves it. A little white sugar and cream is the only addition that can be made, and even this is a concession to our unnaturally sweetened and perverted palates, rather than to the necessities of the case. As for strawberry pie, strawberry dumpling, strawberry pudding, and the whole range of dishes in which strawberries are *cooked*, they should be stricken out of every housekeeper's list, with a single reservation in favor of "strawberry cake," in which, however, the strawberries are *not* cooked, and which is so great a pet with the male as well as female part of every household, that we dare not say a word against it, even if it was not one of our own special weaknesses.

STRAWBERRY SHORTCAKE.

Mix dough as for soda buscuit; that is to say, one quart of sifted flour, piece of butter size of an egg, two tea-spoonsful of cream of tartar, one of soda, a pinch of salt, and sweet milk to form a soft dough. Put cream of tartar in the flour, and soda in *dry* also, and, when thoroughly mixed, roll out half an inch thick and bake in a shallow pan fifteen or twenty minutes; have ready two quarts of fresh, fine strawberries; split the cake, place half the strawberries between and cover thickly with white sugar and cream; put the other half on the top and cover in the same way; send to the table immediately. This is the method of making at the finest city restaurants.

FRUIT FOR DESSERT.

Add a little water to the white of an egg, and beat it well; dip the fruit in and immediately sprinkle it all over with powdered sugar. Then leave it for four or five hours, and serve with custard, loppered milk, or ice corn-starch pudding. Large and fair bunches of red and white currants make a charming dish in this way. Strawberries, blackberries, cherries or raspberries, are either of them suitable.

SUMMER FRUITS MIXED.

Take fine, fresh strawberries, white and red currants, and white or red strawberries; strip them carefully from the stalks, and heap them high on a dessert dish in layers, strewing each layer with sifted sugar. Before serving lay thick cream entirely over the fruit, and gently stir them with a spoon when served. Some use instead of cream two wine-glasses full of Sherry, Madeira or any other good white wine. Either currants or strawberries by themselves, are good, prepared in this way.

RHUBARB, OR PIE PLANT.

This is one of the greatest of spring luxuries, though the quantity of sugar required to be used with it renders it rather expensive. Remove the stringy part and cut up into small slices either for stewing or pies, no spice is required, but sugar may be put in as long as your conscience will let you, and a handful afterwards.

QUINCES FOR THE TABLE.

Bake them; remove the skin, slice them and serve with cream and sugar.

APPLE PIQUE.

Peel and stew some apples, but do not let them break. Place them in a glass dish half full of syrup, and put a piece of currant jelly on the top of each apple.

TOMATOES.

These can be eaten raw, when ripe, with salt, pepper and vinegar or sugar. By pouring boiling water on them, the skin can be taken off, then cut them in pieces and cover them with powdered sugar.

A DESSERT OF CHESTNUTS

Boil Spanish chestnuts very soft and pulp them through a sieve. Beat the whites of eggs with pounded white sugar, to a thick froth pile the chesnuts in a dish, and cover thickly with the whip, just before stirring.

LEMON PASTE TO KEEP.

To one pound of butter, put one pound of loaf sugar, six eggs (leaving out the whites of two,) the rind grated, and the juice of three lemons. Put all in a pan, and let simmer till the sugar is dissolved, and it thickens to the consistency of honey. Put it into pots, and close them air tight.

LEMON FLAVOR.

When lemons are plenty procure a quantity, cut them into thin slices, and lay them on the plates to dry in the oven; when dry put them into a tight bag or close vessel, in the store room, where they are both handy and agreeable for almost anything.

TINCTURE OF LEMON OR ORANGE PEEL.

A fine flavor for cake, sauces, and the like, may be easily, and cheaply obtained, by taking a thin rind off any lemons, or oranges, that may be used, and putting it into a bottle half full of brandy, or proof spirit. A few weeks will suffice to impregnate it very strongly with the flavor.

COUNTRY ICE CREAM.

Any family having ice and milk, can make ice cream without a freezer as follows: Scald two quarts of fresh milk,—if a little cream be added all the better,—stirring in three table-spoonsful of corn starch or arrow root, to give it body. These may be omitted if not at hand. Stir well to keep from burning. Beat up four to eight eggs, according to convenience, and pour the scalding milk on the eggs, stirring well. When cold add sugar and essence of lemon, or extract of vanilla, to suit the taste, and a very little salt. Pour the cold contents into a deep tin pail, or can, holding about three quarts; put on the cover, and set in an ordinary water pail. Pound up ice to the size of hens' eggs and less, some, of course, will be quite fine; pack it around the tin can, mixing in about one pint of either medium or fine salt; pack this till it reaches nearly to the top of the can containing the mixture to be frozen, but be careful none enters it. Now move the tin can or pail around by means of its bail, lifting the cover occasionally to scrape off the frozen cream on the inside, so that other portions may come in contact with the freezing surface. From fifteen to twenty minutes will be sufficient, and the dish may be served up at once or set away, without removing from the wooden pail, in a cool place for several hours, covered with a flannel cloth.

STRAWBERRY ICE CREAM.

Take two pounds of fresh strawberries, carefully picked, and with a wooden spoon rub them through a hair sieve, about half pound of powdered sugar, and the juice of one lemon; color with a few drops of prepared cochineal; cream, one pint. When the sugar is dissolved, ascertain that the sweetness is correct; then freeze. This will make a quart. When fresh strawberries are not in season, take strawberry jam, the juice of two lemons, cream, to one quart. Color, strain, and freeze.

APPLE ICE.

Take nice apples, grate them, make them very sweet and freeze them. Pears, peaches, and quinces can be done in the same way.

MOLASSES CANDY.

Boil slowly a quart of molasses, stirring occasionally. To find when it is done, drop a spoonful of it into some cold water; if it breaks brittle, take it off. Have some flat pans well buttered, pour the candy hot into them, and set it aside to cool. When nearly cool, take it from the pans and stretch it for a long time until it becomes a clear light color. While boiling, it can be flavored according to taste, or mixed with nuts or pop corn. A small piece of alum put in will make it more brittle.

SUGAR TAFFY.

Dissolve three pounds of sugar in a pint of water, in which half a teaspoon of citric acid has been dissolved; boil it, and remove the scum. When it will crack after being dropped in cold water take off, and squeeze and mix in the juice of three lemons or oranges. Boil again until thick as before, then pour into buttered pans, in a thin layer. Mark it off into square blocks before it cools, so that it will break regularly.

LEMON DROPS.

Boil clarified syrup until it will crack when dropped in water; flavor it with lemon, then pour it in small drops on buttered paper, and set aside to get cold.

CHOCOLATE DROPS.

Throw into a well-heated metal mortar, from two to four ounces of the best quality of cake chocolate, broken small, and pound it with a warm pestle until it resembles a smooth paste or very thick batter; then add an equal weight of sugar, in the finest powder, and beat them until they are thoroughly blended. Roll the mixture into small balls, lay them on sheets of writing paper, or upon clean dishes, and take them off when nearly cold. While soft, the tops may be encrusted with white nonpareil comfits.

SYRUPS FOR CANDIES.

To a pint of cold water put two pounds of loaf-sugar, let it dissolve, add the white of an egg and beat the mixture well. Put it on the fire, when it boils up take it off and remove the scum. Put it on the fire again, let it boil up and throw in a few drops of cold water; take it off again and remove the scum, and so continue until no scum rises.

BARLEY SUGAR, (*for Children.*)

Soak a quart of barley over night, in the morning boil it gently in more water, until it becomes a clear and rather thin jelly. Add to this two pounds of sugar, and the juice of a lemon, and boil again, until clear and stiff, so that when poured out in buttered plates or saucers, it will set hard. The white of an egg improves it.

SWEET CAKES.

POUND CAKE.

Beat six eggs to a froth, then add a pound of sugar and half a pound of butter, beat all well together; dissolve half a tea-spoonful of soda in half a cup of milk. Take a pound of sifted flour and rub a tea-spoonsful of cream of tartar through it with your hands; add the eggs, sugar, and butter; stir all thoroughly together, flavor it to your taste, and bake in a quick oven.

SPONGE CAKE.—1.

Three eggs well beaten, one cup of white sugar, one cup of sifted flour, a tea-spoonful of cream tartar, half a tea-spoonful of soda, both put in one cup with two tea-spoonsful of sweet milk, and dissolved. Beat the cake very thoroughly, then add a half tea-spoonful of extract of lemon. Bake in quick oven. This is good enough for a party, yet not expensive.

SPONGE CAKE.—2.

Four, six, eight, or ten eggs, weight of eggs in powdered sugar, half that weight in flour. Beat the yolks ten minutes, mix them well with sugar, and one tea-spoonful of essence of lemon. Beat whites separate, and stir in last.

ALMOND SPONGE CAKE.

Ten eggs, one pound of sugar, half pound of flour, a few drops of lemon. When these ingredients are well beaten, add half-pound of sweet almonds, blanched, and pounded in a white mortar or stout bowl. To blanch them—that is, skin them—pour boiling water upon them. Add a little peach extract, and bake in a brisk oven. This is very rich.

RICE FLOUR SPONGE CAKE.

Make like sponge cake, except that you use three quarters of a pound of rice flour, thirteen eggs, leaving out four whites, and add a little salt.

MRS. V. S SPONGE CAKE.

One tumbler of flour, one of fine white sugar, five eggs, one tea-spoon cream tartar, one half tea-spoon soda. Beat the whites of the eggs to a froth, add the sugar, then the yolks, and lastly, the flour; flavor with lemon, and bake to cut in squares.

A NICE TEA DISH.

This cake is very nice cut in thin slices, and layers of canned peaches, or canned strawberries laid between, sift over the whole powdered sugar. The same receipt makes delicious jelly cake.

A MAGNIFICENT CHRISTMAS CAKE.—1.

Two pounds of flour, two pounds of sugar, two pounds of raisins, stoned and chopped, two pounds of currants cleaned, one pound of citron, cut in strips, one pound of butter, ten eggs well-beaten, four tea-spoonsful baking powder mixed with the flour, a pint of sweet milk, lemon, nutmeg, and allspice to taste, and a little salt. Mix and beat thoroughly. Put in plenty of spice. Bake four or five hours, and then ice. Trim it with holly wreath, and branch.

CHRISTMAS CAKE.—2.

Four eggs, two cups of brown sugar, half a cup of molasses, one cup and a half of shortening, (half butter and half lard), one cup of milk, either sweet or sour, five cups of flour, two large tea-spoonsful of soda, two large tea-spoonsful of ground cloves one grated nutmeg, a tea-spoonful of cinnamon, one pound of chopped raisins, citron. A table-spoonful of brandy improves this. Eggs not to be beaten.

FINE FRUIT CAKE.

Soak three cups of dried apples over night in cold water enough to swell them, chop them in the morning, and put them on the fire with three cups of molasses. Stew until soft, but not pulpy. When cold, mix with them three cups of flour, a cup of butter, three eggs, and a tea-spoon of soda. Bake in a steady oven. This will make two good-sized pans full of splendid cake. The apples will cook like citron, and taste deliciously. Raisins may be added if desired, and salt and plenty of spice—allspice if liked.

PORK FRUIT CAKE.

Take half a pound of fat corned pork, chop it very fine. Mix it with one pound of raisins chopped, five cups of flour; one cup of molasess, two cups of sugar, two eggs, one cup of milk or wine, and one tea-spoonful of saleratus. Spice it with a table-spoonful of cloves, one nutmeg, and half a table-spoonful of cinnamon. This will keep all winter and is better after being kept a considerable time.

A FINE BRIDE CAKE.

Three pounds of fine flour well dried, three pounds of pounded sugar, three pounds of fresh butter, six pounds of currants well washed and dried, two pounds of raisins chopped fine, one pound of sweet almonds, blanched and cut thin, one pound of citron, one pound of lemon peel, one pound of orange peel, quarter ounce of mace powdered and sifted fine, quarter ounce of nutmeg grated, twenty-four eggs, and half pint of fruit syrup. First work the butter to a cream with the hand, then beat in the sugar for quarter of an hour. Let the whites of the eggs be beaten to a strong froth, then mix with the sugar and butter; beat the yolk half an hour at least, and add them; next dust in the flour, beating the cake the whole time; and the other ingredients by degrees, and keep beating until the oven is ready; butter the hoop, and line it also with a buttered paper before putting in the cake. It will take four hours in a moderate oven.

The Almond Icing.—Beat the whites of six eggs to a strong froth, beat two pounds of almonds (which have been pounded in a mortar) with a little rose-water; mix the almonds and eggs lightly together, and add by degrees two pounds of loaf-sugar pounded. When the cake is done, lay this icing upon it, and put it in the oven to brown.

Sugar Icing.—Two pounds of sugar sifted, two ounces of fine starch; beat the whites of five eggs to a strong froth; sift in the sugar and starch, and beat for half an hour; lay this on the almond icing, and spread smooth with a knife. If put on when the cake comes out of the oven, it will be hard by the time it is cold. The cake must be kept in a dry place until wanted for use.

CONNECTICUT ELECTION CAKE.

Ten pounds of flour, five pounds of shortening, equal parts butter and lard salted. Work shortening into flour very fine, no knobs, then add a quart of brewer's yeast. Take enough sweet milk to make it a little softer than biscuit. Work it a long time, until it begins to grow light. If you see the butter round the dish while rising do not be frightened. Let it stand and rise until it cracks open. While it is rising, weigh five and a half pounds of white sugar, break ten eggs in a large dish, work the sugar and eggs together; five pounds of raisins, either seeded or chopped; soak them in two gills of the best sweet cider; two table-spoonsful of powdered mace, two nutmegs, the rind of two oranges, chopped fine. Add citron if you choose. After the cake is raised enough, work in all the above ingredients, and let it stand in a warm place until it rises again. Then bake. This makes twenty large loaves.

INDEPENDENCE CAKE.

Twenty pounds of flour, fifteen pounds of sugar, ten pounds of butter, four dozen of eggs, one quart of wine, one quart of brandy, one ounce of nutmegs, three ounces each of cinnamon, cloves, and mace, two pounds of citron, five pounds each of currants and raisins, and one quart of yeast. Frost it, and dress it with box and rose leaf.

NEW HAVEN COMMENCEMENT CAKE.

One pound of sugar, three quarters of butter, one of flour, one cup of yeast, three nutmegs, two tea-spoonsful of cinnamon, and five eggs. Set to rise over night. In the morning add a tea-spoon of soda, and as much chopped raisins and chipped citron as you choose, and let it stand an hour before baking. A little raspberry vinegar or melted currant jelly will improve it. Ice it.

PLUM CAKE.

Take two cups of sugar, one cup of butter, one cup of milk or butter-milk, one tea-spoonful of saleratus or volatile salts, a gill of brandy, a tea-spoonful of essence of lemon and sufficient flour to make a stiff batter. Beat this well together, add half a pound of raisins stoned and chopped, half a pound of currants, washed and dried by the fire, and one quarter of citron, and bake in a brisk oven.

NEW YEAR'S HICKORY-NUT CAKE.

One pound of flour, one pound of sugar, three quarters pound of butter, six eggs, two tea-spoons of cream of tartar, one of soda, half-cup of sweet milk. Beat the cake thoroughly, and then stir in a small measure of hickory-nuts, first, of course, taking them from the shell. Bake in a steady but not quick oven. This is a very fine cake.

HUCKLEBERRY CAKE.

One cup of sugar, one egg, piece of butter size of an egg, half a cup of milk, one tea-spoonful of soda, two of cream of tartar, a tea-spoonful of any preferred essence, and sifted flour to make a stiff batter. Put cream of tartar in the flour, soda in the milk, and beat thoroughly. Add last a pint of dried huckleberries, and bake in a quick oven. This is cheap and good.

LOAF CAKE.

Stir into two quarts of flour a pint of milk, slightly warmed, and a small tea-cup of yeast. Place it near the fire, where it will rise quickly. When perfectly light, work in with the hand four beaten eggs, a tea-spoonful of salt, two of cinnamon, a wine glass of currant jelly, a grated nutmeg, and some chipped citron. Stir a pound of sugar with three quarters of a pound of butter; when white work it into cake; add another quart of sifted flour, and beat the whole with the hand ten or fifteen minutes, then set it where it will rise again. When of a spongy lightness, put it into buttered cake pans and let them stand fifteen or twenty minutes before baking. Add if you like, a pound and a half of raisins just before putting the cake into pans.

NEW YEAR'S CAKE.

Three and a quarter pounds of flour, one of butter, and a half of sugar, one pint of milk, two tea-spoons of cream tartar, one tea-spoon of soda, caraway seeds.

APPLE CAKE.

Take one pound of white sugar, two pounds of apples pared and cut thin, and the rind of a large lemon; put a pint of water to the sugar and boil it to a syrup; put the apples to it and boil it quite thick. Put it into a mould to cool, and send it cold to table, with a custard or cream poured round it.

CURRANT CAKE.

Beat a pound of fresh butter to a cream; take one pound and a quarter of sugar, and one and a quarter of currants washed and picked, and beat up the whites and yolks of eight eggs; put in the sugar by degrees, then a pound of flour and currants; add a gill of brandy, some candied orange and citron; beat the mixture till very light; and bake it in pans.

FINE ALMOND CAKE.

Boil a pound and quarter of finely sifted loaf sugar to a candy; have ready a pound of sweet almonds well blanched and pounded, adding a little orange-flower water while pounding to keep them from oiling; put them in the sugar with the rind of two lemons grated very thin and as much juice as to make it of a sharp taste. Place this in glasses in the oven; stir them often to keep them from candying; when a little dry put the mixture upon paper in small cakes to harden.

LEMON CAKE.—1.

Rub one tea-cup of butter and three tea-cups of powdered loaf sugar to a cream; beat and stir in the yolks of four eggs, add a tea-cup of milk, the juice and grated peel of one lemon, and the whites of the eggs; then sift in four tea-cups of prepared flour, and bake for about half an hour in two long tins. It can be iced to advantage.

LEMON CAKE.—2.

Beat well together one egg, a small piece of butter, flour, and the rind of a lemon grated with sufficient lump sugar to sweeten it. Roll them very thin, cut them into such shapes as desired, and bake on a tin in a brisk oven.

PICNIC CAKES.

One cup of sugar, one half cup of butter, two eggs, one half cup of sweet milk, one tea-spoonful of cream of tartar, one half tea-spoonful of soda. Mix with sifted flour to the consistency of cookies, cut in strips, which roll in powdered sugar and twist into round cakes. Bake a very light brown.

MRS. BRISTOL'S BREAD CAKE.

Four cups of light dough, two cups of sugar, one cup of butter, three eggs, one tea-spoonful of soda, one nutmeg, raisins. This makes two large loaves, and constitutes a fine, cheap and healthy fruit cake.

"PORTAGE FALLS" CAKE.

Two cups of sugar, one cup of butter, three fourths of a cup of sweet milk, four eggs, the yolks and whites beaten separate; two tea-spoonsful of cream of tartar, one tea-spoonful of soda. Put the cream of tartar in the milk and the soda in the flour. Beat long and well; bake in a mould, in each section of which drop several strips of citron. It should be iced.

POVERTY CAKE.

Two cups of sugar, two cups of sour milk, one tea-spoonful of saleratus, piece of butter as large as an egg, spice to your taste, mix to a batter.

SNOW CAKE.

Take half a pound of butter, half a pound of pounded loaf su-

..., of six eggs, and one pound of arrowroot. Beat the butter to a cream, then add the arrowroot and sugar gradually, beating all the time; beat the six whites separately, in a basin, and when a stiff froth, add to the mixture; put a few drops of any sort of essence either lemon, almond, or vanilla, and beat all for twenty minutes. Then put into a tin and bake in a moderate oven, great care being taken that the outside is not burnt before the inside is done. Some persons cut snow cake into slices before sending it to table, having previously cut off the outside and sifted powdered sugar over each slice.

SMALL SEED CAKES.

One cup of butter, two of white sugar, three eggs, half a cup of seeds, and flour enough to make a stiff paste. Roll it very thin, with sugar instead instead of flour, on the board, and cut it in round shapes. Bake it about fifteen minutes.

CREAM CAKE.—1.

One cup of sugar, one of sour cream, two of sifted flour, two eggs, one tea-spoonful of cream of tartar, half of soda, half of salt. Flavor with essence of almond. It is quickly made, and delicious eaten fresh.

CREAM CAKE.—2.

Mix a quart of flour, a pint or more of sweet cream, to wet it well, a tea-spoonful of saleratus, dissolved in a little sour cream and bake.

CREAM CAKES.

(*Outside.*) Two cups of flour, half-cup of butter, half-pint cold water. Boil the butter and water together, and stir the flour in gradually while boiling. Let it cool; then add five eggs, a pinch of saleratus, and a little salt. Drop the mixture on tins, and bake in a quick oven.

(*Inside.*) One pint of milk, one cup white sugar, half-cup of flour, two eggs. Beat the eggs, sugar, and flour together, and stir them in the milk while boiling. Flavor with lemon or vanilla. Cut a slit in the side of each cake, and put in the filling after the cakes cool.

CORNETS A CREME.

These are little cakes, made of the yolks of four eggs, three ounces of white sugar melted in a few drops of water upon the fire, two table-spoonsful of flour, and a little essence of lemon; this mixture is baked very thin upon buttered pans, and then rolled round into small cornucopias, and filled with a whip of cream and a little powdered sugar.

PORTUGAL CAKE.

Take half a pound of fresh butter, a pound of fine sugar, and four eggs, beat the mixture well till it is light and looks curdling; flavor it with mace, add half a pound of currants and a pound of flour; mix all together, put it in pans and bake in a mild oven.

GLEN VIS CAKE.

Take one large cup of sugar, half a cup of butter, two eggs, half a cup of milk, half a tea-spoonful of soda, one tea-spoonful of cream of tartar, spice, and a proportionate quantity of flour. By using the whites only of three eggs the cake is made finer and whiter.

WARSAW WHITE CAKE.

Take one and a half large cups of flour, mix half of it with two table-spoonsful of melted butter, one tea-spoonful of cream of tarter, and some milk; mix the other half with some milk and one tea-spoonful of soda. Add to these a coffee cup of sugar, beat all together and bake. The milk for cake should always be divided, and the soda dissolved in one portion and the cream of tartar in the other.

SOUTH CAROLINA CAKE.

One small cup of butter, two cups of sugar, three cups of flour, four eggs, half a tea-spoonsful of soda, half a tea-cupful of milk, a little brandy, and a cup of raisins.

CIDER CAKE

One cupful of sugar, one cupful of butter, mix them together, and break in two or three eggs; then add one cupful of flour, one nutmeg, and one tea-spoonful of saleratus; put into it one cupful of cider, or pour the cider foaming over it; then add two cups full of flour; mix the whole well together, and bake it three quarters of an hour.

CONNECTICUT COFFEE CAKE.

Two eggs, two cups of sugar, one cup of coffee (liquid), three fourths cup of butter, three cups of flour, one tea-spoonful each of cloves, cinnamon, and nutmeg, one tea-spoonful of cream of tartar, and one half tea-spoonful of soda.

FRIED CAKES WITHOUT EGGS OR MILK.

Melt a small table-spoonful of lard in a pint of hot water; add a heaping tea-spoonful of salt. Mix in smoothly a tea-spoonful of soda, two tea-spoonsful of cream of tartar, and sufficient sifted flour to make a batter; add a coffee cup of sugar, and a little nutmeg if desired, and work the dough quickly, but thoroughly. Roll it out thin, cut into round cakes and fry immediately.

FRIED CAKES.

Two cups sugar, two cups sweet milk, half-cup butter, two eggs, two tea-spoonsful cream of tartar, one tea-spoon soda, a pinch of salt, spice. Add flour in sufficient quantity to roll in shape, and fry in hot lard.

GINGER POUND CAKE WITH FRUIT.

Three quarters of a pound of sugar, three quarters of a pound of butter, two pounds of flour, six eggs, one quart of molasses, half a pound of currants, quarter of a pound of raisins, three table-spoonsful of ginger, one tea-spoonful of cloves, two tea-spoonsful of cinnamon, three tea-spoonsful of baking powder dissolved in a few spoonsful of milk. Bake one hour.

CRULLERS.

Three eggs, one cup of sugar, half a cup of butter, one cup of milk, three tea-spoonsful of baking powder, nutmeg, cinnamon, and lemon juice to taste, flour sufficient to stiffen. Cut in stripes and fry in lard.

CUP CAKE.—1.

Three cups of flour, one cup of butter, two cups of sugar, four eggs, a tea-spoonful of saleratus, nutmeg, and essence of lemon.

CUP CAKE.—2.

Cream half a cup of butter, with three cups of sugar, by beating; stir in five eggs; dissolve a small tea-spoonful of soda in a cup of sweet milk; add six cups of sifted flour; stir all well together, and if too thick, add a little more milk, without any more soda. Flavor with essence of lemon, and a little grated nutmeg. Stir all well together, and bake in three pans.

MOLASSES CUP CAKE.

Butter one half cup, molasses one cup, sugar one cup, sweet milk one cup, three eggs, three cups of flour, one large tablespoonful of ginger, half tea-spoonful of salt, one tea-spoonful of soda dissolved in molasses. Mix butter and sugar together well first, then add the other ingredients, eggs well-beaten being the last. This is very good.

CAKE WITHOUT EGGS.

One pint of sour milk, a pint and a half or two pints of flour, one pound of raisins, one cup of butter, three cups of sugar, a spoonful of saleratus, and spice to taste. Mix together and bake an hour.

HARD TIMES MOLASSES CAKE.

One large cup of molasses, one cup of sugar, one cup of buttermilk, half a cup of butter, one tea-spoonful of soda, one tablespoonful of ginger, four cups of flour. Good sweet dripping, or part lard, and part butter may be used. When lard is used instead of butter, it should have a little salt worked into it. This is very good.

JENNY'S CAKES.

One cup of sweet milk, one small cup of sugar, two spoonsful of cream of tartar, one spoonful of soda, a very little salt and nutmeg; mix very thin with sifted flour, and bake thin and quick.

MARY'S TEA-CAKE.

Two eggs, beaten well, with one cup of sugar, then add one cup of sour milk, one half cup of butter, or pork drippings, one spoonful of soda, one half tea-spoonful of essence of lemon, and a little salt; mix about as stiff as pound cake, and bake in a loaf.

BIRTHDAY CAKES.

Into a pound of dried flour, put four ounces of butter, four ounces of sugar, one egg, a tea-spoonful of baking powder, and sufficient milk to wet to a paste. Put in currants, and cut in cakes. Sprinkle colored caraway seeds on top, and bake them a light brown.

SOCIETY CAKES.

One quart of sponge, three cups of sugar, one cup of butter, three eggs, saleratus, half a pound of stoned raisins, spice it and bake slowly.

SALLY LUNN.

Six cups of light dough, one-half cup of milk, one-half cup of butter, two eggs, and two spoonsful of white sugar; add flour enough to make it the consistency of thick batter, mix well, and pour in greased cake-pans; let them set in a warm place one-half hour, and bake by a slow fire.

SALLY LUNN BREAD.

One quart of milk, a little soda, three eggs, one tea cup of sugar, piece of butter the size of an egg, yeast sufficient for two loaves of bread. Make a stiff batter. Bake twenty minutes.

CHRISTMAS CAKES FOR GOOD CHILDREN.

Three heaping table-spoonsful of sugar, two heaping table-spoonsful of butter, one egg, two table-spoonsful of corn-starch or maizena, put into three cups of flour, a small cup of sweet milk, a heaping tea-spoonful of cream of tartar, and half of soda, a pinch of salt, a few Zante currants. Roll out in powdered sugar, cut in strips, and twist them round like champagne cakes. Sprinkle over them colored caraway comfits. Bake quick, a light brown.

JUMBLES.

Sift four cups of flour; cream two cups of nice brown sugar, and half a pound—a small tea-cup—of butter is near enough; beat two eggs very light, grate a little nutmeg, add one-half a tea-spoonful of soda in half a cup of sweet milk; add flour enough to roll into cakes; handle as little as possible; bake in a long tin pan, in a quick oven.

WONDERS.

Table-spoonful of butter, one of sugar, one egg, a little spice. Mix stiff, with flour, and boil in lard.

ROCK CAKES.

With a pound of dried flour mix a third of a pound of powdered sugar, quarter of a pound of fresh butter beaten to a cream, three well-beaten eggs and half a pound of dried currants, washed; beat them all well together, and flavor with nutmeg and lemon peel grated, pounded mace and a spoonful of brandy. Prepare the baking plates by sprinkling a little flour on them, and drop the batter on them with a spoon, a spoonful at a time. The batter should be stiff, so that the top of the cakes will remain rough. Stick them with blanched almonds sliced, and bake them in a slack oven until of a light color.

SHREWSBURY CAKE.

Sift three pounds of flour, and a pound of sugar, flavor it with cinnamon and nutmeg; beat three eggs with half a pound of melted butter, so that it will be of a proper consistency to roll into paste; knead it well, roll it out and cut in small cakes, prick them, and bake them in a brisk oven.

NEW ENGLAND DOUGHNUTS.

Two cups of sugar, one half a cup of butter, one pound of flour, one nutmeg, one tea-spoonful of cinnamon, one-half cup of baker's yeast. Mix into a dough, with warm milk, and set it to rise. When light, roll out half an inch thick, and cut into diamonds. Boil in a small iron kettle, in lard which is boiling hot, but must not be allowed to burn. Turn when brown on one side, and take them up with a fish slice.

DOUGHNUTS.

One quart of milk, three eggs, one and one quarter pounds of sugar, three fourths of a pound of butter; add ginger, nutmeg, and a small cup of yeast.

COOKIES.

Two cups of sugar, one half cup of butter, one cup of sweet milk, one tea-spoonful of baking powder, caraway seeds, flour enough to roll. These are deliciously light and tender.

PARTY PUFFS.

Make a rich paste, roll out thin, and cut with a biscuit-cutter. Lay them on a shallow tin pan, which has been buttered, and roll out a puff-paste, which cut of the same size. In the centre of each of the pieces of puff paste cut a hole with a small wine glass, leaving a rim, which place on the top of your first pieces of paste, and bake all together a light brown. Before putting in the oven, brush them over with sweetened white of egg; it greatly improves the appearance. Fill with jelly or sweetmeats of any kind.

ENGLISH BUNS.

Rub well together three and a half pounds of flour, and three quarters of a pound of butter; mix it with sweet milk heated, half a pint of ale yeast, spice, and caraway seeds; knead it into a light paste, and put it before the fire to rise. Then work in three quarters of a pound of sugar, roll it rather thin, cut into buns, place them before the fire to rise again, then bake in a quick oven.

BUNS.

Half a cupful of yeast, one and a half cupsful of sweet milk, or water, half a cupful of sugar, stir to a thick batter; let it rise over night, in the morning add one cupful of sugar, half a cupful of butter, a small tea-spoonful of saleratus; stir as stiff as biscuit; let it stand until light, mould, raise and bake. They are excellent warm, for tea.

GINGER SNAPS.

One pint of molasses, one tea-spoonful of butter and lard, mixed, two even tea-spoonsfuls of soda, dissolved in two thirds of a tea-cupful of boiling water, two table-spoonsful of ginger; mix as quickly as possible, with flour enough to roll out thin, and bake quickly to a light brown. Sorghum molasses is preferred. They will keep any length of time.

GINGER NUTS.

Take three quarters of a pound of butter, a pint of molasses, and half a pound of sugar. Melt them together, and when cold mix it with three pounds of flour, half an ounce of ginger, and a little lemon juice.

SPONGE GINGERBREAD.

One cup of sour milk, one cup of molasses, half a cup of butter, one or two eggs, one and a half tea-spoonful of soda, one large spoonful of ginger, and flour to make it as thick as pound cake; put the butter, molasses, and ginger together, and make them quite warm, then add the flour, milk, and soda together, and bake as soon as possible.

HARD TIMES GINGERBREAD.

Two cups of molasses, one cup of sugar, three parts of a cup of butter, or sweet dripping, a coffee cup of water, a teaspoonful of saleratus, a table or tea-spoonful of ginger. Knead soft, roll half an inch thick. Bake quick.

RICE CHEESE CAKES.—1.

Beat three eggs, the whites separately, and four ounces of white sugar together, then take half a pound of finely sifted ground rice, a quarter of a pound of butter, mix all together, with a small blade of mace finely pounded, and the peel of two lemons, rubbed on sugar. The cheese cakes to be light must be made very quick.

Pour the batter into little tins not quite full, and bake in a brisk oven. Eaten cold.

RICE CHEESE CAKES.—2.

Boil a quarter of a pound of rice till tender in three pints of milk, put in four eggs, quarter of a pound of butter, half a pint of cream, six ounces of sugar, a lemon extract, nutmeg. Beat well, and put in paste in small saucers, or patty-pans, and bake.

ENGLISH CHEESE CAKES.

Take six ounces of potatoes, and the peel of four lemons; boil them together until tender, and then beat thoroughly the lemon-peel, with a quarter of a pound of sugar; and the potatoes with the same quantity of butter, and a little cream or milk, into which an egg has been beaten. Mix all well together, with a few nicely cleaned Zante currants, and bake in patty-pans, lined with rich paste, half an hour. Sift sugar over them.

APPLE CHEESE CAKES.—1.

Pare, core, and boil twelve apples, with enough water to mash them; beat them up very smooth, then add three eggs, the juice of two lemons and some grated peel, quarter of a pound of fresh butter, beaten into a cream and sweetened with pounded loaf sugar; beat all well in with the apples, bake it in a puff paste, and send it up like an open tart.

APPLE CHEESE CAKE.—2.

Pare, core, and boil twelve apples, with enough water to mash them; beat them up very smooth, and add the yolks of six eggs, the juice of two lemons, and some grated peel, a quarter of a pound of fresh butter, beaten into a cream, and sweetened with pounded loaf sugar; beat all well in with the apples. Bake it in a puff paste, and send it up like open tarts. It is well to make a silver cake with these apple cheese cakes, as it makes a fine addition to the table, and uses up the whites of the eggs.

BREAD CHEESE CAKES.

Slice up a large French roll very thin, pour on it some boiling milk; when cold, add four eggs, quarter of a pound of butter melted, some nutmeg, a spoonful of essence of lemon, a little sugar, and half a pound of currants; when mixed together, pour the mixture into puff paste as other cheese-cakes.

COCOANUT CHEESE CAKES.

Half a cocoanut, three ounces of lump sugar in half a quarter of a pint of water, the sugar being first dissolved in the water, and then the cocoanut, grated, to be added; let this boil for a few minutes over a slow fire, and, when cold, add to it the beaten yolks of three eggs and the white of one; put the mixture into tins with puff paste, and bake them in a slow oven.

ALMOND CHEESE CAKES.

The yolks of three eggs well beaten, a quarter of a pound of bitter and quarter of a pound of sweet almonds, and a quarter pound of sifted sugar. The almonds must be pounded, but not very finely. The eggs should be beaten to a cream, and the sugar mixed with them, and then the almonds added. To be put into tartlet tins lined with puff paste.

NEW YEAR'S BISCUITS.

Boil a pound and a quarter of lump sugar, upon which you have rubbed the rind of a lemon, in half a pint of milk; when cold, rub half a pound of butter with two pounds of flour, make a hole in the centre, pour in the milk, with as much carbonate of soda as would lie upon a sixpence, and a couple of eggs; mix the whole into a smooth paste, lay it out upon your baking-sheet in whatever flat shapes you please, and bake them in a very warm oven. The proper way to shape these biscuits is by wooden blocks having pineapples, leaves, and other devices carved on them.

CREAM BISCUIT.

Rub one pound of fresh butter into one pound of flour, make a hole in the centre into which put half a pound of powdered sugar, upon which the rind of a lemon was rubbed previously to pounding, and three eggs; mix the eggs well with sugar, and then mix all together, forming a flexible paste; cut it into round pieces each nearly as large as a walnut; stamp them flat with a small stamp, and bake them in a slack oven.

APPLE BISCUIT.

Boil apples in water until soft, then take them out and rub through a wire sieve; flavor with a drop or two of essence or of of lemon, and, if you like the taste, a drop of the oil of cloves. Add lump sugar equal in weight to the pulp, and grind it with it; roll the sugared pulp into flat cakes about a quarter of an inch thick, and cut them into shapes. Finally dry them in a very slow oven, the heat not being strong enough to bake them or melt the sugar; they may be dried also by the summer's sun. They often require to be partially dried before they can be rolled out. They may, instead of rolling, be dropped on to paper, or put in a ring of paper upon a slightly greased iron plate.

ORANGE BISCUITS.

Grate the rind from five oranges, and put into a mortar with quarter of a pound of sweet almonds, three quarters of a pound of pounded lump sugar, and the whites of one or two eggs, and mix it well together with the pestle until it is very light. Drop the mixture, when ready, in small lumps about the size of a walnut, on doubled paper, laid on a baking tin, and put them into moderately hot oven. Do not drop them too near together on the paper, as they spread while baking. When they are baked take them out, and take them off the paper when they are cold.

MOSS BISCUITS.

Weigh half a pound of flour, to which add an ounce and a half of butter and five ounces of sugar, rub them well together, and mix with one whole and one white of egg, and a tea-spoonful of milk; then add two ounces of ground almonds, which rub well into the paste; afterwards rub the whole through a gauze wire sieve, taking it off in small pieces, which lay upon a lightly buttered baking sheet, and bake them in a moderate oven.

GINGER BISCUITS.

One pound of flour, half a pound of butter, turned to a cream, half-a-pound of white sugar sifted. These to be well mixed; then add the yolks and whites of three eggs, beaten separately, with two ounces of powdered ginger. These last mix gradually with the rest. Roll out thin and cut it into biscuits; bake them on tins in a quick oven.

JUDGE'S BISCUITS.

Break six eggs into a basin, whisk them well for five minutes; put in half a pound of powdered sugar, and whisk again for ten minutes. Add some cararway seeds, if liked, and half a pound of dry sifted flour, mixing all thoroughly. Drop the mixture on paper, each being the size of about a silver quarter dollar and high in the middle. Sift sugar over them and bake them. Remove them from the paper while they are hot. A wooden spoon is the best to stir with.

KING'S BISCUITS.

Put half a pound of butter into a basin and turn it about well. Whisk six eggs well, add half a pound of powdered sugar, whisk another ten minutes, and then mix with the butter, after which stir in six ounces of currants, and an equal quantity of dried flour. After mixing these all well together, drop the mixture on paper and bake in a quick oven, taking the biscuits off the paper while hot.

GRAHAM FIG BISCUIT.

Wash and scald figs and mix with enough Graham flour to make a good dough by much kneading; roll and cut into biscuits half an inch thick, bake quickly.

MACAROONS.

Scald a pound of almonds, let them lie awhile in cold water, then dry them, and mash them together. Moisten them in the white of an egg to prevent them turning into oil, and then take an equal quantity of powdered sugar, and the whites of four eggs. Mix the whole well together, shape them on wafer-paper and bake on thin plates in a mild oven.

COCOANUT CAKES.

Scrape off the rind and grate the nut quite fine, and mix it with half its weight of finely pounded white sugar, and the white of an egg. Drop the mixture on wafer paper in rough pieces, the size of a nutmeg, and bake it in a moderate oven.

ICING.

To ice a good sized cake, put eight ounces of powdered sugar into a mortar with four spoonsfuls of rose water, and the whites of two eggs, beating and straining it. Then whisk it well, and when the cake is almost cold cover it with the iceing evenly, using a feather or knife. Put it in the oven to harden, but not long enough to discolor it, and keep it in a very dry place.

CHOCOLATE ICING.

A cup of milk, a quarter of a pound of good chocolate, one cup of powdered sugar, one tea-spoonful of vanilla. Scald the milk and chocolate, then add the sugar, and pour it on the well-beaten white of an egg. This will ice a good sized cake or pudding. An almond iceing is given in the receipt for a bride cake.

PRESERVED FRUITS AND SWEETMEATS.

CANNING FRUIT.

This new method recommends itself, not only on account of its health, but its economy, especially since the price of sugar has become so enormous as to be almost prohibitory. Properly put up in the right kind of cans, there are many fruits which require no sugar, and even the most acid only a very little, say, one fourth of the weight; it should, however, be of the finest quality.

BLACKBERRIES.

Use the zinc-covered, self-sealing jars, as the covers of these can be screwed down without difficulty, while the jars are in the water, and we have never known fruit to spoil in them.

Fill the jars with fruit and sugar in the proportion of one pound of crushed sugar to four pounds of fruit. Set them in cold water (a wash boiler is as good as any thing for the purpose), which heat to boiling. The jars, by the way, should not be filled to within an inch of the top, and when the boiling process, by expelling the air, has forced the fruit up to the top of the jar, it is exactly the time to put on the cover, and with a small holder in the left hand, to keep the fingers from being burnt, screw it tight down, before taking the jar from the water.

Cherries, raspberries and plums, may be preserved in precisely the same way; peaches and pears also, omitting the sugar, which they do not require, as they keep just as well without.

STRAWBERRY JAM.

Separate the hulls from the berries, for each pound of berries weigh out three quarters of a pound of pounded sugar; put the berries in a deep dish sprinkling the sugar among it, and let them remain ten or twelve hours, then boil them together half an hour very slowly.

RASPBERRY JAM.

This should be made in the same manner as strawberry jam. Let it boil, after it commences to do so, fifteen or twenty minutes; another way is to bruise together a quart of raspberries, and a pint of currant jelly; boil them slowly six or seven minutes, stirring them; then put into close pots. This will keep two years.

STRAWBERRIES IN CANS.

Half a pound of sugar to every pound of berries; scald them together, fill the cans while hot, and seal at once.

DRIED STRAWBERRIES

Put ten pounds of strawberries into a jar, and sprinkle among them four pounds of white sugar. Let them stand until the next day, then scald them and put them back into the jar. On the third day, put another pound of sugar over them and scald them again, pour out on plates, or dishes, and dry them in a cool oven, or the back part of the range. They must be kept in tin canisters, and will make a very good dessert dish in winter.

STRAWBERRY JAM.

Boil the strawberries gently until thick, and very much reduced; add loaf sugar, three quarters of a pound to a pound of fruit, and stir constantly, until it is reduced to a paste. Put in small jars, and cover with egg paper—that is paper covered on the under side with white of egg,—and tie down a second paper over them.

PRESERVED RASPBERRIES.

Take five or six pounds of red, but not too ripe raspberries; pick and put them into a preserving pan, with an equal weight of clarified sugar; when they have boiled up about a dozen times, skim and pour the whole into a pan, till the next day; then drain the fruit and put it into jars; put to the syrup about two glasses of cherry juice, previously strained; boil the sugar again, and pour it over the raspberries; add afterwards about a spoonful of currant juice to each pot, and when cold, lay on brandy paper, and tie them down.

CURRANT AND RASPBERRIES SWEETMEAT.

Take equal weight of red currants and raspberries, and of sugar, three quarters of a pound of best loaf, to each pound of fruit. Cover the fruit with the sugar over night, and the next day boil all together slowly for an hour, skimming if necessary. Put in small jars, and fasten down while hot, with egg, or brandy paper. It will keep well, and makes a delicious sweetmeat.

CHERRY JAM.

Stone four pounds of Kentish cherries, add to them half a pint red currant juice and a pound of fine sugar, and boil all together briskly till the mixture becomes stiff.

GREEN GRAPE JAM.

Put the grapes in a jar, and let them cook in a kettle of boiling water, until they are soft, and can be separated from the seeds. Strain through a fine colander, and to every pound of grape, put a pound of crushed sugar. Boil all together very gently, until a thick jam is formed, and then put in small moulds, or glasses, and cover with egg paper.

PLUM JAM.

Prepare the plums by skinning and stoning them, allow three quarters of a pound of finely pounded loaf sugar to one pound of fruit; lay them in a deep dish over night with the sugar sprinkled among them, and in the morning let them boil twenty minutes, after they have become sufficiently hot to bubble over their whole surface.

PINEAPPLE JAM.

Cut the pineapple into small slices and then into square pieces, removing all the skin and eyes. Allow three quarters of a pound of loaf sugar to a pound of pineapple, and boil them very slowly twenty-five or thirty minutes.

BLACK CURRANT JAM.

Boil together for quarter of an hour after it commences to bubble, stirring well a mixture composed of a pint of juice of red currants, and a pound and a quarter of pounded loaf sugar, to each pound of currants.

PRESERVED CHERRIES.

Stone the fruit, weigh it, and for every pound, take three quarters of a pound of loaf sugar. First dissolve the sugar in water, in the proportion of a pint of water to a pound and a half of sugar. Then add the fruit, and let it boil as fast as possible for half an hour, till it begins to jelly, as it soon thickens by keeping. Put it in pots, cover with brandy paper next the fruit, and then closely from the air.

PICKLED CHERRIES.

Procure white "ox-heart" cherries, leave the stems on, and prepare for eight pounds of fruit, four pounds of sugar, two quarts very best vinegar, a little cloves and double the bulk in cinnamon, mace and ginger root. Boil the vinegar, sugar and spices, skimming thoroughly. Put the fruit in bottles, strain the syrup over it, screw them down, and put them in a kettle of boiling water for ten minutes. When they look like cracking they are done.

PINE APPLE MARMALADE.

Boil together for each pound of grated pineapple a pound of double refined loaf sugar. When it is boiled thick, which will be in about fifteen minutes, if the quantity is small, or more if large, put it in tumblers, and paste over them papers wet with the beaten whites of eggs. Keep it in a dry, cool place.

PRESERVED QUINCES.

Peel and core them, put in the kettle, and cover them with the parings, cores, and considerable water. Cover close and boil till tender; then take out the quinces, strain off the liquor, and to every pint add one pound of loaf-sugar. Boil it a few minutes, skim, put in the quinces, and boil slowly twenty minutes, or until they are clear.

CRAB APPLES PRESERVED.

Weigh the apples, and with an equal weight of sugar make a syrup with apple jelly, and after this is well boiled, prick the crab-apples and put them into it. When they have boiled a few minutes, take them out, and let them drain on a sieve. Put them again into the syrup, when they are nearly cold, and after boiling a few minutes more, drain them as before. Repeat this process a third time, and afterwards place them in glasses or jars, pouring the boiling jelly over them.

BRANDY GAGES.

Take green gages, wash and wipe them dry, prick them on opposite sides and pack them in bottles or jars, with mouths large enough to let the fruit in without pressing. Prepare a very rich syrup, let it cool to blood heat, mix in the proportion of one third syrup to two of brandy, mix thoroughly, fill the bottles, cork, and seal perfectly air tight. If syrup is left, bottle it for future use. If the skins are tough remove them.

PRESERVED PINEAPPLES.

Peel the pineapples, cut out the eyes, slice them and cut out the hard centre. Then boil them till tender; skim the liquid and add to it three quarters of a pound of sugar to a pound of pine apple. Boil it, skim it again and put in the fruit, and boil it till clear of soft, or put in lemons and one pound of sugar.

GREEN FIGS PRESERVED.

Take half ripe figs, and prick them near the stalk, scald them and when half cold throw them into cold water and let them drain. Boil clarified sugar in a covered preserving pan, put in the figs, let them boil three or four times; then take them from the fire, skim them well and put them in a warm place over night. In the morning drain off the syrup, boil it up a dozen times, and when lukewarm pour it on the figs. Let it stand till the next day, drain it off and boil it up again, then add the figs to it, boil them together once in the covered preserving pan, skim again, and put in jars for use.

TO PRESERVE PLUMS OR DAMSONS WHOLE.

Weigh your fruit, and to every pound allow three quarters of crushed sugar. Put into stone jars alternate layers of fruit and sugar, tie down with cloth, and let them stand in an oven after bread has been baked in it, until it is cold. The next day strain off the syrup, boil and clarify it, and pour over the fruit, which in the mean time has been carefully removed to glass jars or china pots. Place over them egg tissue-paper, and over that thick white paper pasted, or bladder tied strongly down.

Another method is to put the plums into water over a slow fire until they begin to peel, keeping them under the water, then take the skins off carefully and put them into a jar with enough thin syrup to cover them completely. Boil the syrup next day, put the plums in, boil gently, allow them to stand till cold; repeat the process, turning them in the syrup till nearly cold. Take the plums out, strain the syrup, add more sugar, skim it, put the plums in again and boil them till they become quite clear, then put them in jars and tie them down with paper.

CURRANTS PRESERVED.

Scald a few of the currants at a time until all are done, put sugar into the juice in the proportion of a pound of sugar to a pound of currants, and boil a few minutes; then put the currants back into the syrup, and boil them up once.

RHUBARB PRESERVED.

Pare half a dozen oranges, remove the seeds and white rind, slice the pulp into a stew pan with the peel cut very small. Then add a quart of rhubarb cut fine, and a pound and a half of loaf sugar; boil the whole down as for other preserves. This is almost equal to Scotch marmalade.

ORANGES PRESERVED.

To preserve oranges whole, grate the rinds slightly, and score them round with a knife, or cut the rinds into scollops or any other pattern, not cutting deep; then put them into cold water for three days, changing the water two or three times a day; afterwards tie them up in a bag, and boil them in water until a pin's head will penetrate their skins easily. Take a pound and a half of white sugar to every pound of oranges, and while they are boiling, put the sugar on the fire with rather more than half a pint of water to each pound. Let it boil a minute or two, and then strain it through muslin. Then put the oranges into the syrup, and boil until the syrup will jelly and is of a nice yellow color; it cannot be too stiff. The syrup need not cover the oranges, but they must be turned so that each part gets thoroughly done.

PICKLING PEARS AND PEACHES.

This is a very nice way of preserving these fruits, particularly for those who like such a relish with cold meats. Select smooth freestone peaches, and medium sized juicy pears, and stick them full of cloves, that is to say, like pins upon a pincushion, heads up; and perhaps half an inch apart. Boil together, either the syrup left from dried fruit, and vinegar, in the proportions mentioned in the receipt for drying plums and small fruit, or seven pounds of good Orleans sugar to one gallon of good vinegar, an ounce of mace, and an ounce of allspice. When it boils, put in the fruit, and let it all boil gently together, until a pin will slip in and out easily. Then take the fruit out in jars, boil the spiced and sweetened vinegar for a few minutes longer, and then pour over fruit and set it away to cool. When cold, fasten thick paper over the lids with paste or mucilage.

DAMSON PLUMS, (*To pickle.*)

To two pounds of plums, take one pound of brown sugar, and one pint of vinegar, tea-spoonful of mace, one of cinnamon; boil them well, and pour it on the fruit hot; when cold, drain it off, boil it and pour it on again, repeating it six times.

PEACHES DRIED WITH SUGAR.

Peel yellow peaches, cut them from the stone in one piece, allow two pounds of sugar for six pounds of the fruit, make a syrup of three quarters pound of sugar and a little water, put in the peaches and let them stay till they are quite clear, take them up carefully on a dish and set them in the sun to dry. Strew powdered sugar over them on all sides, a little at a time, and if any syrup is left remove them to fresh dishes. When they are quite dry lay them lightly in a jar with a little sugar between each layer.

TO DRY PLUMS AND SMALL FRUITS.

A very good method is to pit them, and put in jars, a layer of fruit to a layer of sugar, in the proportion of half a pound of sugar to a pound of fruit. Let them stand twenty-four hours, and then boil them, taking the scum off, as it rises to the surface. When they have boiled ten minutes, take them out of the syrup, drain them, and spread them thin on dishes, or hair sieves, to dry in the sun; they will need turning every few hours, until dry.

The syrup that is left can be used, in the proportion of a large pint to a small quart of good vinegar, for pickling pears or peaches,—the method for doing which is explained in the receipt under that head.

Another method for drying plums, peaches and apples, is to prepare them nicely, by pitting or peeling and cutting, dry them partly, and then lay them in jars, strewing sugar between each layer. Tie them down, and they will keep well, and be delicious for pies, or stewing.

Some people are troubled with insects among fruit, when it is kept a long time. A handful of sassafras bark thrown among it will keep it free from worms.

PRESERVED CITRON.

Pare ripe citron melons, and cut them into half-moon shaped pieces, about half an inch in thickness. Boil in soda water until tender, when a straw will pass through them; skim them out and lay them in weak alum water; let them remain three hours; then put them in cold water for another hour. Then take one quart of water, four pounds of sugar, and the same weight of citron; boil this syrup and remove the scum; when clear put in the citron, let it remain till the sugar has penetrated it thoroughly; then pack it in jars. Boil the syrup until it is ropy, and pour it in the jars. Flavor with extract of ginger. Add to each quart jar a tablespoonful of extract of lemon peel, and seal them as soon as filled, with paper wet in egg.

APPLE SWEETMEATS.

Procure fresh gathered ripe apples, of a fine sort; peel them, take out the cores, and cut them in quarters; place them in a preserving pan with a glass of water; a little lemon or orange peel, and a pound of sugar to a pound and a half of fruit. Let it boil thoroughly, and then put it into preserve pots.

APPLE PRESERVE.

Peel and weigh ten pounds of apples; stew them in a pan, with one pint of water; when they are quite tender put in eight pounds of pounded sugar, two ounces of ground ginger, the juice and grated rind of four or five lemons; let it boil half an hour or more, stirring it all the time, then put it in small jars or moulds.

APPLE BUTTER.

Take ten gallons of new sweet cider, before it has fermented; put it into a brass kettle; if the kettle will not hold all of the cider, put in a part, and set it a-boiling; skim it, and as it boils away keep adding, until you have put in all the cider; boil down to about five gallons. For the ten gallons of cider, take half a bushel of quarters of apples; part quince gives it a fine flavor. Now wash and drain the apples, put them into the boiled cider, and when they are soft, it must be stirred constantly until finished. It requires a stick formed in such a way as to keep moving on the bottom of the kettle, to prevent the apple from sticking and burning. Have a slow fire, and attend carefully to the stirring at the bottom of the kettle. If for winter use, from one to two hours' boiling, after the apples first begin to boil, is sufficient; or a longer time if thought proper. Before taking it from the fire, season with spice, cinnamon and cloves, to suit the taste. Remove the kettle from the fire, dip the apple butter while hot into well glazed crocks, or stone jars; then set away to cool. When cold, cut paper covers for each crock; soak it in apple-jack, lay it inside of the vessel, on the apple butter, and cover it close. A barrel of cider may be boiled down to about ten gallons, observing the same proportions as given above.

TO PREVENT WASTE IN APPLES.

An excellent way to prevent waste in apples, is to pick out all that are beginning to speck, peel, cut up and stew as for sauce, and fill into air-tight cans. As canned fruit is used through the fall and winter, the cans can be re-filled in this way with apples, and in that way they will be preserved for pies or sauce till summer.

PRESERVED PIPPINS.

Pippins and bell-flowers make a delicious preserve. Take half a pound of sugar to each pound of fruit, make a syrup in which boil the fruit till clear, take out the fruit and boil the syrup till thick; add extract of lemon to taste, and pour over the fruit to prevent the necessity of long boiling, which injures the taste and looks of preserves; they can be put while boiling into tin cans and sealed.

PRESERVED CUCUMBERS.

Split the cucumbers and extract the seeds. Let them remain for three days in salt and water. Put them now into cold water, with a small quantity of alum, and boil them till tender. Drain them and allow them to lie in a thin syrup for two days; then take them out, boiling the syrup again, and pour it over the cucumbers, repeating this operation twice more. Now boil some clarified sugar until, when a spoonful of it is taken up and blown through, small sparks of sugar will fly from it; put the cucumbers into this and let them simmer five minutes. Leave them until the next day, when the whole must be boiled up again, and afterwards put by for use.

VEGETABLE MARROW PRESERVED.

Soak the vegetable marrow twelve hours in salt and water, then pare it, remove the seeds and soft part, cut it into small, thick, square pieces. Boil it in water until tender, put in a little prepared cochineal to color it; then strain it. Make a syrup of powdered sugar, boil in it two sliced lemons and a quarter of a pound of whole ginger; when cold, put in the vegetable marrow and let it stand two days. Pour off the syrup, add more sugar to it, boil it again and add it to the vegetable marrow; remove the vegetable marrow, boil-it up several times till the syrup is strong and transparent, and the last time you do so boil the vegetable marrow in the syrup. An equal weight of sugar and vegetable marrow is used in making the syrup.

TOMATO FIGS.

Take pear shaped, or small single tomatoes, scald and skin them, then to half a peck or eight pounds of them, take three pounds of brown sugar. Cook them with sugar over a fire without water, until the sugar penetrates and they are clarified. Take them out, spread on dishes, flatten them and dry in the sun. Sprinkle on a little syrup while drying, after which pack down in boxes treating each layer with powdered sugar; the syrup that is left can be boiled down and bottled for use. They will keep from year to year, retaining their flavor, which is nearly like that of fresh figs.

PRESERVED ARTICHOKES.

Cook them half done, then separate the leaves from the fur and preserve the fleshy part called "the bottom," and turn them still warm into cold water to make them firm. Afterwards put them into the oven four different times, when they will become thin, hard and transparent. They may be eaten raw with salad sauce.

CANDIED ORANGE PEEL RINGS.

Cut some Seville oranges in half, remove the pulp, and let the peel soak for three days in strong salt and spring water. This must be repeated three times, after which the peel should be placed on a sieve to dry. Put one pound of loaf sugar to one quart of water, boil it, and skim it until quite clear. Double the orange peel, and cut it across in narrow strips which, when opened, will, of course, form rings. Let these simmer in the sugar until quite transparent, and then dry them before the fire. Make a syrup of the best loaf sugar using only enough water to dissolve it; and while it is boiling put in the rings, stirring continually until the sugar is candied round them, then put them to dry before the fire or in a cool oven.

PREPARING CITRON FOR CAKE.

Boil the citron in soda water until it is clear or tender, have ready a nice syrup of sugar; put in the citron, and boil until the sugar has struck through it; take it out on plates to dry slowly, sprinkle pulverized sugar on both sides, two or three times until it is dried enough. Then pack it in wooden boxes, with sugar between the layers. It is nearly as nice as bought citron.

FRIED PUMPKIN.

Select the ripest and largest. Peel and stew them dry, then spread out on plates and dry in a cool oven until all the moisture is extracted. It will then be a dry, hard, thin layer, which may be packed away in tin cans, or boxes, in a dry place until required for use. Be careful to *dry*, and not to cook or bake it while in the oven. When required for use, soak it over night in sweet milk.

TOMATO SWEETMEATS.

Scald and remove the skin, slice them thinly and stew them in sugar like other preserves, using the best kind of sugar,— three quarters of a pound, for a pound of tomatoes.

JELLIES. HOW TO MAKE THEM.

APPLE JELLY.

Take one dozen of the largest apples, pare and slice them into three quarts and one pint of water. Put them into a tin pan, and boil them until they become a pulp and one half of the water is consumed. Pour it into a jelly-bag, and after it has done running, press what juice you can from the bag. To every pint of juice add one pound of white sugar; set the juice and sugar on the fire and let them boil twenty minutes skimming it all the time. Add lemon juice and peel to taste. Pour it into tea-cups or jelly-glasses at hand, and turn it out entire. The above quantity of apples will make about three pints of juice. Remember, after you have pared one apple, slice it immediately into the water, and do not pare them all together; moreover, let them lie, or it will render them red, and you will lose a great quantity of the apple juice. Golden pippin apples make the finest jelly. It is necessary to be very careful about over-boiling all fruit jellies, else they soon spoil; fifteen to twenty minutes after the sugar has been added is generally sufficient. It is also important to put jellies and jams into the moulds or jars, the moment they are taken from the fire.

Another method from the French is as follows:—Choose fine-flavored, jucy, ripe apples, peel them, and cut them into quarters, putting them into water as they are cut, to prevent their turning black. When they are all cut, place them in the preserving-pan and put to them just water enough to cover them. Let them cook until they are quite soft; take them out of the preserving-pan, place them in a seive, and let the juice drain from them. Boil the juice with an equal weight of sugar until it will jelly, (when tested by placing a little on a cold plate,) and pour it into the jelly jars. Quince jelly may be made in the same manner. If it is desired to have the apple jelly of a full pink tinge, let a ittle cochineal be put into it, and that will give it color.

MRS. WEBSTER'S WINE JELLY.

Take of American isinglass four ounces; dissolve it in three quarts of hot water; add one half ounce of stick cinnamon, the juice of two, and the peel of one lemon, one and one half pounds of pure white sugar; let it all come to a boil slowly, then add a gill of Maderia wine and let it simmer a while longer; then strain it twice through a jelly bag, and set it to cool; the extract of saffron colors it beautifully.

CRAB APPLE JELLY.

Fill your preserving kettle with apples; then cover with water. Boil until they are very soft. Drain the water off through a cloth, and add to each pint of the water, one pound of white sugar. Let the water come to a boil, before adding the sugar. Then boil five minutes. Turn off into glasses, or small jars, and when cold cover with thick paper.

CIDER JELLY.

Boil new cider to the consistency of syrup, adding a pound of white sugar to a gallon of cider. Skim it. Let it cool, and it will be a beautiful clear jelly, very nice to make drink for the sick or well.

CURRANT JELLY.

Fill a jar with currants, and place it in a kettle of boiling water. When the juice is expelled, strain through a cloth, and to every pint add a pound of white sugar. Boil ten minutes, skimming till it is quite clear. Black currant or grape jelly can be made in the same way.

QUINCE JELLY.

If quinces are high a jelly may be made of the peels and cores, but if the fruit is plenty, boil the whole. Allow one quart of water to ten pounds of quince. Cover the fruit and boil until tender; then pour them into a jelly bag without pressing, and let them drain into an earthen dish, no matter if until the next morning. Allow a pound of the best white sugar for every pint of juice. Place the syrup on the fire in a preserving kettle; as soon as it becomes hot, stir in the sugar, boil a few moments; and put it in moulds.

BLACKBERRY JELLY.

Boil the berry a few moments, then strain it and add one pound of sugar to one quart of juice. Boil it till it becomes a jelly.

WINE JELLY.

To one pint of wine add one ounce of isinglass, half a pound of sugar, and spice to your taste.

RICE JELLY.

Take quarter of a pound of rice flour, and half a pound of loaf sugar, boil them in a quart of water; when they become a glutinous mass strain off the jelly, add wine or lemon juice and let it cool.

TAPIOCA JELLY.

Take four table-spoonsful of tapioca, rinse it thoroughly, then soak it five hours in cold water enough to cover it. Set a pint of cold water on the fire, when it boils, mash and stir up the tapioca that is in the water, and mix it with the boiling water. Let the whole simmer gently, with a stick of cinnamon or mace. When thick and clear, mix two table-spoonsful of white sugar with half a table-spoonful of lemon juice, and a glass of white wine—stir it into the jelly; if not sweet enough, add more sugar, and turn the jelly into cups.

JELLY FROM GELATINE.

To make two quarts, take a two ounce package of the gelatine and soak for one hour in a pint of cold water; add to this one and one-half pounds of sugar, the juice of four lemons, some orange peel, stick cinnamon or other flavoring; when the gelatine is thoroughly soaked, pour on three pints of boiling water and strain immediately through a jelly bag or coarse toweling; next pour into moulds and set aside to cool; in warm weather use a little more gelatine.

CRANBERRY JELLY.

This is made like currant jelly, but it is hardly worth while to make it to keep, when it is so easily made fresh all through the winter.

SAGO JELLY.

A tea-cupful of sago, boiled in three pints and a half of water till ready. When cold, add half a pint of raspberry syrup. Pour it into a shape which has been rinsed in cold water, and let it stand until it is sufficiently set to turn out well. When dished, pour a little cream round it, if preferred.

MEDLAR JELLY.

Take medlars when they are ripe (i. e. when eatable) and put them into a preserving pan with as much water as will cover them; simmer slowly until they become a pulp, then strain through a thin jelly bag, and to every pint of juice add a qurrter of a pound lump sugar. Boil for an hour and pour into jars; when cold it will be a stiff jelly. Medlar jelly made from this recipe, in some degree resembles Guava jelly. It makes a very good addition to a winter dessert.

CALF'S FEET JELLY.

Take well cleaned calf's feet, put one quart of water to four calf's feet, and boil until reduced to one quart; then strain, and when cold, take off the top. In taking out the jelly, avoid the settlings. To the quart, put half a pound of sugar, the juice of two lemons, and clarify this with the whites of two eggs, boil all together a few moments and strain it through a cloth.

GRAPE JELLY.

Take garden grapes before they are fully ripe, pick them, and boil gently with a little water, or small cupful, until the piece flows freely, and the pulp is dissolved. Strain throgh a thin Swiss muslin bag, pressing the pulp through, and boil again for fifteen minutes before adding the sugar, a pound of loaf sugar, to every pint. Boil with the sugar fifteen minutes longer, taking off any skum that may rise. Put in moulds or glasses, and cover with egg paper. Wild grapes will make jelly, but not so firm as the cultivated ones.

FRESH FRUITS.

STRAWBERRIES AND CREAM.

Pick your strawberries over carefully; if they are dusty, wash them, by pouring water over them through a colander. Arrange them in a glass dish, sprinkling a thick layer of powdered sugar over them when it is half full, and another on the top; sugar them only a few minutes before they are to be eaten, and cover with cream or condensed milk, partially diluted, when serving. [See page 186, 187.]

PEACHES.

Peel fine juicy rareripe peaches, cut them up, cover thickly with powdered sugar, and serve with cream, or without.

HUCKLEBERRIES.

Some people like these without sugar, the best way therefore is to pick them carefully, and put them on the table in a glass dish, flanked by a bowl of powdered sugar, and a pitcher of milk, and let every one suit his or her taste. They are delicious eaten in a bowl with bread and milk, and in this way, constitute an excellent summer morning, or mid-day meal.

BLACKBERRIES.

These are best without milk, and may be sugared either before or after putting on the table. Plenty of white powdered sugar is necessary, and a little lemon juice dropped upon the sugar is an improvement.

WHITE AND RED CURRANTS.

Pick them large, and fresh from the stems, and put them either together, or separate into glass dishes; cover then thickly with white pondered sugar an hour before they are wanted, and serve with sugar in a glass bowl. Mixed white and red currants make a very pretty dish, and with plenty of sugar are delicious to eat with custard.

CURRANTS AND HUCKLEBERRIES.

Red currants, and huckleberries mixed, make a delightful and refreshing dish, the sugar should be sprinkled through them half an hour before they are eaten, served with milk, or cream. An excellent breakfast dish; the currants just imparting to the huckleberries the piquant taste that they lack.

CURRANTS AND RASPBERRIES.

These are excellent mixed, and eaten in the same way, much finer to our taste than raspberries alone, although in the absence of currants, no one would object to raspberries, which are the most delicate of all fruit, and are served precisely like strawberries.

CHERRIES.

These are less desirable than other small fruit, *uncooked*, and are liable to be infected with worms. White hearts, fine and smooth, pitted, or only sprinkled whole, with powdered sugar, are however, very nice.

YEAST, BREAD, BISCUITS, Etc.

YEAST.

Take twelve large potatoes, pare and grate them; have two single handsful of hops boiled in one quart of water; strain upon the potatoes; set the pan on the stove, and stir till it scalds; take off, and add one table-spoonful of brown sugar, one tea-spoonful of ginger; when cool, add half a pint of good brewer's yeast if it can be got, if not, take hop or cake yeast to start with, the flour will soon work out. This is always ready, does not sour quickly, and will keep two months in a cool place without needing soda. It should be put into a half gallon jug, corked, and tied down and kept in a cool place. One tea-cupful will raise two large loaves of bread.

CONNECTICUT YEAST.

Put a handful of hops in a bag, boil in two quarts of water with five pared potatoes; when done, sift the potatoes, put with them in a pan one table-spoonful of flour, half cup of sugar, half cup of salt; pour on this the boiling hop water. When sufficiently cool, add yeast enough to ferment it well, then put it in a jug, cork tight, keep in a cool place.

AN EXCELLENT YEAST.

Boil four good sized potatoes, mash or sift fine, then add one half cup of sugar, two-thirds of a cup of salt, one quart of boiling water, then put in one pint of cold water and a cup of old yeast; cover and rise over night; it will then be fit to use; one gill is sufficient for three pints of flour.

POTATO YEAST.

This does not keep long, but it is very nice to use for anything which requires raising. It is made by smoothly mashing a dozen large, mealy, boiled potatoes, into which mix a large handful of white flour and a little salt. Stir in a tea-cup of baker's yeast to make it a batter. When it is raised up light, bottle and cork it tight and put it in a cool place. It may be used without any fear of making bread or biscuit bitter, as is sometimes the case with hop yeast.

YEAST CAKES.

Stir light fresh hop yeast into Indian meal until it becomes the consistency of dough. Make this into thin cakes, and dry on a board in the oven, or where there is sun, and a current of air. Turn twice a day, until thoroughly dried, and then put them in a bag and hang in a cool, dry place. They keep good a long time.

BREAD.—1.

For about three loaves of bread, the night before baking, bake a pint of sifted flour, put it into a pan, sprinkle on two tea-spoonsfuls of cold water; then pour on it very gradually, stirring out the lumps carefully as the flour becomes wetted, a quart of boiling water. Let it stand and get nearly cold, and then add half a pint of potato yeast, mixing it in thoroughly. Let it stand in the room, not where it is too warm, over night, in the morning have ready sufficient sifted flour in the tray, then make a pint of thin cornmeal mush, clear and free from lumps, set it away till it cools, then pour it in a hole made in the middle of the flour. Pour in also the yeast batter instead of wetting, and mix the whole into dough. Knead it and set it away to rise, being very careful to keep it an equal temperature the whole time. When light mold it into loaves; let it stand ten or fifteen minutes in a warm place, then bake about an hour, or until done. It should not be underbaked, and it is just as important that it should not be over-done. It is a common error that over-done bread is healthy. If the crusts are thick and hard they can be moistened up, covering the loaf fresh from the oven with one or two thicknesses of damp cloth. Several thicknesses of wet cloth wrapped around it in this way render it indigestible. In making the batter over night, five or six middling sized potatoes, boiled to a mush, and pulped through a colander, may be added to it.

BREAD.—2.

An easier way of making bread, is to heat two bricks to one hundred degrees or more, and place the pan you make the bread in, on them. Put in the flour and salt; make for three loaves, a pint of corn meal mush, free from lumps; set it away to cool; mix it in the flour with a tea-cup of potato yeast, and make the whole into dough with lukewarm water; the mixing and kneading all being done on the hot bricks. Have well-greased tins, divide the dough into them, set them to rise on the hot bricks by the stove, with a piece of carpet over the bricks to moderate the heat, and cover them well with woolens. Let it rise about two hours, then bake in a steady oven.

GENERAL RULES.

Generally in making bread, one quart of wetting, either of milk or water, is sufficient for five quarts of flour or meal. Ten quarts of flour or meal will make four loaves of about three and a half pounds each, to be baked in quart pans. Water mixed with flour or meal should be about blood warm. When yeast is used, it should be well stirred and diluted with lukewarm water before being added to the flour.

RYE AND INDIAN BREAD

The proportions of rye and corn meal used, may be varied according to the taste. If the largest proportion of rye is used, make the dough stiff; if the largest proportion of corn meal, make the dough softer. The greater the proportion of corn meal, the longer the bread requires baking. The best way to mix the dough is to put the corn meal into a glazed earthen pan; sprinkle salt over it, pour on boiling water, work it till thoroughly wet, and when about milk-warm add the rye flour with the yeast, and as much more warm, but not hot water, as is required. Work the dough until stiff, but not as stiff as flour dough. Put it then in' a deep greased pan, put your hand in warm water and pat down the top, set it to rise in a warm place by the stove in winter, but in the sun in summer. When it begins to crack on the top, which will be in an hour or an hour and a half, put in a well heated oven. To make the bread two thirds of corn meal, take four quarts of sifted corn meal, sprinkle a table-spoonful of salt over it, pour over it two quarts of boiling water, as directed above; when lukewarm add two quarts of rye meal, half a pint of lively yeast mixed in a pint of warm water,—add more warm water if necessary. Bake two or three hours. This makes a loaf weighing seven or eight pounds.

GRAHAM BREAD.

Make a batter of Graham flour in the ordinary way, but mix it rather thin. Let it rise, divide the loaves into tins just as soon as it is light, for it becomes sour quicker than bolted flour; bake an hour and a quarter, or an hour and a half, according to the size of the loaf. A little molasses can be added to the batter if desired.

SWEET BROWN BREAD.

One quart of rye flour, two quarts of Indian meal, one pint of Graham flour, all fresh, half a tea-cupful of molasses or brown sugar, half a pint of potato yeast, and salt. Mix into as stiff a dough as can be stirred with a spoon, using warm water for wetting. Let it rise several hours or over night, then bake five or six hours.

RICE FLOUR BREAD.—1.

Boil a pint of rice soft, add a pint of cream, then three quarts of rice flour; put it to rise in a tin or earthen vessel until it has risen sufficient; divide it into three parts, and bake it as other bread, and you will have three large loaves; or scald the flour, and when it is cold mix half wheat flour or corn. Raised with leaven in the usual way.

RICE FLOUR BREAD.—2.

One quart of rice flour; make it into a stiff pap by wetting with warm water, not so hot as to make it lumpy; when well wet, add boiling hot water, as much as two or three quarts; stir it continually until it boils; when it cools, put in half a pint of yeast and a little salt; knead in as much wheat flour as will make it a proper dough for bread; put it to rise, and when risen, add a little more wheat flour. Let it stand in a warm place half an hour, and bake it. This same mixture, only made thinner, and baked in rings, makes excellent muffins.

MOIST RICE BREAD.

In three quarts of cold milk and water, mix a pint and a half of ground rice. It will be a thin gruel; boil it three or four minutes, and then stir in Graham flour until it is too stiff to stir with a spoon. Let it become lukewarm, add two gills of yeast and salt; let it rise, and bake it an hour.

APPLE BREAD

Mix the pulp from a dozen good-flavored, boiled apples, with twice its quantity of wheat flour, or Graham flour; add salt, yeast, and bake as usual.

PULLED BREAD.

Take the crumb out of a hot loaf of bread, and divide it into rocky looking pieces, by pulling it to pieces quickly with the fingers of both hands; place these pieces on a baking tin, lined with paper, and bake them over again to a light-brown color. Do them in a quick oven to ensure their being very crisp.

PIECES OF BREAD.

These need not be thrown away. Rich bread puddings may be made of them; they may be made into crumb cakes, or dressing for any kind of meat that can be stuffed, is made of softened crusts, butter, herbs, and a beaten egg. In the summer when bread becomes mouldy by keeping, the pieces that cannot be used immediately, can be dried on tins in the oven and used pounded for puddings, or crumb cakes, or to dress a ham, as cracker crumbs. Some have a small board on which to slice bread, and brush the crumbs from it into a box. It is easier to save them than to scatter them over the table or floor.

SHORT CAKE.

Put into a basin twelve ounces of flour, and six ounces of butter, or half the quantity if sufficient for your purpose; take off little bits of butter with your fingers and rub thoroughly into the flour; then moisten it with as little water as possible, only just enough to hold the paste together, as the less water used the shorter the crust will be. Roll out the paste upon a smooth board, of the desired thickness. This quantity is sufficient for the cover of two fruit tarts. While making pastry always endeavor to be in a cool place in summer, and a moderately warm one in winter; use cold water in summer, and water a little warm in winter.

RUSKS.

Three pints of flour, one pint of sugar, a quarter of a pound of butter rubbed in the flour, one table-spoonful of yeast, one pint of warm milk. Set a sponge and put all in. Mix soft. This is good for doughnuts.

BAKED BATTER.

Four pints of cold milk, three table-spoonsful of flour, two crackers pounded fine, a small piece of butter, table-spoonful of sugar, two eggs, a little salt to be eaten with butter and white sugar. Flavor with lemon.

RYE DROP CAKES.

Mix together one quart of milk, two beaten eggs, a piece of butter as large as an egg, two tea-spoonsful of cream of tartar, one tea-spoonful of soda, half a tea-cup of white sugar, and sufficient rye meal to make a thick batter. Bake half an hour.

RICE BISCUIT.

Mix with warm water, a tea-cup of boiled rice, two pounds of flour, two spoonsful of yeast; let it rise, and bake it.

HOE CAKES.

First scald a quart of Indian meal in enough water to make a thick batter; mix in two spoonsful of butter, a tea-spoonful of soda, and two tea-spoonsful of salt. Bake about half an hour in a buttered pan.

FANNY'S BREAKFAST CAKES

In one quart of thick sour milk, stir Graham flour, to make a thick batter, add a little salt, a heaping tea-spoon of soda, and a tea-spoon of melted butter. Make it into drop cakes, and bake.

CORN CREAM CAKE.

Take a quart of milk, or buttermilk, and put a sour thick cream mixed with sufficient bi-carbonate of soda to sweeten it, add corn meal enough to the milk and cream to thicken it to the consistency of pound cake, stirring it in; put it an inch thick in floured pans, and bake it in a quick oven.

MRS. D.'S TEA BISCUIT.

Six tumblers flour, one half pound butter, three tumblers milk, two tea-spoonsful cream tartar, one half tea-spoonful soda; mix soft, bake quick.

CORN BREAD.

One pint of sour milk, one pint of corn meal, one pint of white flour, two even tea-spoonsful of soda, one tea-cupful of molasses or brown sugar, one large tea-spoonful of salt; bake an hour. It is nice and warm for dinner, and moist and toothsome when cold. Good Indian cake is made with buttermilk or sour milk, with a little cream or butter rubbed on the meat, and a tea-spoonful of saleratus.

BREAKFAST JOHNNY CAKE.

Mix over night six or eight table-spoonsful of fine yellow Indian meal, with two of wheat flour, one of corn starch, a tea-spoonful of salt, and water enough to wet thoroughly — milk is better, but is not essential. In the morning add one egg, a tea-spoonful of soda, a table-spoonful of brown sugar, and another of melted butter; beat up well, and bake immediately. This is good enough for " company."

BREAKFAST CORN CAKE.

Three cups of meal, and half a cup of flour, mixed with buttermilk, or sweet milk, and water, over night, and left standing. In the morning add a large tea-spoonful of soda, a table-spoonful of sugar, or molasses, and as much melted butter, together with a lit-

the salt. Bake an hour. It is very nice. A little cold hominy, or farina, mixed smoothly with the meal, improves corn cake without eggs, wonderfully.

CORN MEAL WAFFLES.

Two eggs, yolks well beaten, one table-spoon of butter, one of flour, one tea-spoon of salt, one pint of sweet milk, one pint of meal *twice* sifted, half tea-spoon of soda; add last the whites of the eggs well beaten.

WESTERN JOHNNY CAKE.

One quart of milk, three eggs, half cup of sugar or molasses, tea-spoonful of saleratus, a cup of wheat flour, thicken with Indian meal to a batter. Bake in shallow pans.

BUTTERMILK BREAKFAST CAKES.

A quart of Graham flour, a piece of butter as big as a walnut, a tea-spoon of salt, a tea-spoon of soda, and sufficient good butter. Add enough milk to mix to the consistency of cup cake. Drop the batter by the large spoonful on a buttered pan, and bake quick. They will puff right up, and be ready for the table in fifteen minutes.

RICE PUFFS.

To a pint of flour put boiling water or milk sufficient to make a batter. When it is cold beat four eggs and put in, together with a tea-spoonful of salt. Drop this mixture by the large spoonful into hot fat.

RICE FLOUR PUFFS.

To a pint of the flour, add a tea-spoonful of salt, a pint of boiling water; beat up four eggs, stir them well together, put from two to three spoonsful of lard in a pan, make it boiling hot, and fry as you do common fritters.

RICE FLOUR CAKES.

Take a pint of soft-boiled rice, half a pint of milk and water, to which add twelve spoonsful of rice flour. Divide it into small cakes, and bake in a brick oven.

OAT CAKE.

Melt half an ounce of salt butter or lard, in a pint of boiling water, and having put a pound of oat meal into a basin, pour the water, quite boiling, upon it. Stir it as quickly as possible into a dough. Turn this out on a baking plate and roll it out until it is as thin as it can be to hold together, then cut it out into shape of small round cakes. Make these firm by placing them over the fire on a griddle (a gridiron of fine wire bars) for a very short time, and afterwards toast them on each side alternately before the fire until they become quite crisp. A simpler way is to make a thick paste of coarse oat meal and water, knead it, spread it thin, lay it on a griddle over the fire, turn and brown on both sides.

LEIGHT STREET CRUMPETS.

Mix a quart of warm milk, a tea-spoonful of sugar, and a gill of potato yeast, with sufficient flour or meal to make a rather thick batter. When light add a tea-cupful of sweet cream, let it rise twenty minutes, and bake it as muffins or in cups.

FLOUR AND POTATO ROLLS.

Roil and dry one pound of potatoes, mix them with two ounces of sweet cream and half a pint of milk, and rub them through a wire sieve into a pound and a half of flour. Mix a gill more of warm milk with a little yeast, and add to the flour. Make into dough, let it rise before the fire, form into rolls, and bake quickly.

RICE WAFFLES.

Take a large coffee-cup of well-boiled rice, stir in two eggs and a large table-spoonful of corn starch; add a tea-spoonful of salt, a quart of milk, a table-spoonful of melted butter, and " self-raising " flour enough to make a thick batter. If the flour is not " self-raising," put in a tea-spoonful of cream of tartar, and half of soda. See that your waffle-irons are well heated and greased.

GREEN CORN CAKES.

Mix a pint of grated green corn with a tea-cup of flour, half a tea-cup of milk, half a tea-cup of melted butter, one egg, a tea-spoon of salt, and a little pepper. Drop this mixture on a buttered pan by the spoonful, and bake or fry for ten or fifteen minutes. They are very nice for breakfast.

BUTTER CAKES FOR TEA.

To half a pint of milk, stir in two well-beaten eggs, a tea-cup of cream, half a tea-spoonful of saleratus dissolved in the cream, a little salt, a table-spoonful of melted butter, and sufficient sifted flour to make a thick batter. Drop it in thin round cakes on a buttered pan or griddle, turn them while baking, and bake until browned. Send to table piled on a plate with a little butter on each.

SODA BISCUIT.

Stir into one quart of flour two tea-spoonsful of cream tartar, one tea-spoonful of salt; dissolve in three gills of new milk a tea-spoonful of soda; stir it into the flour quickly, pour all on the board, roll out, cut in small circular cakes, bake in a quick oven.

ENGLISH BREAKFAST CAKES.

Warm a pint of milk and four ounces of good butter till luke-warm; add two beaten eggs, three ounces of sugar and two table-spoonsful of yeast; raise the flour, work the dough, using more flour if necessary; divide into cakes, and let them rise for three quarters of an hour and bake them in buttered tins. When done, cut those to be used into slices, butter on each side and warm them a minute, serving them hot. In using the remainder for another meal, they may be warmed and buttered in the same way.

FRENCH ROLLS.

Warm a pint of new milk, melt two large spoonsful of butter, add a little salt. When cool, sift in one pound of flour, one egg well beaten, one spoonful of yeast. Beat these well together, but avoid kneading. When risen, form it into rolls, handling as little as possible. Bake on tins, and serve.

GRAHAM BISCUIT.—1.

These are quickly made, and very nice for breakfast. Take a

quart of Graham or unbolted flour and mix it to the consistency of drop cake with butter-milk, an even tea-spoonful of soda and a little salt; add a table-spoonful of melted butter, and drop the mixture on a shallow pan. Bake in a quick oven fifteen or twenty minutes.

GRAHAM BISCUIT.—2.

Mix together as for bread one quart of Graham meal, two spoonsful of molasses, one tea-spoonful of lard, two spoonsful of wheat flour, half a cup of yeast, and salt. Let it stand all night to rise, and in the morning put it in muffin rings; let them stand half an hour, and then bake.

SOFT WAFFLES.

One quart of milk, four eggs, one quarter pound of butter, yeast; to be made as thin as pancakes.

MUFFINS.—1.

Mix a quart of wheat flour with half a tea-cupful of potato yeast, two beaten eggs, a heaping tea-spoonful of salt, a pint and a half of luke-warm milk, and two table-spoonsful of melted butter; set to rise, and when very light turn into well-buttered muffin rings, and bake a clear, light brown.

MUFFINS.—2.

Two coffee-cups of milk, three of flour, two eggs, one table-spoon of butter, two tea-spoonsful cream of tartar, one of soda. Take half your milk, half your flour, eggs, salt, butter, and cream of tartar; beat well until smooth, then add by degrees the rest of the milk and flour, and lastly the soda, mixed with a little flour.

HOT CROSS BUNS. (GOOD FRIDAY.)

Take two pounds of flour well dried, rub in half a pound of butter, add four eggs, four spoonsful of yeast, and as much new milk as will make it into a soft dough. Put in while mixing, half a pound of powdered sugar, and half an ounce of caraway seeds. Set it by the fire to rise, and when it is light, divide it into the proper size for buns. Make a cross upon each, and glaze the top with white of egg, and sugar.

DRY TOAST.

Dry bread well and evenly toasted, without being burned, is the best food that can be taken for very acid and irritable stomachs. Nice, fresh-sliced bread toasted, may be well spread with butter and served immediately as a good breakfast dish. Bread a little soured or over fermented is improved, though not cured, by toasting.

DIP TOAST.

Toast bread, and dip it quickly into boiling water; spread it with plenty of butter, and serve immediately, or let it stand in the oven if required to wait.

CREAM TOAST.

Toast slices of stale bread on both sides, and pour on them while hot, sweet cream diluted by an equal quantity of scalded milk.

THE FAMILY OF GRIDDLE CAKES.

BUCKWHEAT CAKES.

Take equal quantities of buckwheat, Indian meal and Graham flour, to make one quart, add half a cup of new yeast, a tea-spoonful of saleratus, a little salt and enough good milk, or luke warm water to make a thick batter. Set it near the fire to rise, and when risen, cook them in a well buttered griddle.

COMMON PANCAKES.

Mix together three spoonsful of flour, two beaten eggs and a little salt, stir in good milk by degrees, and fry them in boiling lard a light brown color. The eggs may be dispensed with, or yeast or snow used in their stead.

SHROVE TUESDAY PANCAKES.

Four eggs, four table-spoonsful of flour, one pint of milk and pint of cream, or quart of milk, and table-spoonful of melted butter; salt to taste, and add just before frying in hot lard, a quarter of a pound of currants.

BREAD GRIDDLE CAKES.

Take pieces of stale bread, soak them in water till quite soft, drain them and rub the bread to a pulp; then add two or three beaten eggs and sufficient milk to make a thick batter, and cook them in the griddle.

SODA GRIDDLE CAKES.

Stir together in one pint of milk, one tea-spoonful of soda, two tea-spoonsful of cream of tartar, sufficient flour to make a thick batter, and fry them on the griddle.

RICE CAKES.

To one tea-cupful of cold boiled rice, put one of flour, one egg, one table-spoonful of corn starch, tea-spoonful of salt, and sour milk, or buttermilk, enough to make a batter; mix smoothly, and at the last add a tea-spoonful of soda and a little melted butter; bake immediately. If sweet milk is used, put in rather less soda and double the same quantity of cream of tartar. Cold boiled hominy can be used in the same way; these are an excellent Spring substitute for buckwheat cakes.

FLANNEL CAKES.

Put two ounces of butter into a pint of hot milk, let it melt; add then a pint of cold milk, four beaten eggs, a tea-spoonful of salt, two table-spoonsful of yeast, and sufficient flour to make a stiff batter. Set it in a warm place three hours to rise, then fry on the griddle.

CREAM PANCAKES.

Mix the yolks of two eggs with half a pint of cream, and two ounces of sugar, fry them on the griddle thin, and serve hot, with grated sugar over them.

ECONOMICAL GRIDDLE CAKES.

A capital and economical way of making griddle cakes, is to keep a stone jar or pitcher, into which put all the scraps, cold hominy, rice, mashed potato, small pieces of bread, in short everything eatable which is clean and good, and can be reduced to a pulp. Into the mixture also put any stray drops of milk that may be left, and when a pint, or more, or less, according to the size of the family, has accumulated, mix it with flour into a batter, sweeten with a tea-spoon of bi-carbonate of soda, or refined saleratus, and reduce still further if necessary, with a little sweet milk. These cakes will be found delicious, and can be made without any eggs, by putting in one or two table-spoonsful of maizena.

INDIAN GRIDDLE CAKES.—1.

Mix together one pint of Indian meal, one cup of flour, a table-spoonful of molasses, a tea-spoonful of saleratus, a little salt and ginger, and sufficient sour milk to make a stiff batter. Bake on the griddle.

INDIAN GRIDDLE CAKES.—2.

In a quart of warm milk mix a quart of Indian meal, a handful of wheat flour, a tea-spoonful of salt and two tea-spoonsful of yeast, and two or three beaten eggs. Let it rise and bake on the griddle. If the batter should sour, dissolve a little saleratus in lukewarm water, stir it in the batter and let it stand half an hour before using.

INDIAN GRIDDLE CAKES.—3.

Scald at night half the quantity of meal to be used; mix the other half with cold water until it is thick batter; add a little salt and set it to rise without yeast. This will make light, crisp cakes in the morning. The skimmings of boiled meat is the best to fry them with. Fry slowly.

RYE GRIDDLE CAKES.

One quart of sweet milk, two eggs one-half tea-spoon saleratus. Pinch of salt, enough rye flour to make batter.

RICE FLOUR CAKES LIKE BUCKWHEAT CAKES.

Mix one quarter of wheat flour to three quarters of superfine rice flour, and raise it as buckwheat flour. Bake it like buckwheat cakes.

TOMATO GRIDDLE CAKES.

Cover sliced ripe tomatoes with a nice batter, and fry them on the griddle.

SCOTCH PANCAKES.

Mix together four table-spoonsful of sifted flour and four well beaten eggs; after these are stirred together awhile, add gradually a pint of milk, season with a little salt and nutmeg. Put a shallow frying pan with a small piece of butter in it, on the fire, and pour into it half a tea-cup of batter. Turn the pan round over the fire for a minute or two, then by taking it off the fire and holding it upright in front of the bars it will rise immediately. When it is done, cut the edges, sprinkle with sugar, and roll up.

THE POUGHKEEPSIE SEER'S INDIAN BANNOCK.

One pint of corn meal, one quart of milk, boil one pint of the milk, and scald the meal thoroughly. Put in a tea-spoon of salt, a table-spoon of melted butter, three well-beaten eggs, and thin batter with the cold milk. Bake brown in shallow pans.

BOILED FARINACEOUS DISHES.

HOMINY AND FARINA.

As a change from griddle cakes, housekeepers will find a dish of boiled hominy, or farina, very palatable, and especially healthful for children. Farina should be mixed thin, about like meal mush, and boiled as long, say an hour. Hominy should be soaked in cold water over night, and boiled for an hour, with a little salt, in the morning. It is eaten with sugar and milk, or butter and sugar. It is a reliable breakfast dish the year round.

HOMINY CAKES.

Mix with cold hominy an equal quantity of white flour until perfectly smooth; add a tea-spoon of salt, and thin off with butter-milk, into part of which a tea-spoon of soda has been dissolved; when of the consistency of griddle cakes, add a dessert-spoon of melted butter, and bake as usual; with maple syrup they are delicious, and the absence of eggs will not be noticed.

SAMP.

Soak a quart of cracked Indian corn, over night, and put it on the fire, first thing after breakfast, with three pounds of beef, not too salt, and one of pork. Cover with water, and let it cook slowly five hours, being very careful not to let it burn.

HASTY PUDDING

Boil water, mix in a little salt, and then stir in gradually so as to prevent lumping, sufficient corn meal to thicken it. It should boil at least an hour, and may be eaten with milk, cream and sugar, or butter and syrup, or sugar.

RYE MEAL MUSH.

Stir gradually in boiling water in which a little salt has been thrown, fresh-ground rye meal. Let it boil about an hour.

INDIAN MEAL GRUEL.

Boil a quart of water in the saucepan, mix in cold water three table-spoonsful of Indian meal and half a table-spoonful of flour, pour in the boiling water gradually stirring all the time; boil twenty or twenty-five minutes, stirring occasionally. Take it off and season sparingly with salt and nutmeg, and add if desired a very little new milk; for a very sick person, the nutmeg and milk, and even the salt, may be omitted. Oat meal gruel may be made in the same way.

MILK PORRIDGE.

Take half a pint of boiling water, mix a large spoonful of flour in a little cold water, stir it into the water while it is boiling, and let it it boil fifteen minutes; then add a tea-cupful of milk, a little salt, and give it one boil.

ENGLISH FRUMETY

Soak half a pint of wheat, and then boil it gently for three or four hours. Beat up an egg in a quart of milk, and mix with it, also a tea-cupful of raisins and currants, a little salt, nutmeg, or cinnamon, and grated lemon peel. Boil all together for another quarter of an hour, and serve. If preferred thinner, more milk can be added.

OLD FASHIONED HULLED CORN.

Shell a dozen years of ripe, dry corn, put it in an iron kettle and cover with cold water; put in the corn a bag of two tea-cupsful of fresh wood ashes, and boil until the corn looks yellow, and tastes strong of the alkali, then take out the bag and boil the corn in the lye over an hour, then pour off the lye, add fresh water, and simmer until the corn swells. If the hulls do not then come off by stirring, turn off the water and rub them off with a towel; add more water and simmer for three or four hours, often stirring to keep it from burning; when it swells out and becomes soft and white, add salt to liking and let all the water simmer away. Eat warm or cold with cream or milk.

BREAKFAST.

BREAKFAST.

A great variety of dishes are unnecessary for breakfast, but see that what you do have, is nicely cooked, and properly served. Unless sickness or some other circumstance prevents, the mistress of the house should always add the finishing touches to the breakfast room, and the breakfast table. The most experienced servant will fail in producing just the right degree of light and sunlight, in getting rid of the last speck of dust, or the latest evidence of ashes, and never thinks at all of transferring a branch of rosebuds, and geranium from the garden to the mantel piece; these belong to the gentler thought, and more refined instincts of the cultivated lady, and such duties are not at all beneath the dignity of the highest in the land.

That the dishes may be well-cooked, and well served, they must be adapted to the other services required on that day. On washing and ironing days, for instance, as little time, and as little of the fire should be used as possible, and care should be taken to save interruption to the important, and principal business of the day.

Broiled chicken, or warmed over chicken, and omeletts, are always nice breakfast dishes, but in cities the prices puts them out of the reach of ordinary people, except on extraordinary occasions. The regular dishes, such as beefsteak, mutton chops, fish, broiled ham, eggs, and warmed over potatoes, are all understood, and in the different kinds and degrees, constitute the daily breakfast probably, of half the world.

There is a very important point however, to which little attention is paid, and that is fruit. "Fruit," saith the old proverb, "is golden in the morning, silver at noon, and lead at night," yet it is only at night, that in this country, we eat it at all, as part of a meal. This is wrong, fruit is a most valuable part of food, it cannot be too highly estimated; more fruit, with less saleratus, and rich greasy compounds, such as butter with meats, gravies, and the like, would take away the occupation of half the doctors, and reduce wonderfully the sum total of dyspepsia and liver complaints.

A distinguished physician has said that one or two tart Messina oranges eaten before breakfast during the three spring months, would cure the worst obstinate bilious disorder; but the cure would undoubtedly be as effectual if they were eaten at breakfast, and the usual amount of pork and melted butter on hot cakes, reduced during that time.

The rule should be to have fresh fruit on the table every morning, as long as it lasts, and then a preparation of dried, canned, or preserved fruits, a small investment in Guava jelly; and that India fruit, for breakfast, will not be thrown away, after your own stock is exhausted, and you begin to tire of apples, and the common dried varieties.

A very valuable adjunct to the breakfast table is the tomato; highly prized as it is, its admirable medicinal qualities are only just beginning to be discovered. Providentially, it is so cheap, and grows so readily and profusely, that the poorest person can luxuriate in its excellence, as well as the richest, and derive all the more benefit from not being able to destroy its virtue with butter, and an excess of condiments.

Tomatoes are an almost soveriegn cure for dyspepsia, and should be on the table, raw or cooked, the year round. Persons habituated to them, soon learn to love them in any form, sliced with a little pepper, salt, and vinegar, stewed, baked, or even fresh from the vines; the least healthful and generally the least palatable mode of serving them, is sweetened, or cooked with sugar.

Mush, hominy, wheaten grits, or some dish of that sort, should be frequently seen upon the breakfast table, such food is excellent for children, and soon becomes very palatable, and highly esteemed by grown persons. Moreover if it is not eaten when first boiled, it is not wasted; it is just as good fried, or used as a basis for griddle cakes.

In some families, warm soda biscuit for breakfast, is the regular thing; this is very hurtful. Good home-made bread, not quite fresh, is best. French bread, baked the day before, next best;

good baker's twist, third best. For a change, warm corn bread, or johnny cake may be made for breakfast, rice cakes, or waffles, and if biscuits, make them from the light dough mixed over night, shortened with a little butter.

When the spring water-cresses come in, there should be thankfulness. Pile them up fresh, green, and crisp, upon a dish in the centre of the table, and eat them with new laid eggs boiled soft, salt, nice Graham bread, and sweet butter. This is a breakfast suited to Lent, and fit for a Republican queen.

BILL OF FARE FOR BREAKFAST.

1. Broiled chicken, toast, omelette, and Guava jelly.

2. Broiled mutton chops, stewed tomatoes, fried potatoes, and Graham drop biscuit.

3. Broiled ham, corn bread, sliced tomatoes, and toast, or bread.

4. Fried ham and eggs, stewed apples, hominy, and home-made bread.

5 Broiled lamb chops, rice cakes, warmed over potatoes, and marmalade.

6. Boiled No. 1 mackerel, potatoes warmed up with butter and milk, sliced tomatoes, and Johnny cake.

7. Fresh eggs cooked soft, fried potatoes, bread, and stewed peaches.

8. (*Lent.*) Soft boiled eggs, water-cresses, and Graham bread.

9. Fried halibut, potatoes, salad, and French bread.

10. Beef hash, corn bread, stewed tomatoes, and toast.

BREAKFAST.

11. Minced veal, toast, rice, waffles, and sliced oranges.

12. Cold roast veal, fried potatoes, apple sauce, and raised biscuit.

13. Broiled lamb chops, hominy cakes, tomatoes, twist bread.

14. Indian slapjacks, pork chops cut thin, and fried brown, fried apples, and Graham bread.

15. (*Easter Sunday Morning.*) Fresh eggs boiled, French bread, and Guava jelly.

16. Broiled salmon, potatoes, baker's twist, and stewed cherries.

17. Broiled shad, fried hominy, potatoes, and salad of watercresses.

18. Fried Indian mush, ham broiled very thin, poached eggs.

19. Broiled partridge, toast, rice cakes, and cranberry jelly.

20. Soused shad, fried potatoes, boiled hominy, and butter-milk Graham biscuit.

21. Broiled mackerel, fried mashed potato, and hoe cake. Plain lettuce or radishes.

22. Sausage cakes seasoned with sage, potatoes boiled in their skins, and "mixed" griddle cakes.

23. Minced chicken, rice waffles, boiled eggs, potatoes warmed over in milk.

24. Veal cutlets, muffins, and fresh strawberries,

25. Fresh mackerel, stewed gooseberries, potatoes, corn bread.

26. Fried blue-fish, fried hominy, twist bread, huckleberries.

27. Veal sweet-bread, toast, tomatoes sliced, potatoes, and fresh peaches.

28. Fried calves' liver, with parsley, and thin slices of bacon, little corn cakes, Graham bread, and blackberries.

29. Cold corned beef, cabbage chopped fine, and warmed over with vinegar and a little beef fat. French bread, and boiled Indian mush.

Birthday Breakfast.

30. Broiled or fricaseed chicken, and cold boiled ham garnished, or chicken pie ornamented, fried potato balls, rice currant fritters, French bread, or biscuit, a dish of fresh, or canned fruit, and high glass dish of fruit, and flowers in centre.

31. Nothing in the shape of beverages has been added, because all families follow their habits and traditions in this respect, and also with regard to butter, etc., and the addition of such accustomed articles in every instance, would be entirely superfluous.

COFFEE, TEA, Etc.

COFFEE.

It is better to buy whole coffee and grind it yourself. Let the coffee pot be clean and free from the smell of stale coffee. Grind sufficient coffee fresh for use at one time, then stir it about with the white and shell of an egg, mixing them thoroughly. Or an egg may be mixed with half a pound of ground coffee, which is to be used as required, and the egg tends to preserve the aroma. Take a table-spoonful of coffee or less for each person, pour upon it as much boiling water as will be required, and boil it up as quickly as possible. Pour out a tea-cupful and put it back again, or pour the whole backwards and forwards several times. Take it from the fire and pour half a tea-cupful of quite cold water into it and let it stand five minutes by the fire; but do not let it boil again, before you transfer it to the coffee pot in which it is to be served. Do not shake it in doing this, as the egg shell and coffee powder will have settled at the bottom, and the liquid ought to be perfectly clear. A little isinglass is sometimes used instead of egg. Many insist that it is quite unnecessary to use the egg at all. Loaf sugar and boiled milk should be served with it, allowing each person to suit their own taste.

COFFEE CREAM.

Some make coffee cream by boiling three cups of coffee after it is made, with a pint of cream and sugar to taste, until they are reduced nearly one half, and so serving it.

DINNER COFFEE.

Take pure Mocha coffee, one table-spoonful to each person, mix with egg and cold water, and boil perfectly clear. Serve without milk, but with loaf sugar, or if you choose with burnt brandy, and sugar, in very small cups.

COLD COFFEE.

Make a quart of good coffee, pour it off clear, and add to it a pint of new milk, a gill of cream, and enough loaf sugar to sweeten it. Set it back on the fire, and let it all come to a boil. This will be delicious cold, or it is good warmed up next day. Bottles of such coffee are sometimes useful to take on a picnic. Use the best lump, or coffee crushed sugar, for coffee, coarse brown spoils the flavor.

CHOCOLATE (*American*).

Procure the best chocolate, grate it, allowing two heaping tablespoonsful to a quart of mixed milk and water. Boil it fifteen minutes, taking off the scum as it rises, and serve with sugar and cream.

CHOCOLATE (*French*).

Break the chocolate in pieces, boil it in a little water, stirring all the time, then add double the quantity of milk, and allow that to boil also, stirring, but not skimming, until it has boiled up thick for several minutes. Add loaf sugar to taste, and serve with cream, or new milk to thin it off, if preferred.

COCOA.

To make good cocoa from the nibs, it should be boiled for three or four hours, and strained when it is taken from the fire. Should any grease rise to the surface after this it must be removed either with writing paper, or by skimming. Sufficient quantity of cocoa may be made at one time to last three or four days, as it will remain perfectly good for that time, and should be merely boiled up when wanted and served with hot milk. In boiling, use a quart of cold water to a quarter of a pound of cocoa nibs, or vary according to taste.

TEA.

"Tea," as a meal is a lost institution in most of our large cities.

More's the pity, for it was the cosiest, and pleasantest meal of the day. Moreover, with it, has gone out early hours, and thrifty habits, attention to home duties, and love of home pleasures. The late breakfasts, which are the rule now, and the six o'clock dinners, not only destroy health, but give the day to gossiping and visiting, to shopping and the promenade, and afford an excuse for daily expensive lunches at fashionable restaurants, which make simple home fare distasteful.

"Tea," in the old-fashioned sense, is still to be met with occasionally in the country, and who that has ever assisted in a pleasant family circle at that most enjoyable of all meals, but remembers it with a longing to experience it once again. The cosy table, the light delicate food, the hot, fragrant beverage in small cups, handled tenderly, as if with a due appreciation of their contents; the leisure which all enjoy after the principal business of the day is over, and the stimulus to lively and agreeable conversation, which the meal affords.

But the *tea* itself must be good; no luke warm infusion, no mere slop, by quantity of which you seek to make up for the quality. One cup of really good, inspiring tea, is worth a gallon of the liquid which well-intentioned housewives sometimes pour out, with the assurance that it is not strong, and will not hurt you. The truth is, that the amount of liquid is a positive injury, while, whatever of virtue the tea possessed, is drowned in it; but there are persons who still insist upon their ancient right to three or four cups, and perhaps the less tea there is in these, the better.

HOW TO MAKE TEA.

Scald your tea-pot for six persons, put in three tea-spoonsful of best green tea, pour a little boiling water upon it, and set it to steep. Put four tea-spoonsful of best black tea in a tin cup with a cover, pour cold water upon it, cover it tight, and bring it to a quick boil; let it boil a minute, and then add it to the green, which should only steep in boiling water, not boil. Fill up with the necessary quantity of boiling water, and it is ready for the table.

It is not known by many persons, that the Oolong and other black teas require boiling, in order to extract their strength and virtue. Those who mourn over poor, weak, modern tea, are advised to try this method.

PLAIN BILLS OF FARE FOR DINNER ALL THE YEAR ROUND.

JANUARY.

Roast turkey, celery, cranberry sauce, boiled onions, mashed potatoes browned, mashed turnips, apples and nuts.

Minced turkey, potatoes boiled in their jackets, cranberry sauce, currant dumplings.

Shank end of a leg of mutton, boiled with rice, mashed potatoes, pickled beets, and mince pie.

Leg of mutton boiled, then roasted, with caper sauce, mashed potatoes, and turnips, stewed tomatoes, and baked apple dumplings.

A good soup made from leg of mutton broth, the shank bone, and fresh beef bone, with bunch of sweet herbs, and vegetables; mutton sliced, and warmed over, roast potatoes, fried parsnips, and mince pie.

Fish chowder, plain boiled potatoes, macaroni, pickled beets, and boiled apple pudding.

Company Dinner.

Vermicelli soup, boiled turkey stuffed with oysters, roast chicken, boiled ham, cranberry jelly, celery, fried potatoes, canned corn, tomatoes, stewed parsnips, cauliflower, macaroni, plum pudding, nuts, oranges, and raisins.

FEBRUARY.

Irish stew, fried parsnips, roast potatoes, pickles, and apple pie.

Boiled corned beef, cabbage, carrots, mashed turnips and potatoes, rice, and raisins with sauce.

Cold corned beef, roast potatoes, macaroni, fried parsnips, pickled beets, and apple pie.

Broiled mutton chops, potatoes boiled in their skins, stewed tomatoes, and tapioca pudding.

Baked pork, and beans, and boiled codfish, with mashed potatoes, and pickles, apple sauce. Baked apple pudding.

Roast leg of mutton, and currant jelly, mashed potatoes, boiled onions, fried parsnips, and bread currant pudding.

Stuffed and stewed prairie chickens, stewed tomatoes, mashed canned corn, and lemon pie.

Extra Dinner.

Tomato soup, boiled salmon trout, with anchovy sauce, roast turkey, cranberry sauce, canned corn, Lima beans, celery, brown mashed potatoes, fried oyster plant pickles, bread and butter pudding, apples, oranges, biscuits and French coffee.

Sunday Dinner.

Oyster soup, roast ribs of beef, cold slaw, succotash of corn and Lima beans, mashed potatoes, fried parsnips, and apple meringue pie.

MARCH.

Beef a la mode, from the upper part of the leg, roast potatoes boiled parsnips, stewed cabbage with vinegar, and apple fritters.

Soup made from shin of beef, and split peas, bacon, and cabbage, boiled potatoes, pickles and apple pie.

Fillet of veal larded, potatoes, fried parsnips, apple sauce and "birdnest" pudding.

Knuckle of veal stewed with rice, fried potatoes, stewed tomatoes and mince pie.

Cold beef, roast potatoes, fried parsnips, cold slaw and "Buffalo" pudding.

Boiled codfish with egg sauce, beef hash, mashed potatoes, cold slaw, and pumpkin pie.

Boiled ham, and spinach, lobster salad, plain boiled potatoes, and rice pudding.

Sunday Dinner.

Baked salmon trout, fricasseed chickens, mashed potatoes, salsify, currant jelly, and bread and butter pudding.

APRIL.

Lamb stew with potatoes and greens, currant dumplings.

Veal cutlets with bacon, spinach, mashed potatoes, sliced fresh tomatoes, and Indian pudding.

Stuffed and baked shad, salad of early lettuce, boiled rice used as a vegetable instead of potatoes, lemon pie.

Roast lamb, mint sauce, new potatoes, sliced fresh tomatoes, spinach and rhubarb pie.

Boiled leg of mutton, caper sauce, greens, mashed potatoes and tapioca pudding.

Cold leg of mutton, with salad and mashed potatoes, roly poly pudding.

"Medley" pie made of a few scraps of cold meat, an onion, apples, sugar and spice, fried potatoes and rice currant fritters.

Sunday Dinner.

Roast chickens, stewed tomatoes, new, or Bermuda potatoes, spinach, canned corn, and lemon meringue pie.

MAY.

Roast lamb, green peas, mint sauce, spinach and potatoes, rhubarb batter pudding.

Boiled blue fish with parsley sauce, fried potatoes, lamb *croquettes*, or balls made of cold meat, done up with an egg, etc., stewed tomatoes and bread pudding.

Irish stew of mutton with greens, and baked beans, sliced tomatoes and currant dumplings.

Veal pot pie, with potatoes, salad and rice, and raisins.

Boiled leg of lamb, caper sauce, stewed tomatoes, mashed potatoes, and rhubarb pie.

Boiled fresh mackerel, green gooseberry sauce, hashed lamb, mashed potatoes, and rhubarb dumplings.

Stewed pigeons, with thin slices of fried bacon, spinach, potatoes, salad and lemon pie

Company Dinner.

White soup, olives, baked blue fish, salad, fillet of veal stuffed, and roasted Bermuda potatoes, sweet potatoes, spinach, stewed tomatoes, jelly, and kidney beans, custard in cups, rhubarb pie.

JUNE.

Stewed rabbit, early potatoes, greens, salad, green gooseberry pie.

Boiled lamb chops, potatoes, kidney beans, sliced tomatoes, and rhubarb batter pudding.

Roast leg of lamb, potatoes, asparagus, and sliced tomatoes. Blanc mange with jelly.

Stewed mutton with rice, early potatoes, salad, gooseberry pie.

Veal pot pie, potatoes, sliced tomatoes, and rice pudding.

Roast chickens, jelly, early potatoes, asparagus, and corn starch pudding, with cream, and fresh strawberries.

Chowder of blue fish, with potatoes, sliced tomatoes, cold boiled ham, and fresh currant pie.

JULY.

Shoulder of veal stuffed, potatoes, asparagus, salad and strawberry pie.

Small ribs of lamb stewed with new potatoes, green peas, tomatoes, and blackberry batter pudding.

Boiled ham, with potatoes, spinach, and dessert of bread and milk, and berries.

Boiled salmon with green peas, and egg sauce, potatoes, salad, and strawberry dumplings.

Corned beef, early cabbage stewed with vinegar, young turnips, potatoes, and cherry pie.

Roast beef, potatoes, asparagus, Lima beans, Indian corn, tomatoes, and green apple pie.

Chops cut off leg of mutton, and cooked with tomatoes, potatoes, kidney beans, and cherry batter pudding.

Roast leg of mutton, green peas, stewed tomatoes, potatoes, and huckleberry pie.

Extra Dinner.

Tomato soup, boiled salmon, with anchovy sauce, salad, roast lamb, green peas, mint sauce, potatoes, stewed tomatoes, succotash of Lima beans and Indian corn. Ice blanc mange, with pineapples, and open currant tart.

AUGUST.

Fillet of veal larded, new potatoes, stewed tomatoes, spinach, and huckleberry pudding.

Cold veal, succotash of corn and string beans, potatoes, salad, and cherry pie.

Veal pie, stewed tomatoes, potatoes, horseradish, and rice dumplings.

Lamb chops with tomato sauce, string beans, and new potatoes, huckleberry, or blackberry pie.

Cold lamb, potato salad, stewed tomatoes, green corn boiled, and cherry pudding.

Roast leg of lamb, mint sauce, new potatoes, new mashed turnips, salad, green peas, and currant, or gooseberry pie.

Dish of pickled cod with melted butter, cold boiled ham, potatoes, salad, corn, and fresh fruit pie, or pudding.

Stewed pigeons, lobster salad, potatoes, asparagus, currant jelly, Lima beans, currant, and custard tarts.

SEPTEMBER.

Roast prairie chickens, with apple sauce, potatoes, and spinach; corn starch pudding, and sliced peaches.

Fillet of mutton slightly corned, potatoes, green corn, new turnips, and currant jelly. Bread pudding.

Cold mutton, mashed potatoes browned, mashed turnips, salad, and blackberry pudding, "Buffalo" style.

Shank end of leg of mutton stewed with rice, stewed tomatoes, fried potatoes, and peach pie.

Sirloin of beef roasted, potatoes, cauliflower, succotash, and tomato salad. Yorkshire puddding.

Cold beef, hot potatoes, salad, or pickles, green corn, and plum batter pudding.

Oyster soup, the beef-bones being used to make the small amount of stock necessary, minced beef with potatoes, stewed tomatoes, string beans, and green apple pie.

Birthday Dinner.

Oyster pie, roast chicken with jelly, potatoes, corn, Lima beans, salad, bread and butter, pudding, and dish of fresh pears, peaches, plums, etc., arranged with leaves, and flowers.

OCTOBER

Mutton chops, with mushroom sauce, potatoes, succotash, and lemon meringue pie.

Boiled mutton, caper sauce, mashed turnips, potatoes, sliced tomatoes, or stewed; any rice pudding.

Broiled beef steak, baked potatoes, tomatoes, and baked apple dumplings.

Irish (mutton) stew, with dish of rice, as vegetables, tomatoes, and fresh apple pie

Vegetable soup, chowder made of haddock, potatoes, salad, and currant dumplings.

Corned beef, cabbage, potatoes, turnips, carrot, and stewed beets, Tapioca apple pudding.

Tomato soup, alamode beef, stewed cabbage, potatoes, Lima beans, celery, and baked rice pudding, with fruit.

NOVEMBER.

Stewed rabbit, with dish of pork and beans, boiled onions, potatoes, and pickles. Apple pie.

Roast haunch of mutton, mashed white turnips, potatoes, and jelly. Pancakes with jelly.

Chicken pot-pie, mashed potatoes, celery, pickled cauliflower, and squash or pumpkin pie.

Ox tail soup, soused fish, cold beans, hot potatoes, pickles, and English roll pudding.

Beef stew, mashed potatoes, fried parsnips, pickled beets, and baked apple pudding,

Roast chickens, mashed potatoes, cold slaw, egg plant, fried in butter, stewed tomatoes, and bread pudding.

Thanksgiving Dinner.

Oyster soup, cod, with egg sauce, lobster salad, roast turkey, cranberry sauce, mixed pickles, mangoes, pickled peaches, cold slaw, and celery; boiled ham, chicken pie ornamented, jelly, mashed potatoes browned, tomatoes, boiled onions, canned corn, sweet potatoes, roasted broccoli. Mince, and pumpkin pie, apple tarts, Indian pudding. Apples, nuts, and raisins.

DECEMBER.

Spare rib of pork, mashed potatoes, apple sauce, and baked apple dumplings.

Ribs of beef, boned and stuffed, potatoes, boiled onions, fried parsnips, and pickled cabbage; pumpkin pie.

Soup, broiled chops, mashed potatoes, apple sauce, and boiled rice, with raisins.

Soup meat, made into a stew with vegetables, and stock spice and sweet herbs, Indian dumplings, potatoes, and apple pie.

Roast turkey, cranberry jelly, mashed potatoes, stewed parsnips, salsify, or vegetable oyster, celery, mince pie, and apples.

Young goose, with onion stuffing, par-boiled, then roasted, mashed potatoes, apple sauce, broccoli, and apple pie, with cheese.

Cold fowl, cold boiled ham, roast potatoes, fried parsnips, maccaroni, cranberry sauce, or pickles, and mince pie with cheese.

Christmas Dinner.

Mock turtle soup, salmon, or baked trout, with anchovy sauce. Roast turkey with necklace of sausages, cranberry sauce, boiled fowls stuffed, with mushrooms, bread sauce. Boiled ham, apple sauce, mashed potatoes, potato balls, boiled onions, egg plant fried in batter, Lima beans, and stewed tomatoes; oyster fritters, oysters vol á vent, celery and pickles.

Dessert. Christmas plum pudding, lemon cheese cakes, tipsy cake, champagne jelly, apples, nuts, raisins, and grapes.

WINES AND DRINKS.

CURRANT CHAMPAGNE.

Ingredients for thirty gallons:—Three bushels, or one hundred and fifty pounds of currants, seventy-five pounds of white Havanna or refined crushed sugar; three pints white brandy, with sufficient pure soft water. The fruit should be gathered in dry weather, when ripe; mash them to break every berry, but not bruise the stems; add a portion of the water, and after stirring well, turn the mass on to a strainer, over a grain sieve, or riddle, rubbing and pressing very gently with the hands. The usual practice of squeezing and wringing through the strainer forces through too much pulp, occasioning too great a degree of fermentation. The sugar should be put into a tub or other open vessel, with the brandy, and the liquor strained on to it. When the sugar is dissolved, strain the whole through a fine hair, or grass cloth, into a strong, sweet cask of thirty-two gallons, and fill up to within two gallons, which leaves sufficient room for the fermentation to proceed, and drive in the bung tight. It is desirable that all parts of the process should go on at the same time, and be finished with all possible dispatch. The sooner the wine is bottled after it is perfectly fine, the more briskness it will exhibit. In producing champagne, it is necessary to give air for a short time, to increase the fermentation and deprive it of a great portion of its sweetness. The white currant is sweeter, and pleasanter flavored, when ripe, for table use, than the red. The wine made from it is nearly colorless, of sweet and pleasant flavor. Bottled before the fermentation has entirely subsided, it makes a fine champagne.

CURRANT WINE.

Bruise ripe currants stripped from the stem, and add to every gallon of pulp, half a gallon of water, first boiled and cold; let it remain in a tub twenty-four hours to ferment; strain it through a hair sieve, not pressing it with the hand, but letting it take its time to run. Then stir well in two pounds and a half of white sugar to every gallon of liquor. Add a quart of best rectified spirit of wine to every six gallons. After it has stood six weeks, bottle it. If it is not very fine empty it into other bottles, let it stand two weeks and then rack it off into smaller bottles.

BLACK CURRANT WINE.

Put the currants, after picking out the stems and leaves, into an open vessel, and cover them with water, keeping an account of the amount; then with a pestle or pounder mash every berry; let them stand for twenty-four hours to dissolve the pulp, then put the mass into a coarse bag and submit them to pressure, when the juice will run freely. After deducting the amount of water, the remainder will be the pure juice; and now, to every gallon of the juice add two of water, including that first put in, and to every gallon of the mixture, add four pounds of crushed sugar. Put it into a cask, reserving sufficient to fill up while fermenting. Put the cask in a moderately cool dry room to ferment; as the refuse works at the bung; fill up with the liquor reserved. When it has ceased working, bung it close for nine months, and it will be fit for bottling and use. This will have much of the flavor of Port wine, and make an excellent article for sacramental purposes. By reducing the quantity of sugar and adding water, it will be a fair imitation of claret wine, for a summer drink.

GRAPE SYRUP.

Pick the grapes from the stems, and to every four pounds of grapes, add a pint of water. Set them over a moderate fire till the grapes are well boiled, keeping the pan, which should be block tin or brass, covered; strain through a hair sieve, gently pressing the grapes; when cool, cover it with a plate and let it remain; till the next day in either wood, or an earthen vessel. Then c: ful-

ly clear it off, and to each pint allow a pound of loaf sugar broken, put the sugar into a pan, adding a pint of water to every four pounds; stir it while cold till the sugar is partly dissolved; then put it on a moderately brisk fire with the pan covered, stirring it often till nearly boiling; watch it carefully that it may not rise too much; let it boil up several times, skim it off quite clean, then pour in the juice, cover the pan until it nearly boils; remove the cover and let the syrup boil fifteen minutes, skimming it well. Pour the syrup into a stone jar, with a little grated lemon, or a few pieces of broken cinnamon, and let it remain one day. Then strain it into bottles, cork, and keep it in a cool place. This is recommended as an unalcoholic wine.

GRAPE WINE.—1.

Crush five gallons of ripe grapes, and let them soak seven days in four and a half gallons of soft water; add to it seventeen and a half pounds of white sugar. Strain it, put it into a clean cask, leave it open until fermentation ceases, then bung tightly.

GRAPE WINE.—2.

Gather the grapes when they are just turning color, or about half ripe. Pound them in a tub with the stalks, and to every quart of pounded fruit, put two quarts of water. Let this stand in a mash tub fourteen days, then draw it off, and to every gallon of liquor put three pounds of loaf sugar; when this is dissolved, cask the wine. After it has worked, bung it securely down, and keep it for six months; then bottle it, and tie down or wire the corks, if it be intended to be kept more than one year.

ELDER WINE.

Take the juice of three gallons of elder berries, which will about equal six quarts. Add twenty-four pounds of sugar, and wash the husks of the berries, in sixteen quarts of water. Boil six ounces of ginger in water, strain and boil a second time. Add this and the juice of the berries, to the water in which the husks have been washed. Cask it, and when the fermentation is over, nto the cask some well-dried spices.

ELDER FLOWER WINE.

Allow a gallon of water, and three pounds of sugar to every quart of the blossoms stripped from the stalks, boil and skim the sugar and water, and pour it over the flowers boiling hot. To every gallon of the liquor add a small table-spoonful of home-brewed hop yeast, and the juice of a lemon; stir it thoroughly together. Let the whole ferment for three days in an open vessel of wood or earthen, the top entirely covered with a thick woolen blanket. At the end of three days, strain it through a sieve and whisk the white of an egg beaten to a froth, through the wine. Put at the bottom of the cask chopped raisins, in the proportion of three or four pounds to every six gallons of wine, pour in the wine, and close the bung. In six months it will be fit to bottle.

BLACKBERRY WINE.

First pour boiling water on the fruit and when cool, bruise it. Let it stand until the berries rise to the top; then drain off the clear liquor, measure it and add two pounds of sugar to every gallon of liquor; stir it well and let it stand open a week or ten days, then draw off the wine and pan it through a jelly-bag. Take half an ounce of isinglass for every three gallons, dissolve it in a little of the wine and mix it through the whole.

RHUBARB WINE.

Chop the stalks, and for fifty pounds of rhubarb, allow thirty pounds of sugar; press the juice, add the sugar and enough water for nine gallons of wine; put it into a cask, cover it with a cloth until it ceases to ferment; plug the barrel for three months, then bottle the wine, or if this is not convenient draw it off into a clean cask that it will fill completely.

GOOSEBERRY WINE.

Take a quantity of ripe, white or yellow gooseberries, bruise them with a pestle in a tub, and to every eight pounds of fruit add one gallon of cold spring water. Stir them and let them stand twenty-four hours; then strain the mash through a fine sieve or a grass cloth strainer. To every gallon of juice add four pounds of white loaf sugar. When all is dissolved, stir it well, and when settled put it into a cask with two quarts of brandy to every ten gallons of juice and half an ounce of isinglass. Set the cask in a cool place, leaving out the bung until the fermentation has nearly ceased. Then draw off into bottles, and cork tight immediately.

GREEN GOOSEBERRY WINE.

Having thoroughly bruised eight gallons of green gooseberries, put them into eight gallons of cold water, and allow them to stand for twenty-four hours; at the end of that time drain the liquor well off through a sieve, and for each gallon add three pounds and a half of loaf sugar; pour the liquor into a cask and put to it one quart of the best gin. After standing for six months it will be ready for bottling.

GINGER WINE.

To every gallon of water put nearly three pounds of loaf sugar, two lemons, and two ounces of ginger, bruised. Boil the sugar and water for half an hour, skimming it, then pour it on the rinds of the lemons and the ginger. When the liquor is milk warm, squeeze in the juice of the lemons, and put in it a little yeast at the same time. Let it work for two or three days, then put it into a cask closely stopped for six weeks. Bottle it with one gallon of brandy to twelve gallons of wine. The pulp of the ginger and lemons must be put into the cask with a little isinglass, to refine the wine; but the pips and white part of the lemons should be removed, as they make it bitter.

BLACKBERRY BRANDY.

Bottle equal quantities of blackberry juice and brandy, allowing a pound of loaf sugar to every gallon. Or, a gallon of blackberries can be put to each gallon of deodorized pure spirits, and the berries dissolved in the spirits. These are very good for bowel complaints.

CHERRY BRANDY.

Crush cherries, and allow one quart to every gallon of spirits. Wild cherries are the proper ones to be used. Rum, brandy, or deodorized pure spirits can be used.

RASPBERRY SYRUP.

Add one quart of vinegar to three quarts of berries, let it stand one day then squeeze it through a cloth. Add a pound of sugar for each pint of juice and boil it twenty minutes.

HOP BEER.

To make fifteen gallons, take twelve ounces of hops, six quarts of molasses, ten eggs. Put the hops in a bag, and boil them fifteen minutes in three pails-full of water. Put in the molasses while hot, and pour immediately into a strong ale cask which can be made perfectly air tight, and put in the remainder of the water cold. Let the mixture stand until cool, and then add the egg. This beer will not ferment in cold weather unless put in quite a warm place. It will keep six or eight months. Three months after it is fermented it is almost equal to ale.

GINGER BEER

Stir up in a gallon of boiling water, one pound of loaf sugar, one ounce and a half of the best ginger bruised, and one ounce of cream of tartar, or, if preferred, a lemon sliced, until the heat falls to that of new milk. Then having poured one table-spoonful of good yeast upon a piece of bread, put it in the middle of the vessel letting it float in the mixture. Cover the whole with a cloth, and let it stand twenty-four hours, after which, strain it and put it into bottles, filling each only about three parts full, cork them tightly, and tie them down. In warm weather this ginger beer will be ready to drink in two days.

TO MAKE A CASK OF GINGER BEER.

Take ten gallons of soft water, and fifteen pounds of loaf sugar, clarified with the whites of six eggs; bruise half pound of white ginger; boil half an hour. Pare off the thin yellow rind of twelve lemons, and pour the liquor when it is boiling, over the lemon peel. As soon as it is cool, mix a gill of good yeast with it, and put it in a cask. Retain two quarts of the liquor, in which dissolve two ounces of shred isinglass; mix it with the wine, and shake well. Let the cask stand open all night; then close the bung, and in three weeks bottle it off. It will be fit to drink in three months.

SPRUCE BEER.—1.

Water ten gallons; sugar ten pounds; essence of spruce quarter of a pound; yeast half pint. Dissolve the sugar and essence of spruce in the water, previously warmed; then allow it to cool a little, and add the yeast as in making ginger beer; bottle immediately in half pint bottles.

SPRUCE BEER.—2.

To a gallon of water, allow an ounce of hops and a spoonful of ginger. Boil it well, strain it, and add a pint of molasses and half an ounce of the essence of spruce; let it cool, pour in a tea-cup of yeast and put it into a clean cask. After it has fermented a day or two, bottle it.

MEAD.

To six gallons of water, add six quarts of strained honey, the yellow rind of two large lemons, pared very thin, and the whites of three eggs beat to strong froth. Mix and boil all together three quarters of an hour, skimming it well. Pour into a tub. When lukewarm, add three table-spoonsful of good fresh yeast, cover and leave it to ferment. When it is well worked, pour it into a barrel with lemon peel in the bottom, and let it stand six months. It will then be ready to bottle.

SHRUB.

Take three quarts of red currant juice, three quarts of good rum, dissolve in it two pounds of lump sugar, stir together and strain through a jelly bag. When it is entirely clear, bottle it.

QUICK BEER.

Fourteen quarts of cold water, one quart of molasses, one quart of hop yeast and four table-spoonsful of ginger; mix it well, strain through a fine sieve and bottle it immediately. In twenty-four hours it will be ready for use.

GINGER POP.

Take three quarters of a pound of white sugar, one ounce of cream of tartar, the juice and rind of a lemon, one ounce of ginger, put the whole into a pan, and pour over it four quarts of boiling water; let it stand till lukewarm, and then add a table-spoonful of yeast. When it has ceased boiling, bottle it off in small soda water bottles or jars. It will be fit for use in twenty-four hours.

IMPERIAL.

Put into a jug that will contain three pints, half an ounce of cream of tartar, the juice of a lemon and the rind pared very thin; pour boiling water over these, and add sugar to taste. When cold, it is fit for use. It is refreshing and wholesome for persons heated from the weather, or feverish from indisposition.

BERRY DRINK.

Put two quarts of ripe, fresh raspberries into a stone or glazed vessel, whose glazing will not be affected by acids, and pour on them a quart of good vinegar. Let it stand twenty-four hours, and then strain out the juice and vinegar. To each pint of this, add a pound of pulverized white sugar, and put it into a porcelain kettle to boil smartly for about half an hour, removing all the scum as it rises. When cold, bottle and seal. Half a gill of this, stirred in a tumblerful of cold water, makes a delicious drink. Strawberries, dewberries, or blackberries can be used in the same manner, only using just as much vinegar as will cover the fruit. Add no alcohol. With bottles well sealed, it will keep two years.

YANKEE CORN DRINK.

To five gallons of cold water, add one quart of sound corn, and two quarts of molasses. Put it into a keg, shake well, and in two or three days it will be fit for use. Bung tight. It may be flavored with essence of spruce or lemon. The corn will last to make five or six brewings; if it becomes sour, add more molasses and water. It is a cheap and simple beer, and is called very good.

A QUICK DRINK.

Take a glass of sherry, a small bit of mint, and some sugar to taste; mix together in a large tumbler, add some pounded ice, and then pour on it a pint of cider; drink it when it effervesces. Half the quantity will generally be found enough, or the ingredients may be divided into two glasses, unless you have a soda water glass.

MILK LEMONADE.

Put one quart of boiling water, the juice of six fine lemons, the peel of three, pared very thin, two wine glasses of syrup, and half a pint of Maderia or Sherry into a covered vessel and let it stand twelve hours. Then boil half a pint of new milk, pour it on the mixture, and run it through a jelly bag until clear. It makes a refreshing drink.

PORTABLE LEMONADE.

Mix strained lemon juice to loaf sugar, in the proportion of four large lemons to a pound of white sugar, or as much as it will hold in solution. Grate the rinds, which add to this. Preserve in a close jar, or large mouthed bottles. Use a table-spoonful for a tumbler of water.

FOURTH OF JULY SHERRY COBBLER.

A large tumbler two thirds full of pounded ice; half a dozen strawberries, a few fine chips from the yellow rind of a lemon, a table-spoonful of powdered sugar; fill with fine Sherry, shake, and take in the usual way.

EGG NOG.

To the yolks of six eggs, add six table-spoonsful of powdered sugar, a quart of new milk, half a pint of French brandy, and a pint of Maderia. Beat the whites up separately, and stir them through the mixture, just before pouring into cup glasses.

STATEN ISLAND LEMONADE.

Take half a dozen fresh lemons, and half a dozen smooth Seville oranges, and rub loaf sugar on the outside, until the flavoring oil is all extracted from the rind; roll them soft, press out the juice, add the sugar to the juice, strain off the seeds, a bowl of pounded ice, a pint of Sherry, and a quart of water. Shake all together very thoroughly. It is a delicious summer drink.

CLARET PUNCH.

A pint bottle of claret, a gill of French brandy, four table-spoonsful of powdered sugar, the juice and thinly cut rind of a lemon, a lump of ice, and a pint of water.

A COOL CUP.

Weigh six ounces of sugar in lumps, and extract the essence from the rind of a large, fresh lemon by rubbing them upon it, then put them into a deep jug, and add the strained juice of one lemon and a half. When the sugar is dissolved, pour in a bottle of good cider, and three large wine-glasses full of Sherry; add nearly half a small nutmeg, lightly grated, and serve the cup with, or without some sprigs of fresh balm or borage in it. If closely covered down, and placed on ice for a short time, it will be more agreeable as a summer beverage.

MAY DRINK. (*German.*)

Put into a large, deep jug one pint of light white wine, to two of red, and dissolve in it sufficient sugar to sweeten it agreeably. Wipe a sound China orange, cut it in rather thick slices without paring it, and add it to the wine; then throw in some small bunches of the fragrant little plant, called woodruff, cover the jar closely to exclude the air, and leave it until the following day. Lemon rind can be used instead of oranges. Serve this to May-day visitors.

OXFORD SWIG

Put into a bowl a pound of sugar, pour on it a pint of warm beer, grated nutmeg, and some ginger, also grated; add four glasses of sherry and five pints of beer, stir it well, and if not sweet enough, add more sugar, and let it stand covered up four hours, and it is fit for use. Sometimes add a few lumps of sugar rubbed on a lemon to extract the flavor, and some lemon juice. If the lemon rind is pared very thin, without any of the white skin left, it answers better, by giving a stronger flavor of the lemon.

Bottle this mixture, and in a few days it will be in a state of effervescence. When served in a bowl fresh made, add some bread toasted very crisp, cut in narrow strips.

SACK POSSET.

Four ounces of fine brown sugar, a pint of sweet wine or sack, and a nutmeg; let them simmer till the sugar is dissolved; beat ten eggs, and put them on the fire to warm with a quart of milk, stir them one way to prevent curdling; when cold mix all together and put it on the fire to warm, but not boil; serve hot.

CHRISTMAS EGG NOG.

Take the yolks of eight eggs and six table-spoonsful of pulverized sugar, and beat them to the consistency of cream; to this add half a nutmeg, grated, and beat well together, then mix one third of a pint of good Jamaica rum, and a wine glass of brandy or Madeira wine; have ready the whites of the eggs beaten to a stiff froth, and beat them into the above mixture; when this is done, stir in three pints of good rich milk. No heat is used.

MILK PUNCH.

Beat up two eggs, well mix them with a quart of milk, adding sugar, nutmeg, and lemon peel, to taste. Boil this gently, and stir it all the time until sufficiently thick. Remove it from the fire for a very few minutes, then add to it a full gill of rum, stirring it all the time it is being poured in.

MILK PUNCH TO KEEP.

Pare six oranges and six lemons, as thin as possible, and grate them afterwards to extract the flavor. Soak the peel for twenty-four hours in a bottle of rum or brandy, closely stopped. Squeeze the fruit on two pounds of sugar, and add to it four quarts of water and one of new milk, boiling hot. Stir in the rum, and run it through a jelly bag until quite clear, then bottle and cork it closely immediately.

COLD PUNCH.

Put into a saucepan a full pint of cold water and one pound and a half of white sugar; let it be on the fire until the sugar is dissolved. Add three bottles of white wine, some lemon syrup, and a little ginger, let it get hot, but not boiling. When quite hot, pour half a bottle of fine rum into it and immediately take it off the fire. As soon as the punch begins to cool, it must be bottled and well corked. It will keep good for some time.

MISCELLANEOUS.

KEEPING GRAPES.

Pick the grapes before they are dead-ripe and when perfectly dry; remove all the defective ones; wrap each bunch well in old paper or cotton, and not allow more than two layers in a box; place in a cold, dry room where they will not freeze.

The French preserve grapes the year round, by coating the clusters with lime. The bunches are picked just before they are thoroughly ripe, and dipped in lime water of the consistency of thick cream. They are then hung up to remain. The lime coating keeps out the air, and checks any tendency to decay. When wantted for the table, dip the clusters into warm water to remove the lime.

In preserving grapes, with cotton, they are sometimes placed gently between layers of cotton in a glass or earthen ware jar. The jar is then corked down and the corks dipped in melted resin, or otherwise rendered air tight.

KEEPING APPLES.

Apples, potatoes, etc., are well preserved in barrels and boxes in a dry cellar, with light and air excluded, and the temperature quite cold without freezing. Apples are sometimes kept excellently in river sand dried in an oven, placing in a large box a layer of sand and a layer of apples, taking care that the apples do not touch each other.

KEEPING PEAS FOR WINTER USE.

Shell the peas, throw them into boiling water with a little salt in it, allow them to boil five or six minutes. Then drain in a colander and afterwards on a cloth until completely dried. Then place them in air tight bottles. Some place them into wide mouthed bottles, not quite filling them, and pour in fried mutton fat so as to cover them. Then cork tightly, securing the cork with resin or with a bladder. When used boil them until tender with some butter and a very little mint. Another method is after they are dried as above, place them on a tin or earthen dish in a mild oven once or twice until they harden, and then place them in paper bags hung in the kitchen.

KEEPING CABBAGES.

When the weather becomes frosty, cut them off near the head, and carry them with the leaves on, to a dry cellar. Break off superfluous leaves, and pick into a light cask or box, stems upward, and when nearly full, cover with leaves. Secure the box or barrel with a lid against rats.

KEEPING CABBAGES IN THE COUNTRY.

Take up the cabbages by the roots, set them closely together in rows up to the head in soil, roots down, the same as it grows; drive in posts at the corners of the bed, and intermediate spaces, if necessary, higher on one side than the other; nail strips of board or lath on these posts; lay upon these old boards, doors, or if you have nothing else, bean poles and corn fodder, so that the roof will be clear of the cabbages, and allow the air to circulate; close up the sides with yard or garden offal of any kind, and the cabbages will keep all winter, fresh and green, and be accessible at all times, or nearly so, the frost not being so severe under this protection as in exposed places. Exclude moisture, but never mind the frost.

KEEPING MUSTARD.

Dissolve three ounces of salt in a quart of boiling water, and pour it hot upon two ounces of scraped horseradish. Closely cover the jar, and let it it stand twenty-four hours, strain it, and by degrees mix it with flour of mustard. Beat them well together for a long time, until the mixture becomes of the proper thickness. Put it into wide-mouthed bottles, and cork it down closely, when it will keep good for many months.

TO PRESERVE PAINT.

Wash white paint with warm water, soap, a soft flannel; do not scrub it with a brush, and wipe it dry with a large, old linen cloth. This will keep it nice for years.

TO KEEP LEMONS.

Keep them in cold water, changed every week. This also adds to the juice.

TO PRESERVE PARSLEY FRESH AND GREEN.

Put it into a strong pickle of salt and water, boiling hot, and keep for use. Or it is good for soup, stuffing, etc., hung up in bunches, in a dry attic or store-room.

TO PRESERVE MUSHROOMS

Put your mushrooms, cut as for stewing, into a saucepan; stew till all the liquor is drawn, and then till all again is absorbed; and when quite dry, put in a good lump of butter, cayenne pepper, and salt. After it has boiled, pour into sweet-meat pots the sizes that will be sufficient for a dish, and well cover them with butter; and they will be, when warmed up and well finished off with a little white sauce, as good as when fresh gathered.

TO KEEP MEAT, GAME, OR POULTRY, IN HOT WEATHER.

If you wish to keep meat a day or two longer, and there is danger of its being effected by the hot weather, sprinkle roughly pounded charcoal over it, and put the same under it; for birds, put a lump of charcoal in the inside, and sprinkle the breast, and under the wings, with the pounded charcoal.

TO REMOVE TAINT FROM MEAT OR POULTRY.

Wash the part affected, with chloride of soda first, and then in fresh water. It should be cooked as soon as possible after being wet. Broiling, or roasting, is the best way to cook meats that have been kept a little too long. If salted, wash it and throw away the brine, then leave it, for a few days in the following composition: Fresh burnt charcoal powdered, twelve parts; common salt eleven parts, saltpetre four parts. Mix and use the same as common salt. Before cooking remove the black color with clear water.

SNOW AS A SUBSTITUTE FOR EGGS.

In making pancakes or puddings, snow is an excellent substitute for eggs; two table-spoonsful of snow stirred in quickly are equal to an egg in puddings or pancakes for making them light. It is explained by the fact that snow contains in its flakes much atmospheric air, which is set free as it melts.

CORN STARCH INSTEAD OF EGGS.

For most cakes and puddings, for which eggs are used, a tablespoonful of corn starch or maizena will be found an excellent substitute for one egg.

EGG PAPER.

Soft, tough paper cut to fit jars, and dipped in a saucer of white of egg, put over steamed jars of fruit or preserves, will keep them better than all the late inventions. When the jars and fruit are scalded hot as possible, it will keep them nicely. For jellies and all kinds of pickles, it makes a cheap, convenient cover. The paper must turn over the rim of the jar.

FROZEN POTATOES.

Frozen potatoes give more starch or flour than fresh ones.

SIZE OF TURNIPS.

Small sized turnips have double the nutritious matter that larger ones have, but the largest ruta bagas are the most nutritious.

TO WASH FRUIT STAINS FROM THE HANDS.

Rub them with sorrel, rhubarb stalks, lemon, apple or tomato skins.

DAMP WOOLEN CLOTHING.

Before putting damp woolen clothing to the fire, rub it with a moist sponge, the way of the nap, until the smoothness is restored; brushing will not remove the roughness, unless this precaution is taken.

DIAMOND CEMENT.

This is the best cement for broken glass, or china, because it is colorless, and perfectly resists moisture. It requires to be liquified by placing the vial in boiling water, and should then be applied with a camel's hair brush.

HOW TO PREVENT THE INROADS OF VERMIN.

On entering a new house, have it thoroughly clean, and every hole and crevice, in cupboard, closet, or room, stopped up with a cement made of putty, and chloride of lime. Before putting carpets, or oil-cloth down, dust the edges of the boards with Lyons' or Persian powder, which will prevent the attacks of moths, and cockroaches. A dollar spent in this way, will be found an excellent investment. Repeat the process, when general cleaning time comes, and with ordinary precaution in cleaning bedsteads, and taking care of furs, you will never be troubled with bugs, moths, or cockroaches.

LOBSTER'S EGGS.

Lobster's eggs boiled, and pounded in a mortar, constitute a perfectly safe, harmless, and beautiful rouge.

TO STRENGTHEN THE HAIR.

Dilute an ounce of borax, and an ounce of camphor in two quarts of water, and wash the hair thoroughly twice a week, clipping the ends occasionally. It will quickly grow long, thick, and even.

TO CLEAR, AND STRENGTHEN THE VOICE.

The best method is in vogue among all distinguished vocalists, viz: swallow the yolk of a raw egg, *whole*, every morning on rising; also avoid pastry, and sponge the throat and chest well with cold water daily.

BUTTER COOLER.

A simple mode of keeping butter in warm weather, where ice is not handy, is, to pour about a pint of water, in a round dish, and place half a brick, or stone the size of half a brick, in the water, and put the plate of butter upon it, then invert a common flower pot over the butter, so that the pot will set down in the water. The porousness of the earthen ware will keep the butter cool. It will be better still if the pot be covered with a wet cloth, the rapid abstraction of heat by external evaporation causing the butter to become hard.

KITCHEN ODORS.

Odors from boiling ham, cabbage, etc., may be prevented by throwing red pepper pods, or a few pieces of charcoal into the pot.

FRUIT SINKING.

To prevent fruit from sinking in puddings or cake, roll it in flour before putting it in.

COCHINEAL.

In using cochineal to give color, they may be broken and tied up in fine muslin, which obviates the difficulty of getting them out when the color is given.

IMPROVING CORN MEAL.

Indian meal is improved by being kiln dried. It may be spread on a dripping pan and heated in the oven.

TO MAKE HENS LAY IN WINTER.

Keep them warm, keep corn by them constantly, but do not feed it to them; feed them with meat scraps, where lard or tallow has been tried, or fresh meat. Some chop up green peppers finely, and feed them. Let them have a frequent taste of green food, a little gravel and lime, or clam shells.

TO FATTEN TURKEYS

Every morning for a month, give them mashed potatoes mixed with buckwheat flour, barley or beans; take away what remains in the evening. After a month, add half a dozen balls made of barley flour, when they go to roost. Give them these eight days successively; turkeys thus fed are fat and good.

HATCHING.

Chickens are hatched in twenty-one days; turkeys, twenty-six; ducks and geese, thirty; pigeons, eighteen.

TO CLARIFY DRIPPING.

Place the dripping in a large pan, pour on about a quart of boiling water, and pass the whole through a muslin or a sieve. Let it get cold, and the dripping can be taken out in a cake; the refuse being at the bottom, will be easily scraped off. If it be not sufficiently clarified, the process must be repeated.

TO CLARIFY MOLASSES.

Common molasses may be clarified and rendered much more palatable by heating it over the fire and pouring in sweet milk, in the proportion of one pint to a gallon of molasses. When the molasses boils up once, the albumen in the milk collects all the impurities in a thick scum upon the top, which must be carefully removed, and the molasses is then fit for use. Bullock's blood is also used for this purpose, but milk is more agreeable in many ways for domestic use.

HOME MADE BREAD.

The quantity of bread is greatly increased by using bran water for mixing the dough. A quart of bran should be boiled for an hour in water, and then strained through a sieve.

IVORY HANDLES.

Ivory handles should not be wet in washing. It is hard to remove stains from ivory, without, at the same time, removing the polish. Muriatic acid removes the polish. If the stain arises from ordinary wear, it may be soaked in strong lime water, and afterwards exposed to the air, repeating the operation until it becomes white. It should not be exposed to the sun, or it will crack. A solution of muriatic acid will remove ink stains; to restore the polish, rub with fine putty powder, or gilder's whiting till the polish returns. Another method to remove stains from ivory handles is to take alum water, boil it and let it grow cold. Then soak the handles in it for an hour, take them out and brush them well with a tooth brush. Dip a clean towel in pure water, squeeze it out and while wet wrap it around the handles, soaked and brushed as above, and leave all to dry gradually. If dried too rapidly out of the alum water, the handles will be injured; if dried slowly, they will become white.

TO FASTEN KNIFE HANDLES.

Handles of knives or forks that have come off by being put in hot water, by mixing powdered resin with chopped hair or tow, chalk, whiting, or quick lime; partly fill the hole with it, heat the spike of the knife or fork and force it in. Melted resin or brick dust, mixed, is also used. Or put a small portion of a quill pen into the handle, heat the blade, put it in the quill in the handle, and press it in firmly.

TO TAKE OFF STARCH OR RUST FROM FLAT IRONS.

Tie a piece of yellow beeswax in a rag, and when the iron is nearly hot enough to use, rub it quickly with the wax and then with a coarse cloth.

RUST ON STEEL IMPLEMENTS, OR KNIVES.

Cover the steel with sweet oil, well rubbing it on. Let it remain for forty-eight hours and then, using unslacked lime finely powdered, rub the steel until all the rust has disappeared.

ROUGH FLAT IRONS.

Rub them with fine salt, and it will make them smooth.

CRACKS IN STOVES.

Ashes and common salt wet and mixed, will stop the cracks in a stove and prevent smoke escaping.

CEMENT FOR METAL AND GLASS.

The following cement will firmly attach any metalic substance to glass or porcelain. Mix two ounces of a thick solution of glue with one ounce of linseed oil varnish, or three fourths of an ounce of Venice turpentine. Boil them together, stirring them until they mix as thoroughly as possible. The pieces cemented should be tied together for two or three days and nights.

POLISHING PASTE.

Cut half a pound of mottled soap into pieces, mix with half a pound of rotten stone in powder; put them into a saucepan with sufficient cold water to cover the mixture,—about three pints; boil slowly till dissolved to a paste.

VARNITH TO PREVENT RUST.

Make a composition of fat, oil and varnish, mixed with four fifths of highly rectified spirits of turpentine. Put this varnish on metal with a sponge.

TO PRESERVE LAMP CHIMNEYS FROM BREAKING.

Place a cloth at the bottom of a large pan, fill the pan with cold water, and place the glass into it. Cover the pan and let its contents boil one hour. Take it off the fire and leave the glass in the water until it is cold.

SOFT SOAP.

Slice up four pounds of white bar soap into four gallons of water, and add a pound of sal soda. Mix, dissolve it thoroughly over the fire, and set aside for use. A smaller quantity can be made in the same proportions.

CREAKING HINGES.

Rub the hinges with a very little soft soap.

ICE ON WINDOWS.

Windows may be kept free from ice, and polished, by rubbing the glass with alcohol, with a brush or sponge.

WATER AND FIRE PROOF CEMENT.

A cement which is a good protection against weather, water and fire to a certain extent, is made by mixing a gallon of water with two gallons of brine, in two and a half pounds of brown sugar, and three pounds of common salt. Put it on with a brush, like paint. A smaller quantity can be made in the same proportions.

RAYS OF THE SUN.

The rays of the sun may be kept from penetrating a window, by applying to it an ounce of powdered gum tragacanth in the whites of six eggs, well beaten.

FIRE PROOF CEMENT.

Two pounds of brown sugar, three pounds of fine salt, one pound of alum; mix thoroughly, put on like white-wash, on roofs of houses, fences, around fire-places, etc.

WATER PROOF PASTE.

Mix oil or lard with fine pieces of India rubber, simmer over a slow fire until thick as paste.

FIRE IN THE CHIMNEY.

Salt put on the fire in the grate below, acts chemically on the flaming soot above, and will often extinguish the fire in a short time; or shoot a gun loaded with powder, up the chimney.

TO DRIVE NAILS.

Common cut nails, or screws, are easily driven into hard wood, if rubbed with a little soap, either hard or soft.

TO REMOVE GREASE FOR PAINTING.

Before painting greasy furniture or a greasy partition, white-wash it over night, and wash all you can of the white-wash off in the morning. This removes the grease for painting.

TO CLEAN MARBLE.

Pulverize a little stone blue with four ounces of whiting, mix them with an ounce of soda dissolved in very little water and four ounces of soft soap, boil the mixture quarter of an hour over a slow fire, stirring constantly; lay it on the marble with a brush while hot, and let it lie half an hour; wash it in warm water with flannel and scrubbing brush, and wipe it dry.

MARKS ON A TABLE.

To remove a whitish mark left by a hot dish or boiling water, pour lamp oil on, and rub hard with a soft cloth. Then pour on a little spirits of wine or cologne water, and rub dry with another cloth.

FURNITURE.

Beeswax and strong lye will clean and polish furniture.

TO GIVE A FINE COLOR TO MAHOGANY.

Let the tables be washed perfectly clean with vinegar, having first taken out any ink stains there may be, with spirits of salts. Use the following liquid:—Into a pint of cold-drawn linseed oil, put four penny-worth of alkanet root, and two penny worth of rose pink, in an earthen vessel; let it remain all night, then stirring well, rub some of it all over the tables with a linen rag; when it has lain some time, rub it bright with linen cloths.

TO CLEAN PAINT.

Smear a piece of flannel with common whiting, mixed to the consistency of common paste in warm water. Rub the surface to be cleaned quite briskly and wash off with pure cold water. Grease spots and other filth will be removed.

SOILED CARPETS.

Sprinkle the carpet with dry Indian meal or wheat bran and sweep it hard.

SCOURING FLOUR.

A pound of soft soap, half a pound of soda and four quarts of water. Boil two hours and stir in a quart of silver sand. Use a small quantity at a time on the scrubbing brush.

CHEAP PAINT.

A cheap paint for a barn or rough woodwork, may be made of six pounds of melted pitch, one pint of linseed oil, and one pound of brick dust or yellow ochre.

APERED WALLS.

Rub the walls with a cloth sprinkled with Indian meal. Or gently sweep off the dust and rub with soft muslin cloth.

TO IRON RIBBONS.

Heat an iron not too hot, turn it on the side and draw the wrong side of the ribbons over it quickly, holding them firmly to the iron.

TO STIFFEN CRAPE.

Hold it over potatoes or rice while boiling, and let it dry by the fire.

TO REMOVE BROKEN SPOTS FROM VELVET.

Hold the wrong side of the velvet over steam, and while damp draw the wrong side across a quite clean stove pipe, or a warm iron several times.

TO CLEAN BLACK LACE VAILS.

These are cleansed by passing them through a warm liquor of ox-gall and water, after which they must be rinsed in cold water, then finished as follows: Take a small piece of glue about the size of a bean, pour boiling water upon it, which will dissolve it, and when dissolved, pass the vail through it, then clap it between your hands and frame it or pin it out, taking care to keep the edge straight and even.

WATER SPOTS IN BLACK CRAPE.

Clap it while wet until dry. Spread the spot on the hand dampening it, if it has previously dried, and slap it with the other till the spots disappear.

TO RENOVATE BLACK SILK.

Sponge it with clear strong cold tea, shake it out, and hang it up to dry, or iron it while damp. Another way is, rip out the seams, rub it with a piece of crape, then put it in cold water twenty-four hours, iron it with a hot iron on the wrong side; be careful not to wring the silk.

TO TAKE OUT MILDEW.

Take your cloth when dry, wet thoroughly with soft soap and salt, mixed. Let it lie a short time, then wash it in a good suds and lay out to bleach. If one operation does not answer two will, and the linen will be clear and clean as ever.

TO TAKE INK OUT OF LINEN.

Dip the portion that is stained in pure melted tallow; then wash out the tallow and the ink will come out with it. Lemon juice, or any acid will generally take out any stain. Or dip the part stained in cold water, fill a basin with boiling water, place a pewter plate on the top, lay the muslin on the plate, put salts of lemon or tartaric acid on the ink spots, rubbing it with the bowl of a spoon, the spots will disappear.

WASHING PRINT OR LAWN DRESSES.

Boil a quart of bran, in a bag, in a gallon of water for an hour; take out the bran and divide the water in which it was boiled, putting one-half to one gallon of warm water, in which the dresses are to be washed the first time, and the other half to a second gallon, in which they are to be rinsed or washed a second time; this process needs neither soap nor starch, and makes the colors and consistency of the goods precisely the same as when new; the extract of bran cleans, sufficiently stiffens, and preserves the colors; dry in the shade and iron on the wrong side.

TO RESTORE LINEN THAT HAS LONG BEEN STAINED.

Rub the stains on each side with wet, brown soap. Mix some starch to a thick paste with cold water, and spread it over the soaped places. Then expose the linen to the sun and air, and if the stains have not disappeared in three or four days, rub off the mixture, and repeat the process with fresh soap and starch. Afterwards dry it; wet it with cold water and put it in the wash.

PAINT SPOTS ON CLOTH, SILK, ETC.

When the stain is not yet dried, lay the cloth on a number of thicknesses of sheet, rub on soap with a tooth brush, then dip the brush in warm water and wash the paint away, the sheet beneath absorbing the water. Then wash the brush, dip it in the water, and with it wash the soap away. Then rub both sides of the material with a dry towel and hang it up to dry. If the paint is dry dip a piece of flannel in spirits of turpentine, rub the stain till removed, then wash out the turpentine quickly with soap and water, or if the color is very delicate with warm water alone, or the turpentine will leave a stain of itself. Spots of paint, or of pitch or tar anywhere, may be removed with spirits of turpentine.

WASHING COLORED MUSLINS.

To set the color of muslin, pour boiling water on the dress before washing, and allow it to remain till quite cold. For washing green or blue muslin, take a little sugar of lead, dissolve it in a gallon of cold water, dip the dress in it, let it remain quarter of an hour, then wring it out and send it to be washed. Have no scars or scratches on your hand, and throw the water away immediately, for the sugar of lead is a rank poison.

TO CLEAN SILK.

Take a quarter of a pound of soft soap, a tea-spoonful of brandy, and a pint of gin; mix all well together, and strain through a cloth. With a sponge or flannel, spread the mixture on each side of the silk without creasing it; wash it in two or three waters, and iron it on the wrong side. It will look as good as new, and the process will not injure silks of even the most delicate color.

TO CLEAN KID GLOVES.

First see that your hands are clean, then put on your gloves, and wash them as though you were washing your hands, in a basin of turpentine until quite clean; hang them up in a warm place, or where there is a current of air, which will carry off the smell of the turpentine.

ANOTHER METHOD.

Put the gloves on your hands, and rub them lightly, but thoroughly, wherever soiled, with a piece of flannel, soaked in benzine. As they dry off, rub them over with pearl powder, and expose them to the air to take off the smell of benzine. This is the way they are cleaned by French cleaners, and if done, before they are too much soiled, they can be made to look very nice by this method.

IRON STAINS.

These may be removed with juice of lemon, or of sorrel leaves, but if these fail, moisten the stain spots with water and rub on a little powdered oxalic acid. Wash the acid off thoroughly soon after it is put on, or it will eat the cloth. Also wash it from your hands, and keep it away from children, for it is poisonous in the mouth. Ink stain may be taken out in this way. It must be noticed however that acids had better only be used on white as they will discharge pink, lilac, and some other colors.

GREASE SPOTS.

An ounce of pulverized borax put into a quart of boiling water and bottled for use, will be found invaluable for removing grease spots from woolen goods.

INK SPOTS IN BOOKS.

Ink on printed leaves of books, may be removed by a solution of oxalic acid in water. The lamp-black of printers' ink is not affected by it.

GREASE ON A LEATHER COVERED BOOK.

To remove this, rub the leather with white flannel briskly, and repeat until it disappears. This will remove grease from anything that will bear rubbing.

TO REMOVE SPERMACETI SPOTS.

First scrape off all you can, then place a piece of brown paper on the garment, or floor, covering the spots, and put a warm iron on the paper until the oil shows through, continue until no oil is drawn by the paper.

MARKING INK.

Put a little lunar caustic (nitrate of silver) into half a tablespoonful of gin, and in a day or two it is fit for use. Wet the linen with common soda and dry it before using the ink on it. The color will be faint at first, but will become durable on exposure to the sun or fire.

GREEN INK

Mix a solution of the neutral sulphate of indigo, with a solution of bichromate of potash, until the desired shade is obtained, then add a little mucilage. A solution of verdigris also forms green ink.

BLUE INK.

Mix in a glass bottle, one ounce of pure powdered Prussian blue, and an ounce and a-half to two ounces of concentrated muriatic acid. After twenty-four hours, dilute the mass with a sufficient quantity of water.

GOLD AND SILVER INKS.

Grind gold leaf with white honey upon a slab of porphyry, with a muller, until it is reduced to an impalpable powder in a pasty condition; this golden honey-paste is then diffused in water which dissolves the honey, and the gold falls to the bottom in the form of very fine powder. Wash off the honey carefully, mix the gold powder with gum arabic mucilage. When used allow it to dry on the paper, when it may be made brilliant by burnishing it with an agate burnisher. Silver ink is prepared in the same way by using silver leaf.

COCKROACHES.

It is said that red wafers, and also the roots of black hellebore will destroy them. They may be caught in vessels partly filled with molasses.

RATS AND MICE.

You can have a little sport, by placing a barrel with a little meal in it where they run, two or three nights, and then fill it a third full of water, and sprinkle the meal two or three inches deep on the top of it. You may find eight or ten in the barrel in the morning if they are plenty. You can use a smooth kettle, filling it to within five or six inches of the top with water and covering the surface with bran, or chaff.

MOTHS.

One ounce of gum camphor, and one ounce of powdered red pepper, macerated in eight ounces of strong alcohol for several days, then strained. With this tincture, the furs or cloth are sprinkled over, and then rolled up in sheets. Or give them a good beating, and do them up tightly in several thicknesses of paper, so that one covers the cracks of the other; or in linen or cotton so that the moth cannot get in.

BED BUGS.

Wash the bedstead with salt and water, filling the cracks where they frequent, with salt. It is preferable to "ointments."

CRICKETS.

Put Sctoch snuff in the holes where they come out.

NOSEGAYS.

Flowers should not be cut during sunshine or kept exposed to the sun, or tied tightly together in bundles. When putting them in water, cut the stems squarely across with a knife, scissors close the tubes through which the water ascends. The water should be changed every day or once in two days, and a thin slice cut off the end of the stalk every time.

TO PRESERVE THE FLOWERS OF A BOUQUET.

Let a spoonful of charcoal powder be added to the water, and the flowers will last as long as they would on the plant, without any need of changing the water or taking any trouble at all.

HOW LADIES CAN MAKE THEIR OWN PERFUMES.

If we spread fresh, unsalted butter upon the inside of two dessert-plates, and then fill one of the plates with gathered fragrant blossoms of clematis, covering them over with the second greased plate, we shall find that after twenty-four hours the grease has become fragrant. The blossoms, though separated from the parent stem, do not die for some time, but live to exhale odor, which is absorbed by the fat. To remove the odor from the fat, the fat must be scraped off the plates and put into alcohol; the odor then leaves the grease and enters into the spirit, which thus becomes "scent," and the grease again becomes colorless. The flower farmers of the Var, follow precisely this method, on a very large scale, making but a little practical variation, with the following flowers: rose, orange, acacia, violet, jasmine, tube-rose, and jonquil.

TINCTURE OF ROSES.

Take the leaves of the common rose (centifolio) and place, without pressing them, in a common bottle; pour some good spirits of wine upon them, close the bottle, and let it stand till required for use. This tincture will keep for years, and yield a perfume little inferior to attar of roses; a few drops of it will suffice to impregnate the atmosphere of a room with a delicious odor. Common vinegar is greatly improved by a very small quantity being added to it.

POT POURRI

Take three handfuls of orange flowers, three of cloves, carnations, or pinks, three of damask roses, one of marjoram, one of lemon thymes, six bay leaves, a handful of rosemary, one of myrtle, half a handful of mint, one of lavender, the rind of a lemon, and a quarter of an ounce of cloves. Chop these all up, and place them in layers, with bay salt between the layers, until the jar is full. Do not forget to throw in the bay salt with each new ingredient put in, should it not be convenient to procure at once all the required articles. The perfume is very fine.

EASTER EGGS.—1.

Immerse eggs in hot water a few minutes, inscribe names or dates etc., on the shell with the end of a tallow candle or with grease, then place them in a pan of hot water saturated with cochineal or other dye-woods; the parts over which the tallow has passed being impervious to the dye, the eggs come out presenting white inscriptions on colored grounds. Or boil the eggs hard and paint subjects on them with a camel's hair brush, or etch them with a steel pen in India ink. Or dye the shells first, then scrape off the dye in any design desired.

EASTER EGGS.—2.

An egg boiled in the coat of an onion will turn to a beautiful brown color. To give a blue color, boil the eggs in powdered indigo with the addition of a tea-spoonful of dilute sulpluric acid. To give an egg a mottled appearance, with bright colors blended, and contrasted, obtain pieces of silk of the brightest colors, cut them into bits an inch long, half an inch wide, add a few chips of logwood and a little tumeric; let the egg be well inbedded in this so that the silk may form a thick layer round it, sow it up in very coarse brown paper and boil it half an hour or more.

FOOD FOR INVALIDS.

The diet for invalids depends so much upon the condition of the patient, that only the most general directions can be given; the special application must be left in every case to the judgment of the nurse.

Neatness, cleanliness, and promptitude are the great requisites in a sick chamber. The best prepared food is spoiled by want of care and punctuality in placing it before the patient.

When persons are ill, their senses are often preternaturally acute; slight marks of neglect which would not be noticed at another time, become extremely offensive; and a few minutes delay, not only seems unpardonable, but is sometimes really injurious. Patience, tact, and natural kindness of disposition are essential qualities in a good nurse, and when to these are added firmness and good judgment, the sum total of excellence in this line has been reached. As a general rule however, one half the nurses injure their patients by absurd restrictions, and the other half by foolish indulgence.

GRUEL.

This simple refreshment is invaluable in sickness, and is made with little trouble and less expense, yet it is scarcely ever prepared exactly right.

One table-spoonful of fine Indian or oat-meal, mixed smooth with cold water and a salt-spoon of salt; pour upon this a pint of boiling water and turn into a saucepan to boil gently for half an hour; thin it with boiling water if it thickens too much, and stir frequently; when it is done, a table-spoonful of cream or a little new milk may be put in to cool it, after straining, but if the patient's stomach is weak it is best without either. Some persons like it sweetened and a little nutmeg added, but to many it is more palatable plain.

PANADA.

Break up three arrow-root crackers into small pieces; pour upon them boiling water and cover close for a minute, then add a tea-spoon of white sugar and a little pure milk. It is an excellent breakfast or supper for a child or an invalid. Instead of the milk, the juice of a lemon may be squeezed in and another tea-spoon of sugar added.

"SOFT" TOAST

Some invalids like this very much indeed, and nearly all do when it is nicely made.

Toast well, but not too brown, a couple of thin slices of bread; put them on a warm plate and pour over *boiling* water; cover quickly with another plate of the same size, and drain the water off; remove the upper plate, butter the toast, put it in the oven one minute, and then cover again with a hot plate and serve at once.

EGG TOAST.

Make a soft toast, and have ready one or more fresh eggs which have been boiled *twenty* minutes; remove the shells, cut them in slices and place upon the toast, with a little butter, pepper and salt; without the butter they may be eaten with impunity by the most delicate invalid, as an egg cooked for twenty minutes is really more easy of digestion than one that is technically boiled soft.

CALVES-FOOT JELLY.

Boil four nicely cleaned calves-feet in three quarts of water until reduced to one, very slowly; strain and set away until cold, then take off the fat from the top and remove the jelly into a stew-pan, avoiding the settlings, and adding half a pound of white powdered sugar, the juice of two lemons, and the whites of two eggs—the latter to make it transparent. Boil all together a few moments and set away in bowls or glasses; it is excellent in a sick room.

A SICK BREAKFAST.

A small waiter, covered with a clean tea-napkin; a cup of nice warm tea, two slices of thin, lightly-browned toast, a tiny pat of sweet butter, and a small saucer of fruit or jelly of some kind. Guava is very nice, if strawberries or other fresh fruits are not in season.

A SICK DINNER.

The thick, tender part of a mutton chop broiled, a roast mealy potato, a little jelly, a slice of Graham bread, and half of an "invalid's cup pudding."

A SICK TEA.

A bowl of cracker panada, or a cup of weak black tea, one or two slices of Graham bread, with a little butter, and fruit if allowed.

INVALID CUP PUDDING.

One table-spoonful of flour, one egg; mix with cold milk, and a pinch of salt to a batter. Boil fifteen minutes in a buttered cup. Eat with sauce, fruit, or plain sugar.

BEEF TEA.

Cut up half a pound rump steak into small pieces, and put it into a bowl of lukewarm water; cover it, and set it where it will gradually heat. In about half an hour, turn it into a lined saucepan, and cover close, and set it on the range to boil; skim it well as it reaches the boiling point, and after boiling up once or twice, withdraw it from the fire and let it simmer gently in a cooler place for an hour. Strain, and season as preferred. In winter this will keep good, in a cellar, several days; but in summer it is required fresh every day, even if kept in a refrigerator. Mutton broth is made in the same way.

SOFT BOILED EGGS.

Fresh eggs for invalids who like them cooked soft, should be put in a pan of *boiling* water, and set on a part of the range where they will not boil, for several minutes. At the end of that time they will be like jelly, perfectly soft, but beautifully done, and quite digestible by even weak stomachs.

INVALID APPLE PIE.

Slice up one or more nice, tart apples in a saucer, sweeten with white sugar, and cover with a moderately thick slice of bread buttered slightly on the under side. When the bread is browned, the apples, if of a tender kind, and thinly sliced, will be done.

ROAST APPLES.

These can nearly always be eaten with safety, when they are eaten with relish. Choose good sized, fair apples of a tart, and juicy, but not sour kind. Rub them off clean, and put them in rather a slow oven, which may increase in warmth, so that they shall be thoroughly done in an hour. When so soft that the savory pulp breaks through the browned skin in every direction, take them out, sift white sugar over them, and carry one at a time on a China saucer to the patient.

LEMONADE.

This is invaluable in fevers, and also in rheumatic affections. Rub the lemons soft, cut them half through the centre and squeeze out the juice, take out the seeds with a tea-spoon. Put two tablespoonsful of white sugar to each lemon, and fill up with cold or boiling water, according as you desire the lemonade, hot, or cold. Two medium sized lemons will make a pint or more of lemonade.

APPLE WATER.

Roast two tart apples until they are soft, put them in a pitcher, pour upon them a pint of cold water and let it stand in a cool place an hour. It is used in fevers and eruptive diseases, and does not require sweetening.

STEWED PRUNES.

These are extremely good in small pox, measles, scarlet fever, and the like, both as food and medicine. Get the box prunes, as they will not need washing, and because they are generally of a much better quality than the open sort. Soak them for an hour in cold water, then put them in a porcelain lined saucepan with a little more water if necessary, and a little coffee crushed sugar. Cover, and let them stew slowly an hour, or until they are swollen large and quite soft. They are excellent as an accompaniment to breakfast for a sick woman.

DRY TOAST.

Cut your slices of bread even, and not too thick. Toast before a clear fire, a nice light brown. Cover with a napkin, and serve quickly while it is hot. Dry toast is not always good for invalids, especially when the bowels are confined, and it is desirable to keep them open. In this case, Graham bread not toasted is much better.

TAPIOCA CUP PUDDING.

This is very light, and delicate for invalids. An even table-spoonful of tapioca, soaked for two hours in nearly a cup of new milk. Stir into this the yolk of a fresh egg, a little sugar, a grain of salt and bake in a cup for fifteen minutes. A little jelly may be eaten with it, if allowed, or a few fresh strawberries.

MILK TOAST.

This is a favorite dish with nearly all sick people when they are getting well. Cut stale baker's bread in rather thin slices, toast a fine brown, and lay them in a deep dish. Meanwhile, boil a quart of new milk, in a lined saucepan, into which you have first put a very little cold water to prevent burning. As soon as it boils, pour it over the toast, cover, and serve quick. For an invalid, no butter should be put in the milk. Some people put in a thickening of flour, but this spoils it to our thinking.

THICKENED MILK.

With a little milk, mix smooth a table-spoonful of flour and a pinch of salt. Pour upon it a quart of boiling milk, and when it is thoroughly amalgamated put all back into the saucepan, and boil up once, being careful not to burn, and stirring all the time, to keep it perfectly smooth, and free from lumps. Serve with slices of dry toast. It is excellent in diarrhea and becomes a specific by scorching the flour before mixing with the milk.

OYSTER SOUP.

Make a little broth of lean veal, or mutton, simmer with it some root, or essence of celery. Strain it, put again on the fire, and when it boils throw in the oysters with their liquor, and a trifle of pepper, and salt. Serve as soon as it comes to a boil on little squares, or sippets of toast.

BROILED TENDERLOIN.

This is a choice piece from a sirloin steak, and is highly enjoyed when the patient is becoming convalescent. Cut out the round piece from the inside of a sirloin steak, boil it quick over a bright fire, upon a small, heated gridiron, turn it, with its gravy, upon a piece of freshly made toast, sprinkle with salt, and pepper, but no butter, place between two hot plates, and serve directly. A tender mutton chop, or half of the breast of a chicken may be served the same way, only the chicken will require longer, and somewhat slower cooking.

MILK AND EGGS.

Beat up a fresh egg, with a grain of salt, pour upon it a pint of boiling milk, stirring all the time. Serve hot, with or without toast. It is good in case of weakness for an early breakfast, or for a traveller before starting on a journey.

FOOD FOR INFANTS.

FOOD FOR INFANTS.

It is a sad, and significant fact, that at least half the children at the present time, are deprived of their proper sustenance, and left to the tender mercies of wet nurses, or the bottle. Between the two evils, it is difficult to say which is the least; but unless a superior nurse can be found—one intelligent, and thoroughly clean in her personal habits—we should say, choose the last, and bring it up by hand.

It is the opinion of the best physicians, and the conviction is borne out by every mother's experience, that the moral, mental, and spiritual, as well as physical condition of a child is greatly influenced during its nursing period. Mothers who nurse their own children know that it is of the greatest importance to the quiet and healthful condition of the child, that they should be free from all sources of agitation, anxiety, and irritability. Overwork, giving way to fretfulness, or being subjected to the unreasonable temper and caprices of others, frequently induces a state of mind that shows itself plainly in the uneasiness and disquiet it produces in the infant, and would be seen with still greater distinctness were women accustomed to trace results more strictly to their causes.

If this is the case with the mother, if her mental and spiritual condition finds itself reflected so minutely in the lights and shadows of the little life which is dependent upon her, why should it not receive a coloring from the milk which it derives from a dull, coarse, appetite-loving wet nurse of the ordinary stamp? Two thirds of these nurses make a necessity of strong tea and coffee, and malt liquor, two or three times a day; they are often anything but scrupulous in their personal habits, and so accustomed to the exercise of a violent will by virtue of their office, as to be unwilling to bear the slightest control or contradiction. These are not the influences which a thoughtful mother would like to have her child drink in with its milk.

We believe it to be a misfortune, the extent of which is not at all realized, when the mother cannot nurse her own child. The mother's milk contains all the elements necessary for its proper growth in every direction, and no substitute can be found for it; but where this is impossible, unless, as before remarked, a very superior nurse can be obtained, it is safer to trust to the simple food, which at least sustain life, and do no hurt if given at right times and in proper quantities, leaving the mental and spiritual activities unimpeded, though probably subject to a slower growth than if aided by the sympathetic magnetism of the mother's nature.

STARCHY FOOD.

Such as arrowroot, sago, corn-starch, and the like, is commonly held to be very healthy and nutritious for infants, yet the experience of every physician, furnishes numerous instances of feeble, sickly children that are so fed, while the number is small that survive it. The reason of this is, that the digestive organs of infants are not sufficiently powerful to convert the starchy matter into nourishment; it therefore only serves to clog, and impede the action of the system, while the little victim is gradually being starved on the trifle of sustenance which it can obtain, from whatever sugar and milk is given with its other food.

ENGLISH "PAP.

English and French babies, when brought up by hand, are fed almost altogether on "pap," which is made, in England, in the following way:

Boiling water is poured on a small piece of the crumby part of white, light bread. This is covered up for a moment, and then the water poured off. The softened bread is then put in a little porcelain stewpan, with a trifle more of water, and allowed to boil up, and it is then a pulp. A lump of white sugar and a little cold milk, added, brings it precisely up to the ideas of most young

Britishers, who grow very stout and healthy upon it. This is excellent food where the mother is capable of partly nursing her child.

French pap is made of flour instead of bread, which is decidedly objectionable, as it is not only less agreeable, but much less easily digested.

COW'S MILK.

A diet of cows' milk exclusively is not good; it is too rich and very provocative of eruptive diseases. But if the bottle is preferred to spoon-feeding, half of *one* good cow's milk may be given, diluted with half of boiling water and sweetened slightly with white sugar.

An excellent change from this consists of a thin strained gruel from the best prepared barley, with a little milk and sugar added.

A little sugar is necessary in infants' food, but be particularly careful not to make it *sweet*, as this provokes continual thirst, as well as disorders the child's stomach.

INFANT'S BROTH

After the baby is three months old, it may occasionally be treated to a little clear chicken, or mutton broth, made in the following way. Cut up a pound of lean mutton into small pieces, and put them into a small jar, cover them with cold water, set the jar in a kettle of warm water, let it come to boiling point, and simmer the mutton until the strength is extracted. One pound of meat should make a quart of broth—simmer at least six hours—strain and put in a trifle of salt, but no other spice. Treat part of a chicken in the same way, for chicken broth.

BABY PUDDING.

Grate a little stale bread, pour some boiling milk upon it, cover, and when it becomes a pulp, stir into it the yolk of an egg, and a grain of salt. The quantity should fill a tea-cup, in which boil it fifteen minutes.

ESSENTIALS.

Warm, sensible clothing, quiet, with food and sleep at regular intervals are the essentials to health and comfort of babies.

FOOD FOR YOUNG CHILDREN.

The great danger in feeding young children lies not so much in the food, as in its preparation, or want of preparation. A hard indigestible potato is bad for them, and a little tender, stewed meat is good, but if the potato were mashed, and mealy, and the meat hard, and tough, the case would be just the reverse.

The principal danger is in their swallowing indigestible substances, and whether these are hard apples, or lumpy potatoes, tough meat, or sour bread, rich cake, or hickory nuts, makes very little difference, the irritation, and derangement produced is the same.

Meat for children under the age of ten years, should be cooked very tender, and cut up very small, or given in the form of soup. Potatoes should be mashed, apples roasted, or stewed, and if bread and milk could form their breakfast, and some kind of mush, with milk, their supper, they would be all the better for it, for the rest of their lives.

CHILDREN'S PIE.

Cover the bottom of a pie dish with slices of bread and butter, cover it with fresh berries, sprinkled with sugar, or with stewed fruit, fresh or dried. Set it in the oven fifteen or twenty minutes. Sift a little sugar over it, when it comes out.

BROWN MUSH FOR SUPPER.

Stir into a quart of boiling water, a tea-spoonful of salt, and Graham flour enough to make it as thick as Indian mush. Let it boil gently half an hour, keeping it covered. Eat it with cream, or milk, and sugar.

BREAD AND MILK.

Cut, or break stale bread up into small pieces, and let them come to a boil in milk. It makes an excellent breakfast for children with a slice of toast, or without.

CRANBERRIES.

Should be stewed soft, strained through a colander, which will pass every thing but the skin; boild up a second time with the sugar, and set away to cool. They may then be eaten with impunity by the most delicate children.

LADIES' LUNCHES.

These are not at all difficult, and the less fuss and preparation there is for them, the better; they may of course be made very elaborate, but in this case, it has become the fashion for ladies to engage a private room and lunch, for a certain number of guests, at a stylish restaurant, the hour, and extensive preparation, interfering with domestic economies, and regulations of the household, if allowed to take place at home.

Ordinarily however, "ladies' lunches," are simple affairs, delicate, *recherche*, and more famous for the wit they evoke, and the enjoyment they create, than for the dishes, which are not unfrequently quite incongruous. "I will come," says one, "if you will have some of your delicious chicken salad;" "and I," says another, "if you can persuade your cook to make an omelette," "and I,—I want a cup of your chocolate," exclaims a third.

But whatever be the bill of fare, let it be such, that the presence of the hostess will not be required in the kitchen, nor a large attendance of servants in removing dishes.

Many of the pleasantest lunches are quite impromptu; one or more ladies call,—gentlemen nearly always lunch down town, in cities,—and the hostess without ceremony invites them to share her mid-day meal. In such a case, no apology is necessary for very simple fare, the friendliness of the invitation being worth much more than variety, and costliness of dishes.

A dish of poached eggs and boiled ham, will answer for such an occasion, or delicate rice cakes, added to the cold ham, and chickens or sliced tomatoes with tender broiled lamb chops; all dishes easily and cheaply prepared, and sure to be appreciated. A box of sardines is useful to have on hand, but we do not consider them healthful eating, and recommend them only in case of emergency.

To a ladies' lunch, not more than six or eight guests should be invited, and the food should be all placed on the table at one time, tea, coffee, or chocolate being served from a side table by a servant.

BILL OF FARE.

Roast chicken garnished, ham sandwiches, pancakes with jelly, French rolls, potato balls, or *croquettes*, wine jelly, lady cake, tartlets, and oranges.

Lobster salad, mixed pickles, French bread, cold tongue, marmalade, meringues, oranges, and claret punch.

Chicken pie, compote apples, or apples stewed whole; cold ham garnished with sliced lemon and parsley, bread, biscuits, pickled cucumbers, tartlets, sponge cake with a custard poured over it, and whip on top of it, making floating island; and bottled peaches, or strawberries.

Potted salmon, and pigeon pie, currant and raspberry jelly, delicate biscuits, celery or salad of lettuce, cheese cakes, cocoanut cake, and fresh fruit in season.

Cold roast turkey, pickled oysters, cranberry jelly, celery, French rolls, small English mince pies, (made without meat), jelly cake, and grapes, or preserved pineapple.

Cold pigeons which have been stuffed and roasted, little oyster patties, or *vol au vente*, blackberry jelly, and pickled cauliflower, with slices of red beet root; blanc mange, with tarts, and cream, fruit cake, with grapes, and wine.

A STAG SUPPER.

A stag supper is one to which only gentleman are invited, and it is necessary, therefore, to pay particular attention to the dishes which gentlemen usually prefer. The centre of the table should be occupied by a large punch-bowl, filled with claret punch, and set in a deep reservoir, containing blocks of clear ice. At the top of the table should be a cold roast turkey with a string of sausages round its neck; at the bottom, a boiled turkey, stuffed with oysters. On one side of the table should be a large chicken pie, ornamented with pastry, on the other, a pair of roast ducks, one stuffed with onions, the other with prunes. At opposite corners, tureens of pickled oysters, a cold boiled ham, and cold tongue, garnished with slices of lemon, and green parsley. French bread, pickles, pineapple, cheese, sardines and champagne jelly, wherever it is possible to put them; also oval dishes of lobster salad, potted meat sandwiches, and pickled salmon. Celery, grapes, apples, oranges, ice cream, and cream cakes, or Charlotte Russe. Beverages, according to taste and means.

NEW YEAR'S TABLES, PARTIES, Etc.

It does not come within the scope of this work to give directions for the getting up of elaborate and expensive entertainments. People who do these things, generally have a professed cook, or have their table supplied from some fashionable restaurant. We propose only to furnish useful hints to plain housekeepers with limited resources, and shall therefore not go beyond those simple means of entertainment that are within the power of most American families.

NEW YEAR'S TABLE

The custom of receiving calls is becoming so very general out of New York city, that a few hints on the method of setting the table for the occasion may not come amiss.

What is called a substantial table, is out of fashion now, excepting among old-fashioned people, but it must still be remembered that as it is the taste of *gentlemen*, and not of ladies that are to be consulted on this day, sweets, cake and the like, should be subordinated to chicken salad, pickled oysters, potted salmon, sardines, and the like, which gentlemen generally greatly prefer.

An average table displays one handsomely ornamented cake, raised high on a china, glass or silver *plateau*, in the centre, supported by bouquets of flowers. All the dishes are cold, of course, and may be decorated with little bits of evergreen, with flowers or with lemon in slices. Small biscuit sandwiches made of tongue and ham, or ham and potted veal, are very good. Pickled oysters, are indispensable, and sardines, and chicken, or lobster salad, will be found very popular. Jellies, fruit, one or more baskets of mixed cake, and whatever is thought requisite in the way of confectionery, should be arranged tastefully so as to produce the best effect. A dish of oranges ornamented with tufts of green moss, and sprigs of scarlet geranium looks very nice.

It would be much better if no wines were offered New Year's day, —if beverages were limited to coffee, lemonade, and cold water; but as most persons seem to think otherwise, it would be Quixotic to attempt here to stem the tide of fashionable opinion. Cherry, old Bourbon, and claret punch are in great demand where they are to be found. Coffee is always served from a side table.

A FAMILY DINNER. BILL OF FARE FOR TEN.

Soup is not considered so indispensable to even elegant dinners in this country, as in England and France; though it is *generally*, even here, the first course. For our family dinner party however, we have no soups; but we have two kinds of fish,— baked salmon trout, with anchovy sauce, and boiled white fish, with caper sauce. We have, also, small side dishes of lobster and chicken salad; pickles, and glass dishes of white, crimped celery, and cranberry jelly. The fish is followed by a roast turkey with its necklace of sausages, or a roast fowl, and dish of stewed pigeons,; and these are accompanied by an army of vegetables, sauces, and gravies. A boiled ham makes it appearance, but it is chiefly ornamental. The next course is plum pudding, and then comes a dessert of white, and black grapes, oranges, apples, and nuts, Charlotte Russe, or cream puffs, and finally, coffee. Sometimes we have wine, and sometimes we don't, at family dinners.

A SMALL SUPPER PARTY. BILL OF FARE FOR FIFTY PERSONS.

Have at one end of the table a tureen of pickled oysters, at the other, a large dish of chicken salad. Side dishes should contain neat slices of ham, tongue, cold chicken, and sardines, ornamented with sprigs of parsley, slices of lemon, red beet root, cut in stars, or the curled leaves of celery. Chicken salad may be garnished with egg rings, and celery hearts, cut in shapes, and stuck all over the surface. Two pyramids of ice cream will occupy the spaces next to the top and bottom dishes, and will be followed by two handsome baskets of cake, which will just leave room for a pyramid of confectionery, or a high glass dish of fruit in the centre. Filling up the corners, will be glass dishes of jelly, Charlotte

Russe in forms, and little dishes of pickles, and plates of biscuit everywhere; there should also be at least two dishes of mottoes, and two of almonds and raisins. Care should be taken to have abundance of plates, saucers, spoons, and napkins. Hot coffee should be served round at the beginning, and champagne punch at the close; or if not that, claret punch. It is a good idea to have an immense punch bowl of iced lemonade, for the guests to go to whenever they choose.

REFRESHMENTS.

For sociables, receptions, and small evening companies, refreshments are generally handed round, and are of a very simple character. A variety of cake with jelly, and ice cream, are perhaps the most frequently employed, with or without wine. Coffee, and little biscuit sandwiches, with cake, and fruit, are sometimes substituted.

At simple receptions, a cup of tea, or coffee, and a little cake, or biscuit is all that is required.

Do not, however, confine yourself to lady-fingers, or any of the polite forms of starvation. If you have only tea and cake, let the tea be good, and the cake good; and allow your visitors the privilege of having their cups refilled.

A CHILDREN'S PARTY.

Let the children give a party at least once a year, and make out a programme of amusements for them; a magic lantern is very useful, in addition to games and dancing. Let the children themselves principally do the honors, it will teach them how to receive and entertain guests.

It is best to have a table set for the children, and make the refreshments as light and simple as possible. Little baked custards in cups, apple snow, ice cream, baskets of kisses, lady-fingers, and "christmas cakes for good children" [see Sweet Cakes], small apple tarts, oranges, and mottoes, with water and lemonade, constitute a sufficient, and to juveniles, a most attractive variety. It is still better if the mottoes are not given them to eat, but are fewer in quality, and sufficiently handsome to carry home as a *souvenir*. The party should close with a lively game before twelve o'clock, so that the little ones may be at home by midnight at least.

A CHRISTMAS PARTY.

A Christmas party, which includes a Christmas tree, is the most delightful of all parties; it is not particularly fashionable, and it is particularly unceremonious, but on that account all the more enjoyable.

At first sight, a Christmas tree, with a gift for every person invited, would seem to involve great expense, but it need not, if people will content themselves with furnishing the tree with such gifts as their means will admit. Twenty-five dollars will purchase a large tree, decorate it with flowers and lights, and supply pretty and amusing gifts for fifty or more persons. Fifteen or twenty dollars more, will supply all the refreshments, in the shape of cake, and ice cream, and home made jellies, or fruits needed. An improvised Santa Claus distributes the gifts by lot at a certain hour, then follows refreshments, and the evening closes with dancing, and perhaps a game of blind man's buff.

Of course, family and other Christmas trees, may be made as elaborate and expensive in their furnishing, as means will allow; we have only thrown out the suggestion, to show how cheaply it may be done.

WASHING DAY.

WASHING DAY.

This is the dreaded event of every household, large, and small; it is proverbially associated with wretchedness and discomfort, and many have been the plans, methods, and receipts, which have been imposed upon housekeepers, through their desire to relieve themselves of this constantly recurring source of trouble and annoyance.

Such efforts, are mostly vain, and useless however, sometimes worse—positively injurious. Clean clothes are a luxury, that must be paid for in some shape or other—and no substances have been discovered, and few machines invented, to rival the stout arm, and strong hand of the professional wash-woman.

Never use soda to soften water, it rots the clothes in proportion to its strength; buy crude borax by the pound, and put in half an ounce for an ordinary washing; it whitens, and cleanses, and softens, wonderfully, and injures nothing. The women of Holland, whose washing is proverbial, use borax.

Use a really good brand of soap well dried—not the soft, gelatinous, yellow bars, which melt away in a moment, and really stain rather than cleanse the clothes, and always destroy the hands.

Have the clothes soaked over night in warm water, rubbing all creased and soiled places with soap, and they will require only one washing, and that not a laborious one, before boiling. Boil quick, rinse thoroughly, wring through a first-rate clothes wringer, (the barbarism of wringing by hand, is now happily at an end) and bring them in, and fold them as soon as they are dry. Fine shirts, ruffles, and linen, and cambric under clothing, are much injured by being exposed an unnecessary length of time to frost, wind, or dust.

TABLE-CLOTHS, NAPKINS, ETC.

These articles, and any others that are likely to be disfigured with fruit, or coffee stains, should be kept back from the general soaking, in order to undergo special treatment. Put these in a small tub by themselves—and pour a kettle of *boiling* water upon them—not hot, but boiling, hot water sets stains, boiling water takes them out clean. When the water has cooled a little, wash them thoroughly, and boil them, the stains will have probably all disappeared, but if they should prove very obstinate, lay them on the grass wet, when the sun is hot, and they will vanish.

WHITE FLANNELS.

White flannel garments, such as petticoats, underskirts and drawers, baby flannels and the like, require also to be put in boiling water. The very best way to wash white flannels is by machine. Put in the flannels, pour in boiling suds, mild, let them stand a few minutes, then grind them out. Pour the suds away, put the flannels in again, and pour over them a kettle of *clear* boiling water with a pinch of crude borax in it, and grind them out of that. This finishes the process, and makes them beautifully soft and clean, with little labor, and no danger of shrinkage.

ZEPHYR GOODS AND COLORED FLANNELS.

Colored flannel dresses, sacks, Garibaldis and other articles of knitted wool, such as baby socks, knitted sacks and the like, should all be washed in cold water, in which a little crude borax has been dissolved, and with fine white soap, white Castile is best, but don't take colored Castile, as that may stain. The process will be found very easy, and perfectly satisfactory; the dirt will come out in the cold water without any trouble; there will be no shrinking, and the color will remain bright in the colored woolens, or fancy borderings.

TO WASH LACES AND NEEDLEWORK.

Fine handkerchiefs, collars, undersleeves, chemisettes and edgings should never be put into the large " wash," they should be kept till a sufficient number has accumulated, and then on a rainy day, when visitors are not expected, collect them, mend carefully every little hole, soap them and put them in a clean, bright tin pail that will cover down close, and fill up with cold water with a pinch of borax in it. Let them come to a slow boil, then squeeze them out; if they are very yellow, and very dirty, the operation may have to be repeated. Rinse and dry; in the meantime pour a little boiling water over a few lumps of loaf sugar, and if you wish a yellow tinge add a table-spoonful of clear liquid coffee, instead of starch; lay the articles straight out in clean, dry towels, and by the time the last one is folded up, the first will be ready to iron. Point lace can be washed in this way to look like new.

BLONDE LACE, TO WASH.

Very old point, or blonde lace, can be washed successfully in the following way. Wind the lace smoothly round a bottle, and a strip of old linen outside of it, so as to cover it. Let it lay in the bottom of a wash tub while the first and best clothes are being washed, and transfer it to the top of the clothes while they are boiling. Thence take it and lay it in boiling water, which has been slightly colored with liquid coffee, and sweetened with loaf sugar. Press out the moisture, and dry near a fire, or in the sun, and iron carefully while still damp.

MUSLIN, LAWN, OR PRINT DRESSES.

An excellent, and sure way to wash lawn, print, or muslin dresses, is to put one or two quarts of bran in a bag, and boil it in two or four gallons of water. When the strength is extracted, take out the bag, and wash the dresses in the bran water. It will act both as soap and starch, cleansing and stiffening them perfectly, without any danger to their color. Once rinsing is sufficient, in water into which some of the bran water has been poured.

COLORED STARCH.

Colored starch is the latest and greatest novelty in the laundry line. It is made in pink, buff, the new mauve, and a delicate green, and blue will soon be produced. Any article starched with the new preparation is completely colored—dyed we should have said, but as it washes out, and the garment that was pink to-day may be green to-morrow, and buff afterwards, we can hardly say "dyed." It is intended especially for those bright but treacherously colored muslins, that are costly, wash out, and perplex their owners. If the pattern has been mauve, they only need the mauve starch; if green, green starch; and they can be rendered one even and pretty shade, thus becoming not only wearable again, but stylish.

HOW TO STARCH SHIRTS, AND OTHER THINGS.

Put into a thin muslin bag, a quarter of a pound of "best" starch. Soak it for ten or fifteen minutes in three pints of pure, soft water, into which drop a minute quantity of fine French "blue." Squeeze all the starch out of the bag, and dip the shirts, and those articles that require to be very stiff first. Afterwards it can be thinned for children's aprons, and such things as only require to go through water starch. This quantity will stiffen three or four dozen miscellaneous articles, which will be ready for ironing immediately. One trial will convince the most sceptical that this method is infinitely better, less laborious, and more economical than boiled starch.

SAVING SOAP.

Pour on half a pound of washing soda two quarts of boiling water, take half a pound of soap, cut up fine in a saucepan, and pour over it two quarts of cold water; let it boil, and when perfectly dissolved, add it to the other. Mix it well upon the fire, set it away to get cold, and it will look like jelly. Soak your clothes over night, rub them out of the water, put half a pint of your saving soap into your boiler, with *cold* water, and put your clothes into the cold water, let all come to a boil together, then take out the linen, and rinse thoroughly. This will keep clothes a splendid color, with half the usual labor.

THE DAIRY.

THE COWS.

Attend very particularly to the food and drink of the cows; and see that they have clean pasture of timothy, or herds grass, and have pure, clean, water to drink. If cows are suffered to run where they can find such things as leaves, garlic, and weeds, they will often eat them, and drink stagnant water; all of which tend to give a bad flavor to butter.

THE MILK ROOM.

The milk room is much cooler when situated on the north side of the house, where it is not exposed to the hot sun through the whole day; or the shade of large tall trees is very beneficial. The object should be to have it as cool as possible, without being damp. The room and utensils should be kept as clean and sweet, as hot and cold water and pure air, can make them. Close watchfulness of the milk is required; if it stands too long, it will make bad flavored butter, less of it, and will require more labor to churn and work it. Strain your milk into shallow pans; it should not stand over thirty-six hours; if your pans have no legs, that raise them a little from the shelves, place small blocks of marble or wood, under them, so that the air can circulate under them. When washing dairy pans, and pails, always put cold water in them first and wash thoroughly; add a little warm water if you prefer it.

MAKING BUTTER.

Cream should not be kept more than two days in summer, and if there is sufficient cream to churn daily, it is better to do so. Skim the milk before it becomes very sour; pass a silver spoon handle around the edge of the pan, lift the cream with a perforated skimmer, and put it immediately into the cream crock; stir the cream two or three times each day briskly until it is ready to churn, when usually it will come quickly. Churning should be done, during warm weather, early in the morning in a cool place; the dasher ought to be moved slowly and regularly at first, and then more brisk until the butter separates from the milk; when it is gathered, wet the bowl and ladle, first with a little warm water, and then put plenty of cold or ice water to them; pour out the water and take up the butter; drain off as much of the butter-milk, as possible, pressing the butter a moment gently with the ladle.

Scatter a handful of salt in the bowl before putting in the butter; then throw a little salt upon the butter, and mix it in; drain off all the water, and make indentations in the butter with the ladle, fill them with nice salt, and set the bowl in a cool place. At evening, when the butter is hard, work it gently, without breaking the grain, and squeeze out all the milk that can be removed without too much pressure. Salt to the taste, and let it stand until morning, then finish it, making it into rolls, or packing it. When it is finished and becomes hard or set, every working over or changing from one vessel to another injures it, rendering it soft, and pasty, and breaking the grain. It will never again be as firm or nice in flavor, and will not keep sweet as long. If the butter is for packing, put it in the firkin as soon as possible, from the air. Pack close until nearly full, for room should be left to pour on enough nice brine to cover the butter. This is made by pouring boiling water upon salt, and when it is cold, straining it through a cloth. Pour enough of this brine upon the butter to cover it, say a quarter of an inch, or half an inch in thickness; this kept upon butter entirely excludes the air, and keeps it sweet and good as when first packed. If it is to be sent away, pour off the brine, saturate a cloth in it, lay it on the top, and cover it with a thick layer of salt.

JEWISH RECEIPTS.

These are all original and reliable,—the contribution of a superior Jewish housekeeper in New York.

WHITE STEWED FISH.

Put on as much water to boil as is required to cover six or eight steaks of striped bass, boil in it one onion, sliced thin, a little ground ginger, salt, black pepper and a small quantity of whole red pepper. When these are done put in your slices of fish; when boiled take them up carefully, drain them and lay in a dish. Beat up six eggs, to which add a little nutmeg, a little cayenne pepper, and some parsley chopped fine. In a separate bowl strain the juice of three or four lemons, to this add one half pint of the liquor in which the fish has been boiled, which must be strained; when this is done, take the liquor which is mixed with the lemons and throw it into the eggs, beating them all the time. Take a china or iron saucepan, into it put the sauce, set it on a gentle fire, stirring it all the time until it thickens a little, it must on no account be boiled as it will curdle; then throw the sauce over the fish and put it to cool. Chicken can be served in the same way.

BROWN FRICASSEE CHICKEN.

Take a chicken, cut it up in pieces and fry them brown, either in the best sweet oil or rendered fat. Then take six onions, slice them and cover them in a frying-pan with enough oil or fat to fry them; when soft take the cover off, so as to let them brown, then scald and peal two tomatoes, cut them up and put them in the pan with the onions to simmer a little. Put the fried chicken into a saucepan with the onions etc., add a little thyme, pepper, salt and a few grains of allspice, and enough hot water to make a rich gravy; cover it up and let it cook for half an hour or an hour, according to the tenderness of the chicken; a very small piece of garlic and mace can be added when cooking, if liked.

A GOOD PUDDING.

Take one half pound of bread crumbs, six ounces of white sugar, pour over it one half pint of boiling milk, let it stand till nearly cold, then work into it one fourth pound of fresh butter until it becomes very white. Then add four eggs, one at a time, stirring; it must be well beaten between each; then add the rind grated, and the juice of a lemon; take a mould, butter and paper it well, then ornament it with candied peel and raisins, according to fancy. Pour into it the ingredients, put a paper over the top, also tie in a cloth, and let it steam gently for two hours. Serve it with arrow-root, or custard sauce.

PURIM FRITTERS

Take a loaf of baker's bread, cut off the crust and cut in slices of one half inch thick; put them in a dish and soak them in cold milk, but not so long as to allow them to mash; when soaked, take them out and drain them. Beat eight eggs very thick, and pour a little of the egg over each slice of bread, so as to penetrate them; then take each slice of bread and dip it into the eggs that are beaten, and fry a light brown color, in rendered butter, from which the salt has been extracted; when this is done sprinkle over the fritters a little powdered cinnamon, and serve with a syrup made of white sugar.

CODFISH FRITTERS.

Take two pounds of salt codfish, put to soak in water; when fresh enough, boil and drain; pick out the bones, and pound the fish fine in a mortar; to this add chopped parsley, pepper, a little nutmeg, and a table-spoon of butter. Take three or four onions, chop fine and fry them in butter; scald and peel two tomatoes, and let them simmer with the onions; mix this with the fish thoroughly, add six eggs well beaten, and fry in small fritters a light brown color.

LEMON PUDDINGS.

To be added to four eggs, well-beaten, one fourth pound of loaf sugar and two ounces of butter which have been previously well mixed together, then the peel of two lemons and the juice of one, and bake either in cups or pie dish.

A RICHER LEMON PUDDING.—1.

Six yolks and two whites of eggs to be well-beaten, and then added to three ounces of butter and one fourth of sugar, the juice of one lemon and the rind of two, which must be taken by rubbing a lump or two of loaf sugar upon it.

LEMON PUDDING.—2.

One fourth pound of fine boiled bread crumbs added to the above, and a little more sugar to taste, and boil in a form.

APPLE PUDDING.

Grate one half pound of apples, mix with four eggs well-beaten, and six ounces of sugar, and bake in a form and turn out.

ALBERT SANDWICHES.

Take one half pound of butter, melt it to an oil before the fire, add one half pound light weight of flour, and one half of pounded loaf sugar; mix well together, add six eggs *well beaten*, and then beat all well together, either flavor with a few pounded almonds or the rind of lemon rubbed on sugar; put this mixture on well buttered tins about a third of an inch thick, and bake in a quick oven; it must be taken out when it is a very pale color, and loosened whilst it is hot, from the tin, the edges always get too dark, but they are cut off. When nearly baked, sprinkle pink sugar over half the quantity. When cold cut in diamonds and put sweatmeats between, like sandwiches; arrange them nicely in the dish and put whipped cream, flavored with vanilla, and the least bit of sugar, in the middle. The vanilla is best grated. Perhaps you will find it easier to put the mixture on buttered papers laid in tins.

MERINGUES.

Take the whites of eight eggs quite fresh and just broken, beat them with a whisk till as firm as possible. Have ready prepared eight table spoons of *ground* not *powdered* sugar, which mix with the egg as quickly as possible, so as not to give time to melt. Have ready a piece of board and sixteen pieces of white paper; put a tablespoon of the mixture on each paper in the shape of an egg; make it thick but not too spread out, smooth them off nicely, and sprinkle with sugar, *blow off what sugar falls on the paper*, and then put board and all into the oven; *watch them well* and take them out as soon as firm. Have ready another piece of board with clean papers, roll off the meringues on to them, making them stand on their tops; take out a little of the inside with a tea-spoon, and put them back in the oven *or the board* for the inside to get firm, fill with whipped cream flavored with vanilla and some sugar, and join the two halves together to form an egg.

The papers must neither be buttered or have sugar on them, and they must not be baked without boards.

BREAD AND BUTTER PUDDING.

When you make a bread and butter pudding, put only the yolks inside, and whip the whites; sweeten and flavor, and when the pudding is baked, put this on the top, and put it in the oven again for a few minutes, to crisp, and you will find it a great improvment.

SALLY LUNN

Three table-spoons butter, two table-spoonsful sugar, two cups milk, scant four cups flour, five eggs, one tea-spoon soda, two tea-spoons cream of tartar. Bake twenty-five minutes. Eat hot, spread with butter.

ANOTHER METHOD IS AS FOLLOWS.

One pint of flour, piece of butter half as large as an egg, one egg, two table-spoonsful sugar, one tea-cup milk, one tea-spoonful cream of tartar, one half tea-spoonful soda, one tea-spoon salt. Bake twenty minutes.

CUP CAKE.

One cup of butter, two sugar, three cups flour, five eggs, one teaspoon soda, dissolved in tea-cup of milk. Two tea-spoonsful cream tartar, flavor to fancy.

HICKORY NUT CAKE.

Three cups flour, two cups sugar, two eggs, one half cup butter, one pint hickory nuts, one half cup milk, one half tea-spoon soda.

MARMALADE.

Twenty-four yolks of eggs, one half pound white sugar, clarify, boil, and strain; add one table-spoonful beaten sweet almonds to the syrup, while boiling. When the syrup cools, pour the eggs, which must be well beaten, with a spoon gently. Keep stirring on a gentle fire, till it becomes thick.

ORGENT.

Two pounds sugar; clarify and make thick, three ounces sweet almonds, one ounce bitter almonds, well beaten fine, one quart water to the almonds, stir up well, and then squeeze; add them to the syrup, and boil; when cold add orange flower and rose water according to taste.

COCOA NUT PUDDING.

One pound of ground cocoa nut, one pound of crushed sugar made into a syrup, one half pint water, six eggs.

Throw the cocoa nut in the syrup, when boiling, and let it cook say ten minutes, stirring it occasionally to keep from burning; when *perfectly cold* throw in your eggs, and beat them well in, then bake for fifteen to twenty minutes.

CUP CAKE.

One cup butter, two cups sugar, five cups flour, one nutmeg, four eggs, a little saleratus

SWEET CRACKERS.

One pint flour, three fourths cup sugar, two spoonsful of cinnamon, one fourth pound butter, a little salt.

Roll very thin; bake quick; mix all up in a dough with sweet milk.

ALMOND PUDDING.

Pound together half a pound of sweet almonds and six or seven bitter almonds, mix with half a pound of sifted sugar, a little fine orange flower water, and the yolks of ten and the whites of seven well-whisked eggs. Mix thoroughly, and bake in a quick oven half an hour, or until it is sufficently firm to turn out of the dish; sift sugar thickly over it or pour round it a rich syrup flavored with orenge flower water; serve hot or cold.

LEMON DUMPLINGS.

Three fourths pounds of flour, one half pound moist sugar, the juice of two lemons, the grated rind of one, one half pound of chopped suet, all well mixed together with very little water; make with it six dumplings. To boil without ceasing, for one hour, and be eaten as soon as served with melted butter, well sweetened, and the rind of one lemon in it, or any other sweet sauce will do.

LIGHT PUDDING.

Beat five yolks with sugar to suit, add two tea-spoons very full of flour, the juice and grated rind of one lemon; lastly add the five whites beaten well to frost, and bake immediately; it takes about half an hour to cook; grease the dish, serve a sauce with it if liked.

TOMATOES FOR WINTER USE.

See that your tomatoes are quite fresh, else they will break the bottles when they ferment. Pour scalding water over them, and take off the skins. It is usual to remove all the green parts, though some housekeepers think it is not necessary. Put them over the fire in a tin, or china lined saucepan, and let them boil half an hour. Have your cans ready, fill them full, and screw them tight; they require no seasoning till you are ready to use them. Then add pepper, salt, thyme, sweet marjoram and onion. Too much seasoning spoils the taste of the tomato, but a little of these herbs is an addition; also add grated bread crumbs and butter; they are much improved by putting them in a deep dish; season as above, and spread thin slices of bread and butter, or grate the bread, and add the butter; put them in the oven and bake till brown.

PICKLED CUCUMBERS

Put them in a wooden or stone vessel, pour over strong salt and water boiling hot, put a weight on to keep them under the pickle. After three days pour it off, boil and turn it over them again; stand three days again; then take them out and let them lie one night in plain cold water; next day put them over the fire, but do not let them boil, allowing one table-spoonful of alum to a gallon of vinegar; mace, cinnamon, pepper corns, white and black, mustard seed and grated horseradish. One table-spoonful of each to every gallon of vinegar, and one tea-spoonful of tumeric. Fold a double piece of linen and a soft thick brown paper, and tie the jars tight; throw in the vinegar, keep in a dry place. A bladder and linen cloth are nice to be over the pots.

THE END.

INDEX.

GENERAL PRINCIPLES OF COOKING.

HOUSEKEEPING.

	Page.
Cake Box,	12
Children, label them,	12
Chamber, Mantel and Toilet Covers,	12
Dusters,	10
Fire, to put out,	13
Household management,	6
Household memoranda,	9
Kitchen Furnishing,	5
Kitchen Holders,	10
Looking Glasses, to clean,	12
Mattresses,	14
Mending,	10
Night Clothes,	13
Paper and String,	10
Pay as you go,	13
Piece Bags,	10
Packing away clothes,	11
Rainy Days,	11
Scorch, to take out,	12
Sheets,	13
Table, To clean a	13
Wash Rags,	12

HINTS ON ECONOMY.

Apples, to save specked,	14
Buckwheat Cakes,	15
Cheap Dishes,	15
Children eating between meals,	17
Children eating gravy,	15

	Page.
Corners and holes,	16
Examine Safes, Refrigerators, &c.,	16
Family Worship,	16
Morning Dresses,	16
Outside Garments,	14
Pickle and Preserve Jars,	14
Provide for Monday,	14
Purchase things in season,	14
Rise early,	15
Saturday Night,	15
Servants, fewer the better,	16
Stew for family dinner,	15
Sweeping, preparing for,	16
Table, serve neatly,	17
Tea-leaves on carpets,	15

THE USE OF FUEL.

Grate Fires,	18
Kitchen Ranges,	18
Parlor Heaters,	19
Spring Fuel,	19

SOUPS.

Asparagus Soup, with green peas,	27
Artichoke Soup,	27
Barley Soup,	29
Brown Gravy Soup,	26
Bread Soup,	31
Baked Soup,	32
Broth, Scotch Mutton	33
Broth for an Invalid,	33
Carrot Soup,	29
Common Soup,	22

INDEX.

	Page.		Page.
Concord Soup,	25	Beef Croquettes,	39
Calf's Head Soup, brown,	26	Boiled Beef,	84
Chicken Soup,	26	Brisket of Beef for Christmas,	
Colandered Soup,	29	cured,	34
English Pea Soup,	28	Broiled Beef steaks,	35
Fish Soups,	23	Braised Beef,	36
French Soup,	30	Brisket of Beef stuffed,	36
Gumbo,	24	Boiled Leg of Mutton,	41
Green Pea Soup,	28	Broiled Mutton Chops,	42
Gourd Soup,	30	Broiled Cold Mutton,	43
German Pancake Soup,	32	Breast of Veal, stuffed,	47
Hotch Potch,	33	Breast of Veal, stewed,	47
Inexpensive,	32	Blanquette of Veal,	49
Jenny Lind's Soup,	31	Beefsteak, mock,	49
Jardiniere Soup,	32	Boston Pork and Apple pie,	52
Mock Turtle Soup,	25	Bacon Omelet,	53
Onion Soup, with milk,	30	Bacon Egg-cap,	53
Onion Soup, with water,	31	Boiled Ham,	54
Oyster Soup,	27	Broiled Ham,	54
Oyster Mouth Soup,	27	Beef Tea,	298
Parsnip Soup,	29	Cured Beef to eat cold,	35
Pea Soup, without meat,	28	Cold minced Beef,	40
Pea Soup, green,	28	Cold Mutton broiled,	43
Pea Soup, English,	29	Croquettes, mutton,	44
Pumpkin Soup,	30	Cutlets, veal,	48
Rabbit Soup,	24	Cheese, veal,	51
Stock from Bones,	21	Cutlets, pork,	52
Stock without Meat,	21	Curing Hams,	53
Stock, Bran	21	Dried Beef cooked,	40
Stock, Cowheel	21	English pork or raised pie,	52
Stock, four quarts of Brown	22	Egg-cap, bacon,	53
Stock, four quarts of White	22	Fillets of beef,	37
Soup or Stock from one pound		Fillets of Beef with Anchovy,	38
of beef,	23	Fillets of Beef with Forcemeat,	38
Sorrel Soup, without meat,	23	Fried Mutton Chops,	43
Spring Soup,	24	Fritters, veal,	46
Sheepshead Soup,	25	Hashed Beef,	40
Soup, Jardiniere	32	Hamburgh Pickle for Beef,	39
Soup, inexpensive,	32	Hunter's Beef,	38
Soup for Invalids,	24	Hung Beef,	39
Tomato Soup,	31	Hashed Mutton,	44
Vermicelli Soup,	31	Hashed mutton with mushroom.	45
Winter Soup,	23	Hash, the Epicure's	45
White Soup,	25	Hams, to cure,	35
		Ham, boiled,	54
MEATS.		Ham, sugared,	54
		Ham, potted,	54
A-la-mode Beef,	35	Ham, broiled,	54
Beef Balls,	39	Ham and tongue toast,	55

INDEX.

	Page.		Page.
Joint of Mutton roasted,	42	Roast quarter of lamb,	42
Keeping Beef,	41	Roast joint of mutton,	42
Knuckle of veal,	48	Roast fillet of veal,	47
Knuckle of Veal with rice,	48	Roast pig,	51
'Leg of Mutton in four meals,	41	Roast pork,	51
Leg of Mutton, broiled,	41	Stewed beef,	34
Leg of Mutton, roasted,	41	Spiced beef,	37
Leg of Mutton with Oysters,	42	Shoulder of lamb, roasted,	42
Loin of Veal,	48	Savory mutton chops,	43
Leonis Favorite dish,	49	Stew, Western	43
Loaves, Westphalia	54	Shoulder of veal,	46
Mock Duck,	36	Stewed loin of veal,	46
Meat Pie for Lunch,	39	Stewed breast of veal,	47
Minced Beef, cold,	40	Spare rib of pork,	51
Mutton chops broiled,	42	Sugared ham,	54
Mutton chops fried,	43	Tough beef,	41
Mutton chops with cucumbers,	43	Veal, shoulder of	46
Mutton chops, savory,	43	Veal, stewed loin of	46
Mutton broiled, cold,	43	Veal, breast of stuffed	47
Mutton Pudding,	43	Veal, breast of stewed	47
Mutton croquettes,	44	Veal, roast fillet of	47
Mutton, hashed,	44	Veal, loin of	48
Minced uncooked Mutton,	44	Veal, knuckle of	48
Mutton hashed with Mushrooms,	45	Veal cutlets,	48
		Veal minced with maccaroni,	48
Minced Mutton,	45	Veal fritters,	49
Minced Mutton with Cucumbers,	45	Veal, blanquette of	49
		Veal rolls,	49
Minced Veal with maccaroni,	48	Veal, minced,	50
Mock Beefsteak,	49	Veal omelette,	50
Minced Veal	50	Veal olives,	50
Ox cheek stuffed and baked,	36	Veal cheese,	51
Omelette, veal,	50	Westphalia loaves,	54
Olives, veal,	50		
Pudding, mutton	43	SECONDARY MEATS.	
Pig, roast,	41		
Pork, roast,	41	Baked Irish Stew,	56
Pork, spare rib of	52	Boiled Tongue,	57
Pork cutlets,	51	Balls, Grandmother's Breakfast,	58
Pork and Apple pie, Boston	51		
Pork pie, English or raised	52	Brain Cake,	61
Pork and potato pie,	52	Brawn,	62
Pork relish,	53	Cold Meats, to cook,	59
Potted Ham,	54	Cowheel,	59
Quarter of lamb, roasted,	42	Cowheel fried,	60
Quarter of lamb as a savory dish,	46	Calf's Head Cake,	60
		Calf's Head Hash,	61
Roast leg of mutton,	41	Dalma, Turkish	59
Roast shoulder of lamb,	42	Fried Tripe,	62

	Page.
Grandmother's Breakfast Balls,	58
Hash, Savory Winter	59
Hash, Calf's Head	61
Head and Hinge, Lamb's	61
Irish Stew,	56
Lamb's Head and Hinge,	61
Meat Omnium,	57
Pie, Yale Boat,	56
Risibles,	58
Stew, Irish	56
Stew, baked Irish	57
Sweet Breads,	57
Sausage meat and Sausages,	58
Savory winter hash,	59
Sheep's Trotters,	60
Sweetbread, Liver, and Heart,	60
Stewed Tripe,	62
Tongue, boiled	57
Turkish Dalma,	59
Toad-in-the-hole,	59
Trotters, Sheep's	60
Tripe,	62
Tripe Fried,	62
Yale Boat Pie,	56

FISH.

	Page.
Boiled Fish,	64
Boiled White fish,	65
Broiled White fish,	65
Boiled Salmon,	65
Broiled Salmon,	66
Broiled Shad,	67
Baked Shad,	67
Boiled Bass, Rock fish, etc.	68
Baked Cod, Black fish, Haddock, &c.,	69
Boiled Whitings,	69
Codfish and potatoes "picked up,"	68
Cod, Blackfish, Haddock, &c., baked,	69
Cod, Haddock, etc., fried,	70
Cod or Salmon cutlets,	70
Chowder, Fish,	72
Cakes, Fish,	73
Cod, Salt stewed,	73

	Page.
Cape Cod Chowder,	73
Cod Fish and Potatoes,	68
Fried Fish,	64
Fried Shad,	67
Fried Mackerel,	68
Fish Roes, in cases,	70
Fricasseed small fish,	70
Fry, Trenton Falls,	70
Fish and Maccaroni,	71
Fried Smelts,	71
Fresh Herrings,	71
Fish, to dress a second time,	72
Fish Pudding,	72
Fish Cakes,	73
Haddock baked and fried,	69
Herrings, fresh,	71
Kippered Salmon,	66
Mackerel, fried,	68
Mackerel, soused,	68
Maccaroni, Fish and	71
Pudding, Fish,	72
Roes, fish in cases,	70
Salmon, boiled,	65
Salmon, broiled,	66
Salmon and Salad,	66
Salmon, to kipper,	66
Salmon, pickled,	66
Shad, broiled	67
Shad, fried	67
Shad, baked	67
Shad maitre d' hotel,	67
Soused Mackerel,	68
Souchy or Soodjee, water	69
Salmon Cutlets, or Cod	70
Small fish fricasseed,	70
Smelts, fried	71
Second time, To dress fish	72
Salt Cod, stewed	73
Salt Cod and Potatoes,	73
Trenton Falls Fry,	70
White fish broiled,	65
White fish boiled,	65
Whitings boiled,	69
Water Souchy or Soodjee,	69

OYSTERS, SHELLFISH, EELS, ETC.

	Page.
Boiled Eels,	79

INDEX.

	Page.		Page.
Boiled Lobster,	79	Stewed,	83
Balls, Lobster	80	Toast,	83
Collared Eels,	78	To know them,	82
Crabs and Crayfish,	80		
Crab and Lobster Cutlets,	80	**FOWLS AND GAME.**	
Eels Fried,	78		
Eels Spatched,	78	Alice Cary's Minced Chicken,	91
Eels Collared,	78	Boiled Fowl,	85
Eels Stewed,	79	Broiled Fowl,	86
Eels Boiled,	79	Boiled Goose,	86
Eel pie,	79	Broiled Partridge	92
Fried Oysters,	76	Birds, Small	94
Fried Eels,	78	Chicken Fricassee,	86
Loaves Oyster	76	Chicken Stewed,	88
Lobsters,	79	Cold Chicken Fried,	88
Lobster, to boil	79	Chicken, vol-au-vent of,	88
Lobster Salad,	80	Chicken with Cheese,	89
Lobster Sauce,	80	Chicken Puffs,	89
Lobster and Crab Cutlets,	80	Chicken Loaf,	89
Lobster Balls,	80	Chicken Pot Pie,	89
Lobster Curry,	81	Chicken Pie,	89
Maccaroni, Oysters and	77	Chicken Pie, Thanksgiving,	90
Muscles, stewed	78	Chicken Pie, Aunt Abby's	90
Oyster Etiquette,	75	Chickens, Prairie,	91
Oysters Stewed,	75	Chickens Prairie, Roast and	
Oysters Scalloped,	75	Stewed,	91
Oysters Fried,	76	Chicken, Minced, Alice Cary's	91
Oyster Pies,	76	Crab, Imitation,	93
Oyster Patties,	76	Croquettes of Fowl,	93
Oyster Loaves,	76	Duck, roast	85
Oysters and Maccaroni,	77	Duck with Green Peas,	87
Oysters for Lunch,	77	Duck, New York Mock	87
Oysters Pickled,	77	Devilled Turkey Legs,	91
Pie, Oyster	76	Fricassee, Chicken	86
Patties, Oysters	76	Fried cold Chicken,	88
Pickled Oysters,	77	Forcemeat for Roast Turkey,	
Pie, Eel	79	Veal, &c.	94
Stewed Oysters,	75	Goose boiled,	86
Scalloped Oysters,	75	Goose, Roast	87
Stewed Muscles,	78	Game Patties,	93
Spatched Eels	78	Grouse, Roast	94
Stewed Eels,	79	Hashed Fowl,	92
		Hare or Rabbit, Stewed	95
		Imitation Crab,	93
MUSHROOMS.		Pot pie Chicken,	89
		Pie, Chicken,	89
Fricasseed,	82	Prairie Chickens, Roast and	
Loaves,	83	Stewed	91
Powder,	82	Partridge, Broiled	92
Pickled,	82		

INDEX.

	Page.		Page.
Partridge Salad,	92	Mushroom Catsup,	103
Partridge Pie,	92	Oyster Sauce,	98
Pigeon Pie,	93	Onion Sauce, brown	98
Patties, Game	93	Rice Sauce,	97
Roast Turkey,	85	Sauce for made dishes,	101
Roast Duck,	85	Sauce for boiled Turkey, or	
Roast Fowl,	86	Capon,	101
Roast Goose,	87	Sauce for roast Chicken,	102
Roast Prairie Chicken,	91	Sauce for boiled Fish,	102
Roast Grouse,	94	Sauce, Fish to keep a year	102
Rabbit Stewed,	95	Sauce for Venison,	103
Rabbit in Slices,	95	Sauce for roast Beef,	103
Roast Rabbit,	96	Tomato Sauce,	98
Stewed Turkey with Celery	87	Turkey's Egg Sauce,	100
Stewed Chicken,	88	Tomato Catsup,	104
Stewed Prairie Chicken,	91	Vinegar Plant,	104
Small Birds,	94	Vinegar, easy cider	105
Stewed Hare or Rabbit,	95	Vinegar of Marjoram,	105
Turkey, Roast	85	Vinegar for Souse,	105
Turkey, Stewed with Celery	87	Vinegar for Soused Fish,	105
Thanksgiving Chicken Pie,	90	Vinegar, clove	105
Turkey's Legs, Devilled	91	Vinegar, tarragon	105
Vol-au-vent of Chicken,	88	Vinegar, savory	105
Venison Pasty,	95	Vinegar, celery	105
Venison Puffs,	95	Vinegar, green mint	106
Venison Steak,	95	Vinegar, raspberry	106
		Vinegar, black currant	106
		Vinegar, Chili	106
MEAT SAUCES		White Sauce,	97
		Walnut Catsup,	104
Asparagus Sauce,	100		
Bread Sauce,	97	RELISHES.	
Brown Onion Sauce,	98		
Batter, French	101		
Berkshire Sauce,	101	Anchovy cheese,	109
Butter, Drawn	103	Custard, savory	108
Browning for Sauces,	103	Cheese, anchovy	109
Caper Sauce,	98	Cheese, omelet	109
Cranberry Sauce,	99	Cheese, fondu	109
Celery Sauce,	100	Cheese, potted	110
Catsup, Tomato	104	Cheese, pot	110
Catsup, Mushroom	108	Entrement, a German	107
Catsup, Walnut	104	Fondu, straw	110
Drawn Butter,	103	Maccaroni,	110
Egg Sauce,	98	Maccaroni, timball of	111
French Batter,	101	Pot Cheese,	110
Horseradish Sauce,	99	Relish, a cold	107
Mint Sauce,	100	Sandwiches,	107
Mild Mustard,	101	Sandwiches, dressing for	107
Made Dishes, sauce for	101	Tomato Toast,	108

INDEX.

	Page.
Tomato Omelet,	108
Toast, savory	108
Toasted Cheese,	108

PICKLES.

Asparagus,	118
Beets,	113
Beans, French	114
Barberries,	117
Barberries, sweet	117
Blackberries,	118
Cucumbers,	112
Cabbage,	114
Cabbage with sweet pickle,	115
Cabbage, red	115
Cucumber,	112
Green tomatoes,	113
Green pickle,	113
Gherkins,	116
Lemon,	116
Mustard,	113
Mangoes,	115
Mushrooms,	118
Onions,	114
Onions, Portugal	114
Oysters,	77
Piccalilli,	116
Roots,	117
Salmon,	69
Tomatoes,	113
Tomatoes, green	113
Walnuts,	118

SALADS.

Chicken,	120
Carrot,	120
Chow-chow,	123
Cabbage and Vinegar,	123
Cold Slaw,	123
Chow-chow Pickle,	123
Chow-chow, a handy	124
East India Salad,	121
Fish,	121
Hotch Potch,	122
Lobster,	121
Lettuce,	122
Potato,	122

	Page.
Poet's salad,	122
Spring Salads,	120
Salad for Cold Lamb,	121
Suffolk Salad,	122
Tomato Salad,	122
Tomato Soy,	123

EGGS.

Asparagus and Eggs,	127
Apples and Eggs,	127
Boiled,	125
Buttered,	125
Cheese and Eggs,	127
Fried with Ham,	126
Fancy Omelet,	127
Herring and Eggs,	127
Mushrooms and Eggs,	127
Omelet,	126
Omelet, Puff	126
Omelet with Kidneys,	126
Omelet with Herbs,	126
Poached,	125
Pickled Eggs,	128
Preserve Eggs, to	128
Scrambled,	125

VEGETABLES.

Artichokes, Jerusalem,	133
Artichoke Fracis,	133
Asparagus,	135
Beans, French	135
Beets, Young Boiled	135
Beans, Lima,	137
Beans, Pork and	137
Broccoli,	138
Corn, Green,	131
Corn, green on the Ear,	132
Corn Oysters,	132
Cucumbers, Stewed,	138
Carrots, Boiled,	137
Carrots with Parsley,	137
Cabbage, Boiled,	138
Cabbage, Buttered	138
Cabbage Relish,	138
Cabbage red, Relish,	138
Cabbage, red, Stewed,	138
Cabbage, French	139

INDEX.

	Page.		Page.
Cauliflowers,	134	Apple, sweet	146
Cauliflower, Rarebit,	140	Apple, green	146
Dandelions,	139	Apple, English	147
Egg Plant,	134	Apple, Dried	149
Green Corn,	131	Apple, mock	149
Greens, Spring	132	Apple, invalid	299
Onions, Boiled	136	Custard,	145
Onions, Portugal, Stewed	136	Custard, apple	145
Onions, Portugal Fried	136	Cherry, Plum, or Gooseberry,	147
Odors from Boiling Vegetables,	282	Cocoanut,	148
		Corn Meal,	149
Potatoes, Boiled	129	Fruit,	147
Potatoes, Mashed	129	Gooseberry, etc.	147
Potatoes, Fried	129	Grape,	148
Potato Shavings,	130	Huckleberry,	147
Potatoes, Stewed	130	Lemon,	145
Potatoes, Baked	130	Lemon cream, Kitty May's,	146
Potato Pie,	130	Mince,	144
Potato Cakes,	130	Mince, English	144
Potato Pudding,	131	Mince, Mrs. D's.	145
Potatoes a-la-creme,	131	Mock apple pie,	149
Potatoes Scalloped,	131	Plum, Cherry, or Gooseberry,	147
Peas, Green	136	Pumpkin,	148
Parsnips, fricasseed	136	Plum, dried	149
Parsnips, Fried	136	Rhubarb,	148
Parsnips, Boiled	136	Squash,	145
Succotash,	132		
Squash Fritters,	132	PUDDINGS.	
Squash, Boiled	133		
Sea Cale,	133	Apple, English,	150
Salsify, or Vegetable Oyster	133	Apples,	151
Spinach,	139	Arrowroot,	156
Turnips, Mashed	134	Apple Linnie's,	156
Tomatoes, Stewed	135	Apple and Sago,	156
Vegetables to boil green,	131	Apple and Rice,	158
Vegetable Marrows,	139	Apple Dumplings, Boiled	166
Vegetable Marrow Tart,	139	Apple Dumplings, Baked	166
		Apple Fritters,	166
PASTRY, (INTRODUCTORY.)		Buffalo,	150
		Bird's Nest,	153
Puddings and Pies,	141	Bread, little Birthday,	154
Potato Pie Crust,	143	Batter, Little,	155
Puff Paste,	143	Baden,	158
Pies, Crust for Raised	144	Bread,	162
Pies, Meat Suet, Crust for	144	Bread and Fruit, Mrs. Stowe's	162
		Citron,	154
PIES.		Cherry,	155
		Cornstarch, Ice,	159
Apple custard,	145	Chester,	162

INDEX.

	Page.		Page.
Corn,	164	Sago,	159
Currant Dumpling, Little	164	Suet,	161
Corn, Nantucket	165	Sally Lunn,	163
Dandy,	163	Tapioca,	159
Deacon's Apple Indian	164	Tapioca, Cup, Invalid	159
Dumplings,	166	Victoria,	152
English Roll,	154	Washington,	153
Exhibition,	191		
Editor's Favorite,	163	PUDDING SAUCES.	
Fruit,	153		
Fig,	153	Brandy,	169
Fruit, Minnie's	154	Cherry,	168
Fritters, Apple	166	Excellent,	168
Huckleberry, Indian	155	Hard,	168
Hunting, Liecestershire	161	Lemon Brandy,	169
Howitt's, Mrs.	166	Maple Sugar,	168
Indian Fruit,	152	Rose Hip,	169
Indian Huckleberry,	155	Sweet Liquid,	168
Indian, Baked	157	Wine,	169
Ice, Cornstarch	159		
Ice,	164	DESSERT DISHES.	
Indian, Boiled	165		
Indian, Plain	165	Apple Charlotte,	171
Invalid Cup,	300	Apple Custard,	172
Lemon,	155	Apple Souffle,	173
Lemon Dumplings,	167	Almond Blanc mange,	176
Minnie's Fruit,	154	Arrowroot Blanc mange,	176
Nursery,	163	Apples, Love	177
Orange,	155	Apple Tart,	178
Poor Man's	151	Apple Meringue,	178
Plum, Aunt Mary's	156	Apple, Snow	179
Plum, Boiled Yankee	159	Apple Marmalade,	179
Plum, Mrs. Croly's Christmas	160	Apples, Baked	179
Plum, Baked	160	Apples, Stewed	180
Prune or Damson,	160	Apple Cream,	180
Plum, English	160	Apples, Dried Stewed	180
Plum with Snow,	161	Apples, Pippin Stewed	180
Plum, Small and Light	164	Apples, Ginger	180
Poet's,	165	Apples, Floating Island of	181
Pastor's,	165	Apple Snowballs,	181
Rice, Boiled	157	Apples, Compote of	181
Rice,	157	Apple Cream, Nina's	181
Rice, Portuguese	151	Apples, Mother's Surprise	181
Rice, French	158	Apple Cheese,	182
Rice, Apple and	158	Apple Sauce, Saratoga	182
Rice Flour,	158	Apple or Gooseberry Trifle,	183
Saratoga,	152	Apple Pique,	188
Snow,	152	Apple Ice,	190
Seville,	158	Blanc Mange, Almond	176

INDEX.

	Page.		Page.
Blanc Mange, Tapioca	176	Green Gooseberries, Compote of	184
Blanc Mange, Arrrowroot	176		
Blanc Mange, Rice Flour	177	Gooseberry Fool,	185
Blanc Mange, Whole Rice	177	Italian Cream,	174
Blanc Mange, Ground Rice	177	Icing for Tarts,	183
Barley Sugar for Children,	191	Ice Cream, Country	189
Cream Puffs,	170	Ice Cream, Strawberry	190
Custard,	171	Ice Apple,	190
Custard, Boiled	171	Kisses, Chocolate	171
Charlotte, Apple	171	Lemon Sponge,	172
Chocolate Kisses,	171	Lemon Cream,	174
Chocolate Cream Custard,	172	Love Apples,	177
Custard, Apple	172	Loppered Milk,	186
Custard, Raspberry	172	Lemon Paste, to keep	189
Custard, Rice	172	Lemon Flavor,	189
Cream, Orange	173	Lemon or Orange Peel, Tincture of	189
Cream, Lemon	174		
Cream, Vanilla	174	Lemon Drops,	191
Cream, Italian	174	Meringues,	175
Cream, Tea	174	Meringue, Lucy Stone's bread	176
Cream, Rock	175	Mashed Tarts,	178
Charlotte Russe,	175	Marmalade, Apple	179
Cream, Apple	180	Meringues, Apple	178
Compote of Apples,	181	Mother's Surprise,	181
Cream, Nina's Apple	181	Milk, Loppered	186
Compote of Peaches,	184	Molasses Candy,	190
Compote of Rhubarb,	184	Orange Cream,	173
Compote of Red Currants,	184	Orange Fritters,	185
Compote of Green Currants,	184	Pasties,	170
Compote of Green Gooseberries,	184	Puffs, Cream	170
		Pippins, Stewed	180
Cherry Cheese,	184	Pears, Baked	182
Chestnuts, a Dessert of	188	Pears, Scalded	182
Candy, Molasses	190	Peaches, Compote of	184
Chocolate Drops,	191	Pineapple Fritters,	185
Dessert, a nice and cheap	186	Prunes, Stewed	185
Dessert, Fruit for	187	Preserve, Good Common	185
Dessert of Chestnuts,	188	Quinces for the Table,	188
Eugene Russe,	175	Rice Custard,	172
Fruit Tarts,	178	Raspberry Custard,	172
Floating Island of Apples,	181	Rock Cream,	175
Fritters, Pineapple	185	Rice Flour Blanc Mange,	177
Fritters, Apple	175	Rice, Whole Blanc Mange,	177
Fritters, Orange	185	Rice, Ground, Blanc Mange	177
Fruit for Dessert,	187	Red Robbin,	177
Fruits, Summer Mixed	188	Rhubarb Tart,	183
Ginger Apples,	180	Rhubarb, Compote of	183
Gooseberry or Apple Trifle,	183	Rhubarb,	188

INDEX.

	Page.		Page.
Souffle, Strawberry or Apple	173	Currant,	197
Souffle, Sweet	173	Cream,	199
Souffle, Omelet	173	Cornets a Creme,	200
Strawberries,	186	Cider,	200
Strawberry Shortcake,	187	Connecticut Coffee,	201
Sugar Taffy,	190	Crullers,	201
Syrup for Candies,	191	Cup,	202
Sugar Barley, for Children	191	Cup Cake, Molasses	202
Tea, Cream	174	Cake without eggs,	202
Tapioca Blanc Mange,	176	Christmas, for good children	203
Tarts, Mashed	178	Cookies,	205
Tarts, Fruit	178	Cheese Cakes, Rice	207
Tart, Apple	178	Cheese Cakes, English	207
Trifle,	183	Cheese Cakes, Apple	207
Trifle, Gooseberry or Apple	183	Cheese Cakes, Bread	207
Tart, Rhubarb	183	Cheese Cakes, Cocoanut	208
Tarts, Icing for	183	Cheese Cakes, Almond	208
Tomatoes,	188	Cocoanut,	211
Tincture of Lemon or Orange Peel,	189	Doughnuts,	205
		Fruit, a fine	194
Taffy, Sugar	190	Fruit, Pork	194
Vanilla Cream,	174	Fried, without eggs or milk	201
		Fried,	201
SWEET CAKES.		Glen Vis,	200
		Ginger Pound with fruit,	201
Almond Sponge,	192	Ginger Snaps,	206
Apple,	197	Ginger Nuts,	206
Almond, fine	197	Gingerbread, Sponge	206
Apple cheese cakes,	207	Gingerbread, Hard times	206
Almond cheese cakes,	208	Ginger Biscuits,	209
Apple biscuit,	209	Graham Fig Biscuits,	210
Bride,	194	Hickory-nut, New Years	196
Bread, Mrs. Bristol's	198	Huckleberry,	196
Birthday,	203	Hard times, molasses	202
Buns,	205	Independence,	195
Bread cheese cakes,	207	Icing, Almond	194
Biscuits, New Years'	208	Icing, Sugar	195
Biscuits, Cream	208	Icing, Chocolate	211
Biscuits, Apple	209	Icing,	211
Biscuits, Orange	209	Jenny's	202
Biscuits, Moss	209	Jumbles,	204
Biscuits, Ginger	209	Loaf,	176
Biscuits, Judge's	210	Lemon,	197
Biscuits, King's	210	Molasses Cup,	202
Biscuits, Graham Fig	210	Molasses, Hard times	202
Christmas, a magnificent,	193	Mary's Tea,	203
Christmas,	193	Macaroons,	210
Connecticut Election,	195	New Year's Hickory-nut,	196
Commencement, New Haven	195	New Years,	197

15

	Page.		Page
New Year's Biscuit,	208	Citron Preparing, for Cake	223
Orange Biscuit,	209	Figs, Green Preserved	216
Pound,	192	Green Grape Jam,	214
Pork, Fruit	194	Green Figs Preserved,	216
Plum,	196	Jam, Strawberry	212
Picnic,	198	Jam, Raspberry	213
"Portage Falls,"	198	Jam, Cherry	214
Poverty,	198	Jam, Green Grape	214
Portugal,	200	Jam, Plum	214
Party Puffs,	205	Jam, Pineapple	214
Rock,	204	Jam, Black Currant	215
Rice Cheese Cakes,	206	Oranges, Preserved	217
Sponge,	192	Plum Jam,	214
Sponge, Almond	192	Pineapple Jam,	214
Sponge, Rice flour,	193	Pineapple Marmalade,	215
Sponge, Mrs. V's.	193	Pineapples Preserved,	216
Snow,	198	Plums or Damsons Preserved	217
Small Seed,	199	Pickling Pears and Peaches,	218
South Carolina,	200	Pickling Damson Plums,	218
Society,	203	Peaches Dried with Sugar,	218
Sally Lunn,	203	Plums and Small Fruits Dried,	219
Shrewsbury,	204	Pippins, Preserved	221
Tea dish, a nice	198	Pumpkin, Fried	223
Tea, Mary's	203	Quinces, Preserved	215
Warsaw White,	200	Raspberry Jam,	213
Wonders,	204	Raspberries, Preserved	213
		Rhubarb, Preserved	217
		Strawberry Jam,	212
PRESERVED FRUITS AND SWEETMEATS.		Strawberries in Cans,	213
		Strawberries, Dried	213
		Tomato Figs,	222
Apple Sweetmeats,	220	Tomato Sweetmeats,	223
Apple Preserve,	220	Vegetable Marrow, Preserved	221
Apple Butter,	220		
Apples, to Prevent Waste in	221	JELLIES.	
Artichokes, Preserved,	222		
Blackberries,	212		
Brandy Gages,	216	Apple,	224
Canning Fruit,	212	Apple, Crab	225
Currant and Raspberry Sweet-		Blackberry,	226
meat,	214	Crab Apple,	225
Cherry Jam,	214	Cider,	225
Currant Black, Jam	215	Currant,	225
Cherries, Preserved	215	Cranberry,	226
Cherries, Pickled	215	Calf's feet,	226
Crab apples, Preserved	216	Gelatine,	226
Currants, Preserved	217	Grape,	227
Citron, Preserved	219	Medlar,	227
Cucumbers, Preserved	221	Quince,	225
Candied Orange Peel Rings	222	Rice,	226

INDEX.

	Page.
Sago,	227
Tapioca,	226
Wine, Mrs. Webster's	225
Wine,	226

FRESH FRUITS.

	Page.
Blackberries,	229
Cherries,	230
Currants,	229
Currants and Huckleberries,	230
Currants and Raspberries,	230
Huckleberries,	230
Strawberries,	229

YEAST BREAD, BISCUIT, &c.

	Page.
Bread,	232
Bread, General Rules,	233
Bread, Rye and Indian	233
Bread, Graham	234
Bread, Sweet Brown	234
Bread, Rice Flour	234
Bread, Moist Rice	235
Bread, Apple	235
Bread, Pulled	235
Bread, Pieces of	235
Baked Batter,	236
Butter Cakes for Tea,	240
Breakfast Cakes, English	240
Biscuit, Graham	240
Breakfast Cakes, Fanny's	236
Biscuit,	240
Biscuit, Mrs. D's Tea	237
Breakfast Johnny Cake,	237
Breakfast Corncake,	237
Buttermilk Breakfast Cakes,	238
Buns, Hot Cross, Good Friday	241
Corn Cream Cake,	237
Corn Bread,	237
Corn Meal Waffles,	238
Crumpets, Laight St.	239
Green Corn Cakes,	239
Hoe Cakes,	236
Johnny Cake, Breakfast	237
Johnny Cake, Western	238
Muffins,	241
Oatcakes,	239

	Page.
Rusks,	236
Rolls, French	240
Rice Biscuit,	236
Rye Drop Cakes,	236
Rice Puffs,	238
Rice Flour Puffs,	238
Rice Flour Cake,	238
Rolls, Flour and Potato	239
Rice Waffles,	239
Shortcake,	235
Soda Biscuit,	240
Soft Waffles,	241
Toast, Dry	242
Toast, Dip	242
Toast, Cream	242
Yeast,	231
Yeast, Connecticut	231
Yeast, Excellent	231
Yeast, Potato	231
Yeast Cakes,	232

GRIDDLE CAKES AND FARINACEOUS DISHES.

	Page.
Buckwheat,	242
Bread,	243
Bannock, Poughkeepsie Seer's	245
Common,	242
Cream,	243
Economical,	244
Frumety, English	247
Flannel,	233
Gruel, Indian Meal	246
Hominy and Farina,	245
Hominy Cakes,	246
Hasty Pudding,	246
Hulled Corn,	247
Porridge, Milk	246
Rice,	243
Rice Flour,	245
Rye Meal Mush,	246
Shrove Tuesday,	243
Soda,	243
Scotch,	245
Samp,	246
Tomato,	245

BREAKFAST.

	Page.
Bills of Fare for Breakfast,	250

INDEX.

TEA, COFFEE, ETC.

	Page.
Coffee,	253
Cream Coffee,	253
Cold Coffee,	254
Chocolate, American	254
Chocolate, French	254
Cocoa,	254
Dinner Coffee,	253
Tea,	254
Tea, to make	255

DINNER.

	Page.
Plain Bills of Fare for Dinner all the year round,	256
January,	256
February,	257
March,	257
April,	258
May,	259
June,	259
July,	260
August,	260
September,	261
October,	262
November,	263
December,	264
Birthday Dinner,	262
Thanksgiving Dinner,	263
Christmas Dinner,	264

WINES AND DRINKS.

	Page.
Black Currant,	266
Blackberry,	268
Blackberry Brandy,	269
Berry Drink,	272
Currant,	266
Currant, Black	262
Cherry Brandy,	269
Corn Drink, Yankee	272
Claret Punch,	274
Cool Cup,	274
Christmas Egg nog,	275
Cold Punch,	275
Elder,	267
Elder Flower,	268
Egg Nog,	273
Egg Nog, Christmas	275
Grape,	267
Grape Syrup,	266
Gooseberry,	268
Green Gooseberry,	269
Ginger,	269
Ginger Beer,	270
Ginger Beer, Cask	270
Ginger Pop,	272
Hop Beer,	270
Imperial,	272
Lemonade, Milk	273
Lemonade Portable,	273
Mead,	271
Milk Lemonade,	273
May Drink,	274
Milk Punch,	275
Oxford Swig,	274
Portable, Lemonade	273
Quick Beer,	271
Quick Drink,	272
Rhubarb,	268
Raspberry Syrup,	270
Spruce Beer,	271
Shrub,	271
Sherry Cobbler, 4th July	273
Staten Island Lemonade,	273
Sack Posset,	275

MISCELLANEOUS.

	Page.
Apples, to keep	227
Butter Cooler,	281
Bread, Homemade	283
Bed Bugs,	293
Bouquet, to Preserve	293
Cabbages, to Keep	278
Cornstarch instead of Eggs,	280
Cement, Diamond	281
Cochineal,	282
Cornmeal, Improving	282
Cement for Metal and Glass,	284
Cracks in Stoves,	284
Creaking Hinges,	285
Cement, Water and Fire Proof	285
Chimney, Fire in	286
Carpet, Soiled	287
Crape, to Stiffen	288

INDEX.

	Page.		Page.
Crape, Water Spots in Black	288	Marks on Table,	286
Cockroaches,	292	Mahogany, To give fine Color	287
Crickets,	293	Mildew, to take out	288
Damp Woolen Clothing,	280	Muslins, Washing	290
Diamond Cement,	281	Marking Ink,	291
Drippings, to clarify	283	Moths,	292
Eggs, Snow Substitute for	280	Nosegays,	293
Eggs, Corn Starch instead of	280	Peas, To keep for Winter Use	277
Egg paper,	280	Parsley, to Keep	279
Easter Eggs,	294	Potatoes, Frozen	280
Frozen Potatoes,	280	Polishing Paste,	285
Fruit Stains, to Wash From Hands	280	Paste, Water Proof	286
		Paint, To clean	287
Fruit Sinking,	282	Paint, Cheap	287
Flatirons, Rust on	284	Papered Walls,	287
Flatirons, Rough	284	Paint Spots on Cloth, Silk, &c.	289
Fire in Chimney,	286	Perfume, Home made	293
Furniture,	287	Pot Pourri,	294
Floors, Scouring	287	Rust on Knives,	284
Grapes, Keeping	277	Rough Flatirons,	284
Grease, to Remove	286	Rust, Varnish to Prevent	285
Grease Spots,	291	Rays of Sun,	286
Grease on a leather covered Book,	291	Ribbons, To Iron	228
		Rats and Mice,	292
Hair, to Strengthen	281	Roses, Tincture of	294
Hens, to make lay	282	Snow Substitute for Eggs,	280
Hatching,	283	Soft Soap,	285
Handles, Knife to Fasten	284	Silk, To Renovate Black	288
Ivory Handles,	283	Silk, To Clean	290
Ice on Windows,	285	Spermaceti Spots,	291
Iron Stain,	290	To keep Grapes,	277
Ink Spots on Linen,	289	To keep Apples,	277
Ink on Books,	291	To keep Pears,	277
Ink, Marking	291	To keep Cabbages,	278
Ink, Green, Blue, Gold and Silver	291	To keep Mustard,	278
		To keep Lemons,	279
Kitchen Odors,	282	To keep Parsley,	279
Kid Gloves, to Clean	290	To preserve Mushrooms,	279
Lemons, to Keep	279	To keep Meat, Game, &c. in Hot Weather,	279
Lobster's Eggs,	281		
Linen, To take Ink out of	289	To remove taint from Meat,	279
Linen, To Restore Stained	289	Turnips, Size of	280
Mustard,	278	To Wash Fruit Stains from Hands,	280
Mushrooms, To Preserve	279		
Meat, Game, &c., To keep in Hot Weather	279	To Make Hens lay in Winter,	282
		To fatten Turkeys,	282
Meat, To Remove Taint from	279	To Clarify Drippings,	283
Molasses, To Clarify	293	To Clarify Molasses,	283
Marble, To Clean	236	To fasten Knife Handles,	281

INDEX.

	Page.
To take off rust from Flatirons,	284
To prevent Lamp Chimneys Breaking,	285
To drive Nails,	286
To Remove Grease,	286
To Clean Marble,	286
Table, Marks on	286
To give fine color to Mahogony,	287
To Clean Paint,	287
To Scour Floors,	287
To Iron Ribbons,	288
To Stiffen Crape,	288
To remove broken Spots from Velvet	288
To Clean Black Lace Veils,	288
To Renovate Black Silk,	288
To take out Mildew,	288
To take Ink out of Linen,	289
To wash print or lawn Dresses,	289
To wash Colored Muslins,	290
To restore Stained Linen,	289
To Clean Silk,	290
To clean Kid Gloves,	290
To remove Spermaceti Spots,	191
To Preserve Bouquets,	293
Tincture of Roses,	294
Vermin,	281
Voice, to Clear and Strengthen	281
Varnish to prevent Rust,	288
Velvet, to remove broken spots	288
Veils, To Clean	285
Woolen Clothing, Damp	280
Windows, Ice on	285
Water and Fire Proof Cement,	285
Water Proof Paste,	286
Water Spots in Black Crape,	288

FOOD FOR INVALIDS.

Apple water,	299
Breakfast, a sick	298
Beef Tea,	298
Broiled Tenderloin,	301
Dinner,	298
Eggs, soft boiled,	298
Gruel,	296
Jelly, Calf's foot	297
Lemonade,	299
Milk and Eggs,	301

	Page.
Milk thickened,	300
Oyster Soup,	301
Panada,	297
Pudding, Invalid	298
Pie, Apple	299
Prunes, stewed	299
Pudding, Tapioca cup	300
Roast Apples,	299
Soup, Oyster	301
Toast, Soft	297
Toast, Egg	297
Tea, a sick	298
Toast, Dry	300
Tapioca Cup pudding,	300
Toast, Milk	300

FOOD FOR INFANTS AND CHILDREN.

Bread and milk,	305
Baby Pudding,	304
Brown Mush for supper,	305
Cow's milk,	304
Children's Pie,	305
Cranberries,	305
English Pap,	303
Essentials,	304
Infant's Broth,	304
Pudding, Baby	304
Pie, Children's	305
Starchy Food,	303
Young Children, Food for	305

LADIES LUNCHES.

Bill of Fare,	307

NEW YEAR'S TABLE, EVENING REFRESHMENTS, PARTIES, ETC.

New Year's Table,	309
A Family Dinner Party,	310
A small Supper Party,	310
Refreshments,	311
A Children's Party,	311
A Christmas Party, -	312

INDEX.

WASHING DAY.

	Page.
Washing Day	313
Blonde Lace, to wash	315
Colored Starch,	315
Laces and Needlework,	314
Muslin, Lawn or Print Dresses,	315
Saving Soap,	316
Shirts, how to starch	316
Starch, Colored	315
Table Cloths, Napkins, etc.,	314
White Flannels,	314
Zephyr Goods and Colored Flannels,	314

THE DAIRY.

	Page.
Cows,	317
Milk Room,	317
Making Butter,	317

JEWISH RECEIPTS.

	Page.
Crackers, Sweet	328
Chicken, Brown fricassee	319
Cake, Cup	322
Cucumbers, Pickled	325
Dumpling, Lemon	324
Fish, White stewed	319
Fritters, Purrin	320
Fish, Codfish fritters	320
Meringue's	321
Marmalade,	323
Orgent,	323
Pudding, a good	220
Pudding, Lemon	321
Pudding, rich Lemon	321
Pudding, Apple	321
Pudding, Bread and Butter	322
Pudding, Sally Lunn	322
Pudding, Light	324
Pudding, Cocoanut	323
Pudding, Almond	324
Pickled Cucumbers,	325
Sandwich, Albert	321
Tomatoes for Winter use,	224

www.ingramcontent.com/pod-product-compliance
Lightning Source LLC
Chambersburg PA
CBHW031848220426
43663CB00006B/536